Learning English

W0348688

Compact Course 1

NEU

für den schulischen Englischunterricht

von
Lutz Brede, Beate Brenner-Kotzur,
Dieter Firmenich, Angelika Hauß,
Philip Hewitt, Loni Löffler,
Arno Paland, Alexander Saccaro,
und Ernst Weidl
sowie
Paul Aston und Douglas K. Stevenson

Ernst Klett Schulbuchverlag
Stuttgart Düsseldorf Berlin Leipzig

Stephanie Kraus

Learning English – Compact Course 1 – NEU

für den schulischen Englischunterricht

von
Lutz Brede, Homburg; Beate Brenner-Kotzur, München; Dieter Firmenich, Duisburg; Angelika Hauß, Weinheim; Philip Hewitt, Stuttgart; Loni Löffler, Allmersbach im Tal; Arno Paland, Mülheim/Ruhr; Dr. Alexander Saccaro, Freiburg i. Br.; Ernst Weidl, Augsburg
sowie
Paul Aston, York; Dr. Douglas K. Stevenson, Essen

Beratende Mitarbeit:
Berthold Hütten, Goch-Gaesdonck; Paul Kaufmann, Lohn/CH; Hans-Georg Steiffert, Goch-Gaesdonck

Visuelle Gestaltung:
Dieter Gelsheimer, Rödermark; Dieter Gebhardt, Asperg; Herbert Horn, München

Sprachcassetten
Zur Verbesserung der Aussprache empfiehlt es sich, die Begleitcassetten zu diesem Lehrwerk zu verwenden.

S: *1 Compact-Cassette* für Schüler und Lehrer mit den obligatorischen Dialogtexten der Units 1–8. Beide Seiten besprochen. Klettnummer 58147.
Lieferung durch jede Buchhandlung oder, wo dies auf Schwierigkeiten stößt, zuzüglich Portokosten per Nachnahme vom Ernst Klett Schulbuchverlag, Postfach 1170, 7054 Korb.

L: *1 Compact-Cassette* für Lehrer mit den Texten von Unit 9, den fakultativen Texten, Liedern, Hörverstehenstexten und Ausspracheübungen. Beide Seiten besprochen. Klettnummer 58148.
Lieferung direkt an Lehrer, Schulstempel erforderlich.

Zeichenerklärung

⟨ ⟩ Stücke in Winkelklammern sind fakultativ.

[ ] Die in rechteckigen Klammern stehenden Pensen können in Bundesländern, in denen ihre Behandlung nicht vorgesehen ist, als fakultativ angesehen werden; in Bayern jedoch sind sie obligatorisch.

S: Das Stück ist auf der Cassette für Schüler und Lehrer (Klettnummer 58147) verfügbar.

L: Das Stück ist auf der Cassette für Lehrer (Klettnummer 58148) verfügbar.

Over to you: Übungen, die den Schülern erlauben, über sich, ihre eigene Situation und ihre Meinung zu sprechen.

Role Play: Rollenspiele, in denen wichtige Redemittel wiederholt und erweitert werden.

⇆ Dialogübungen, in denen Sprechabsichten zusammengefaßt werden.

1. Auflage 1 4 3 2 | 1994 93 92
Alle Drucke dieser Auflage können im Unterricht nebeneinander benutzt werden; sie sind untereinander unverändert. Die letzte Zahl bezeichnet das Jahr des Druckes.

© Ernst Klett Schulbuchverlag GmbH, Stuttgart 1991. Alle Rechte vorbehalten.

Redaktion: Redaktionsdienst Stuart Amor, Stuttgart
Stuart Amor M.A., Marilyn Blažeković-Hall, Inge Spaughton, David Williams

Umschlag: Dieter Gebhardt, Asperg
Satz: Setzerei Lihs, Ludwigsburg; Repro: Repro Maurer, Tübingen
Druck: Appl, Wemding. Printed in Germany
ISBN 3-12-581400-6

Inhaltsverzeichnis

* Es werden bei jeder Lektion nur die wichtigsten kommunikativen Ziele der Texte bzw. Übungen aufgeführt. Eine vollständige Übersicht über die Lernziele und ihre Wiederholung gibt das Lehrerbuch.

UNIT 1

This is Bristol.
It is in England.

Welcome to Bristol!

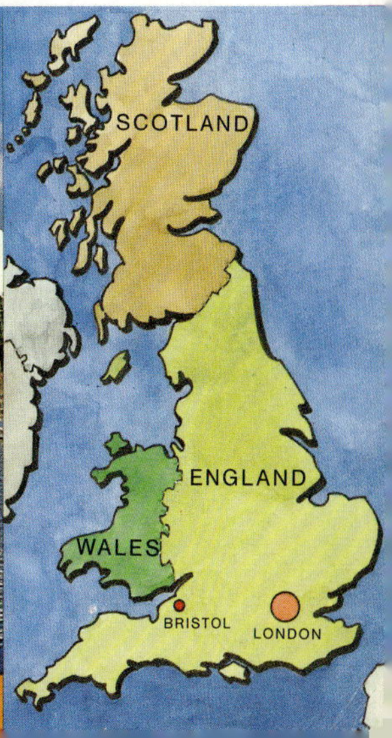

A Welcome to Bristol

a)

b) *Teacher:* Tanja Schulz?
Tanja: Here.
Teacher: Mr and Mrs Benson, this is Tanja.
Mrs Benson: Hello, Tanja.
Mr Benson: Welcome to Bristol.
Tanja: Hello, Mr and Mrs Benson.
Mrs Benson: This is Jenny.
Tanja: Hello, Jenny.
Jenny: Hello, Tanja.
Mr Benson: Is this your suitcase?
Tanja: Yes, it is.
Mrs Benson: And is this your bag?
Tanja: No, it isn't. *This* is my bag.
Mrs Benson: Jenny, put the bag in the car, please.
Jenny: OK.

c) 1. Hello, my name's David.
I'm English.
I'm from Bristol.
And *you?*
What's *your* name?
Where are *you* from?

2. My name's Tanja.
I'm German.
I'm from Hanover.
And *you?*
...

3. My name's ...
I'm German, too.
(Swiss/...)
...

Go on.

1 Ask and answer, please

a) 1. Is Jenny from Bristol? — Yes, she is.
2. Is David from Bristol, too? — Yes, he ...
3. Is Bristol in England? — Yes, it ...
4. Is Hanover in England? — No, ...
5. Is Mrs Benson German? — No, she isn't.
6. Is Tanja from Stuttgart? — ...
7. Is Mr Benson from Bristol? — ...

David	–	he
Jenny	–	she
Bristol	–	it

b) 1. Are you from Germany/ Switzerland/...? — Yes, I am./ No, I'm not.
2. Are you English? — ...
3. Are you German? — ...
4. Are you ...? — ...
5. Are you from Hanover? — ...
6. Are you from ...? — ...

2 This is ...

1 2 3 4 5

Jenny Mr Benson Tanja David Mrs Benson

1. This is Jenny. She's from ....
She's .... She isn't .... *Go on.*

I'm	=	I am
I'm not	=	I am not
he's	=	he is
he isn't	=	he is not
she's	=	she is
she isn't	=	she is not
it's	=	it is
it isn't	=	it is not
My name's ...	=	My name is ...
What's ...?	=	What is ...?

B Upstairs, downstairs

a) *Jenny:* Here we are, Tanja. This is our house.
Tanja: It's nice.
Jenny: Come in. Your room's upstairs. – Here it is. And this is *my* bedroom.
Tanja: Is this David's bedroom?
Jenny: No, it isn't. His bedroom's here. This is the bathroom.
Tanja: OK. Oh! Where's the toilet, Jenny?
Jenny: It's next to the bathroom. It's this little room here.
Tanja: Thanks.

b) *Mrs Benson:* Jenny! Tanja! Where are you?
Jenny: We're upstairs, Mum.
Mrs Benson: Where's Tanja?
Jenny: She's in her room.
Mrs Benson: Come downstairs, please. It's tea-time.

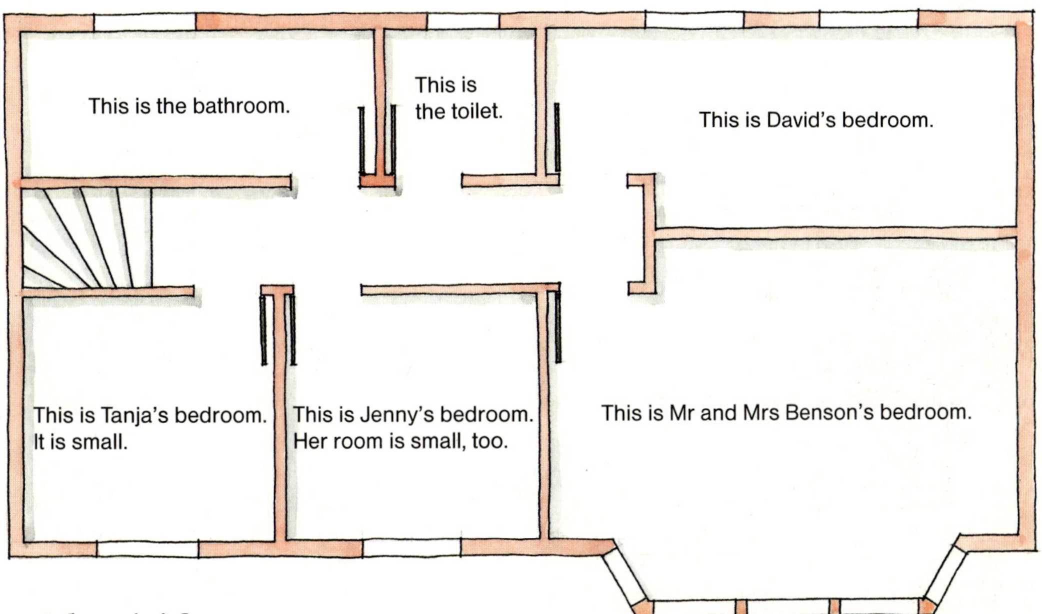

1 Where is it? *Answer, please.*

1. Where's Tanja's bedroom? – It's ... .
2. Where's Jenny's bedroom?
3. Where's the bathroom?
4. Where's David's bedroom?
5. Where's the toilet?
6. Where's Mr and Mrs Benson's bedroom?

2 Ask and answer

Is David's room downstairs?
Is Mrs Benson in Jenny's room? *Go on.*

Where	's	Tanja's bedroom	?
	↓	↓	
Where	is	her bedroom	?
Where	's	David's bedroom	?
	↓	↓	
Where	is	his bedroom	?

3 Where?

Where's	Jenny Mrs Benson Tanja Mr Benson Tanja's suitcase	?	She's He's It's	in her car. in Bristol. in upstairs in	 her room. her bedroom. the bathroom.

4 Look, listen and say

[eɪ]	n**a**me D**a**vid suitc**a**se s**a**y O**K**	[əʊ]	n**o** hell**o** g**o** **O**K **o**ver	[u:]	t**oo** y**ou** s**ui**tcase

C Tanja's room

Tanja is in her bedroom. It is not a big room. There is an old desk in her room. There is an apple and an orange on the desk. The apple and the orange are on a plate. There is a new book on the desk. It is an English book about Bristol. There is a notebook and an exercise book on her desk, too. And a pen and a pencil. There is a nice card on the book. It is from Mrs Benson. It is for Tanja.

Welcome to Bristol, Tanja.
This book about Bristol is for you.
The notebook, the exercise book, the pen and the pencil are for you, too.
Pamela Benson

1 Is there a book on Tanja's desk?

Is there	**a** / **an**	book pencil bag notebook apple orange English book …	on Tanja's	book? desk? suitcase?	Yes, there is. No, there isn't.

2 Look, what's this?

What's this? – It's a book.
Is it an English book? – Yes, it is.

What's this? – It's an apple.
Is it a big apple? – No, it isn't.

English?

big?

small?

old?

small?

new?

3 In your classroom

What's this?	It's	a / an	German book. notebook. small/big/new … apple/orange. exercise book. old …

4 Look, listen and say

a) [ð] [θ]

"**Th**is is **th**e ba**th**room."
"**Th**anks."

b) [ðə]

The pen is for Tanja.
The book is on **the** desk.
…

[ðɪ]

The apple is on Tanja's desk.
The orange is on a plate.
…

D Tea-time

Mrs Benson: Come downstairs, please. It's tea-time . . . .
Jenny: Is David here?
Mrs Benson: No, he isn't. He's late.
Mr Benson: Sit here, Tanja. A cup of tea?
Tanja: Yes, please.
Mrs Benson: Here you are.
Tanja: Thanks.
Mrs Benson: Sugar?
Tanja: No, thanks.
Mrs Benson: Tea or milk, Jenny?
Jenny: Tea, please.
Mrs Benson: A sandwich or a piece of cake, Tanja?
Tanja: A sandwich, please.
Jenny: A piece of cake, Mum.
Mrs Benson: Here you are.
Jenny: Mmm! This cake *is* nice. Listen! David's here.
Mrs Benson: We're in here, David.
Mr Benson: Come in and meet Tanja.
David: Hello, Tanja. I'm Jenny's big brother.

1 Tea for David

OVER TO YOU

Mr Benson: A cup of . . . , David?
David: Yes, ...
Mr Benson: Here . . . are.
David: . . . .
Mr Benson: A . . . of cake or a sandwich?
David: A . . . , please.
Mr Benson: . . . .
David: Mmm! This . . . is . . . .

2 Look, listen and say

[s]
Sit here.
Thank**s**.
It'**s** my **s**uitca**s**e.
. . .

[ʃ]
sugar
she
Engli**sh**

[z]
He'**s** late.
plea**s**e
She'**s** German.
. . .

[s-z]
Mr**s** Ben**s**on i**s** up**s**tair**s**.
Mr Ben**s**on i**s** down**s**tair**s**.

E Tanja's house

Tanja: Look, this is our house in Hanover.

Jenny: It's big! Who's this in front of the house, Tanja?

Tanja: It's me, of course. And this is my mum and dad. They're in Switzerland in this photo.

Jenny: And who's this behind the tree in *this* photo?

Tanja: My little brother, Thomas. – Here he is on his bike with his friend Tobias.

Jenny: How old is he, Tanja?

Tanja: Thomas? He's ten. Tobias is ten, too. Look at this photo. It's mum and dad in the garden with Mr and Mrs Lohmeier. They're under the tree with their dog. And this is me in my room with my cat Kitty.

Jenny: She's lovely. How old is she?

Tanja: She's three.

Who's this?	–	It's me.
		It's my brother.
		It's my mum and dad.
		This is my mum and dad.

1 Who and where?

Look at the picture on this page and ask your partner.

- Who's this?
- It's Tanja. / It's Mr and Mrs Lohmeier. / … .
- Where is she / are they / is he?
- She's/They're/He's/in/in front of/behind … .

2 Where are they?

			in	her	room.
Where's	Tanja?	She's	in front of	their	garden.
Where are	Mr and Mrs …?	They're	behind	his	house.
	Thomas?	He's	on	the	tree.
			under	a	bike.
					…

3 Bristol and Hanover *Please complete.*

a) Hello, I'm Jenny. David is … brother. Here he is on … bike. This is … house in Bristol. Mr and Mrs Benson are … mum and dad.
This is Tanja's house. … house is in Hanover. And this is … brother Thomas and … friend Tobias. Tanja and … brother Thomas are in the garden. Mr and Mrs Lohmeier are in the garden, too, with … dog.

I	→	my
you	→	your
he	→	his
she	→	her
we	→	our
you	→	your
they	→	their

b) – Is David in … room?
– No, …'s in Bristol on … bike.
– And where's Tanja? Is … in … room?
– No, …'s in the garden with … book about Bristol.
– And where are … mum and dad?
– …'re in Bristol with a friend.

c) Look at this photo, Jenny. This is Thomas and me. …'re in front of … house in Hanover. This is … mum and dad in … garden. And this is me. …'m in … bedroom with … cat.

F Kevin

Kevin: Hello. Aren't you Jenny's German friend?
Tanja: Yes, I am. My name's Tanja, Tanja Schulz.
Kevin: My name's Kevin, Kevin Brown. I'm Jenny's neighbour, and this is my dog Red.
Tanja: Hello, Red. You're a lovely dog. How old is he?
Kevin: He's three.
Tanja: My cat's three, too.
Kevin: Where's Jenny? Is she at home?
Tanja: No, she isn't. She's in .... Oh no, look. Here she is.
Jenny: Hello, Kevin. This is my German friend Tanja from Hanover. Are your mum and dad in the house, Kevin?
Kevin: No, they aren't. They're in town. Is David at home, Jenny?
Jenny: Yes, he is. He's upstairs in his room. Come on, Tanja. We're late. Bye, Kevin.
Kevin: Bye, Jenny.
Tanja: Bye, Kevin.
Kevin: Bye-bye, Tanja. ... Hm! She's a nice girl!
Red: Woof!

1 Who, where, how old?

Example: *Tanja* is Jenny's German friend.
Who is Jenny's German friend?

1. Kevin is *in the garden.*
2. Red is *three.*
3. *Jenny* is Kevin's neighbour.
4. Tanja's cat is *three.*
5. David is *in his room.*
6. *David* is Jenny's brother.
7. Tanja is *from Hanover.*
8. Jenny's mum and dad are *in town.*

2 Where's Red?

- Where's Red?
- He's in the garden.
- Where's the cat?
- It's behind the tree.

Go on.

3 Complete the dialogue

Kevin: Aren't you Jenny's German friend?
Tanja: … .
Kevin: … ?
Tanja: Tanja Schulz. …?
Kevin: Kevin Brown. Where are you from?
Tanja: … . Is this your dog?
Kevin: … . His name's Red.
Tanja: How old …?
Kevin: He's … Where's …?
Tanja: He's upstairs in … .
Kevin: … Mrs Benson … ?
Tanja: No, … . … in town.

4 A quiz

1. Where is Bristol?
2. Who is Tanja?
3. Where is Tanja from?
4. Is David German?
5. Is Tanja's room big?
6. Is there a new desk in her room?
7. What is Mrs Benson's first name?
8. How old is Tanja's cat Kitty?
9. Who is Thomas?
10. How old is Thomas?
11. Where is Kevin's house?

5 Red's best friend

Please complete.

Hello, my …'s Red. My best … is Kevin Brown. Our … is in Bristol. It's a … house. There's a nice big … behind the house. Bristol is in …, and I'm an … dog.
Jenny Benson is … neighbour. She's a nice … . … brother is David Benson. David's … is in … of our … . David is … in Kevin's … . Tanja, Jenny's German … is … Hanover. She's a … girl, too.

⟨6 Listening comprehension: In Jenny's room⟩

Listen and answer.

1. Mrs Benson is upstairs. – No, … .
2. Jenny is in town.
3. There is a piece of cake for Jenny.
4. There is milk and cake for Tanja.
5. Jenny is in her room.
6. Red is under Jenny's desk.
7. Jenny's pen is under her desk.
8. There is a picture of Jenny and Red on her desk.

Man's best friend

UNIT 2

A 10 York Road

a) Bristol and Hanover are big cities. Hanover is a city in Germany and Bristol is a city in the West of England. Filton is a suburb of Bristol. This is a picture of York Road in Filton. There are a lot of streets like York Road in the suburbs of Bristol.

Look at the houses on the left. Number 10 is Mr and Mrs Benson's house. The house on the right next to it is Mr and Mrs Brown's house. There are some cars in York Road but there are no buses or lorries. It is a quiet street.

Look, listen and say: Plurals

[s]	[z]	[ɪz]
street**s**	suburb**s**	hous**es**
cup**s**	apple**s**	orang**es**
…	…	…

Go on.

Singular		**Plural**	
street	–	street**s**	[s]
suburb	–	suburb**s**	[z]
bus	–	bus**es**	[ɪz]
house	–	hous**es**	
[haʊs]		[ˈhaʊzɪz]	
cit**y**	–	cit**ies**	[ɪz]

b)

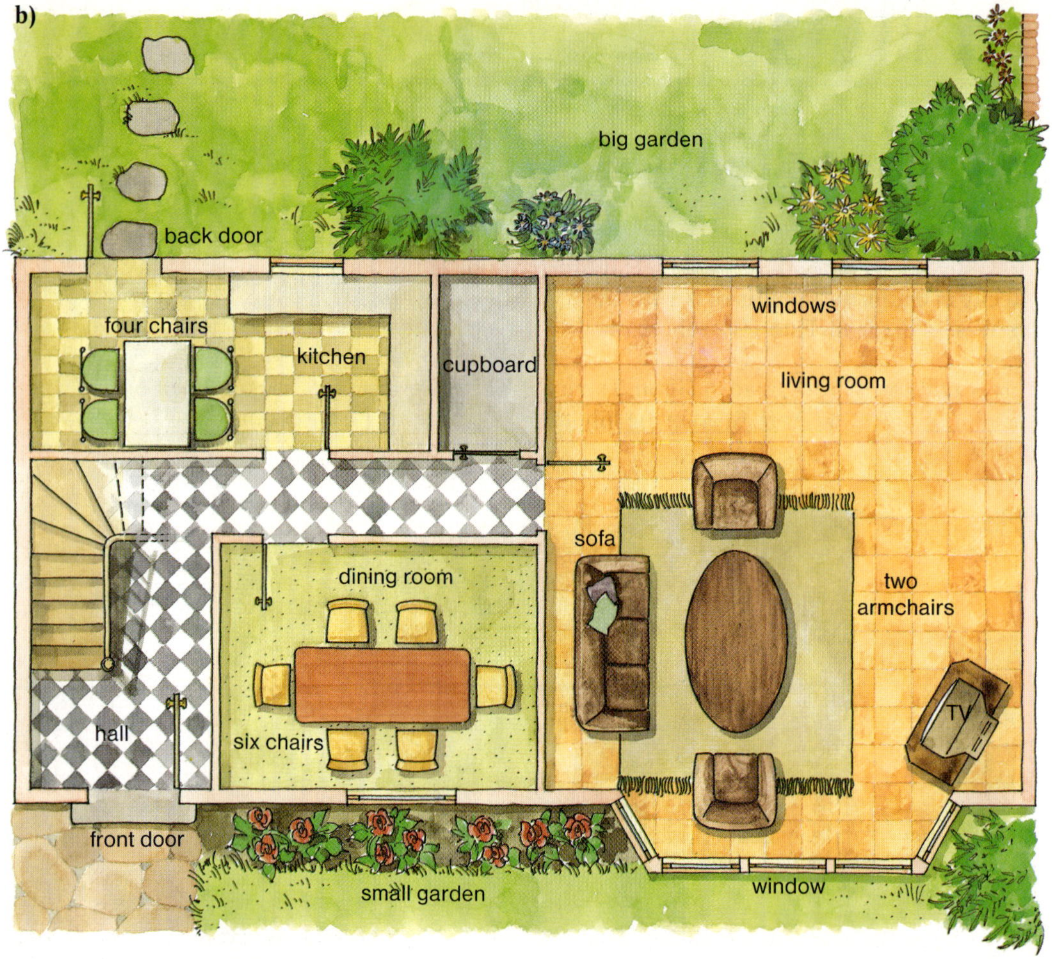

Where is . . .? Where are . . .?

Look at the picture.

Where is	the dining room? the kitchen? the big garden? the living room? the small garden?	It is	on the left. on the right. next to ... in front of ... behind ... ...
Where is Where are	the big table? the TV? the sofa? the four chairs? the six chairs? the two armchairs?		It is in ... They are in ...

Now make up a text about the rooms in the house.

There are three rooms downstairs: ... *Go on.*

c) Jenny's bedroom is upstairs next to Tanja's room. Jenny's bed is a sofa, too. Beside her sofa there are two chairs and a small table with her radio, her cassette recorder and her saxophone on it.
There is a place in the corner for her clothes and a small cupboard for her shoes, but there is no wardrobe. There is a shelf on the wall for her school books, and there are three shelves on the left for her other books and things.
There are four posters on the walls, but there is only one picture. It is a nice room but it is not very big.

⚠ shelf – shelves

Is there . . . ? Are there . . . ?

	a wardrobe	in Jenny's room?	Yes, there is.
Is there	two chairs	on the walls?	No, there isn't.
Are there	two shelves on the left	upstairs?	Yes, there are.
	...	...	No, there aren't.

B In Bristol and Hanover

a) Tanja's room in York Road is upstairs. Her bed is in the corner and there is a desk under the window.
Tanja has got a small cupboard for her clothes but she has not got a wardrobe.
There is a shelf for her books on the wall and she has got a small table next to her bed. She has not got a cassette recorder in her room but there is a radio on the table beside her bed. There are some big posters on the walls.
The room has only got one window and it is not very big but it is a nice, quiet room.

b) *Mr Benson:* How many rooms have you got in Hanover, Tanja?

Tanja: We've got three bedrooms, a living room, a kitchen and a bathroom.

Mr Benson: Have you got a big room?

Tanja: No, I haven't. My mum and dad have got a big bedroom. My bedroom's only small but there are some nice things in it – my radio and my new cupboards. I haven't got a lot of pictures on my walls but I've got one or two big posters.

Mr Benson: Is there a TV in your bedroom?

Tanja: In my bedroom? No, there isn't. We've only got one TV. It's in the living room.

Mr Benson: Haven't your parents got a TV in their bedroom? *We* have.

Tanja: No, they haven't. Have a lot of English people got a TV in their bedroom, Mr Benson?

Mr Benson: Oh, yes. And Thomas? Has he got a nice room?

Tanja: Yes, he has. He's got a lot of posters on the walls.

1 In Bristol (a)

Yes or no?

Tanja has got a desk behind the door.
No, she has got a desk under the window.

1. Tanja has got a big cupboard for her clothes.
2. She has got a wardrobe.
3. She has got a shelf for her books.
4. She has got a cassette recorder in Bristol.
5. Tanja has not got a radio in her room.
6. The room has got two windows.

I've got	– I have got
you've got	– you have got
he's got	– he has got
she's got	– she has got
it's got	– it has got
we've got	– we have got
you've got	– you have got
they've got	– they have got
I haven't got	– I have not got
she hasn't got	– she has not got

2 In Hanover (b)

1. Has Tanja got nice things in her room?
2. Has she got a TV in her bedroom?
3. Have her mum and dad got a big bedroom?
4. Has Tanja got a cassette recorder in her room?
5. Have her mum and dad got a TV in their bedroom?
6. Has Thomas got a nice room?
7. Has Thomas only got one poster in his room?

Yes, he has. / No, he hasn't.
Yes, she has. / No, she hasn't.
Yes, they have. / No, they haven't.

3 What have they got?

Look at the pictures. What have they got? Ask your partner.

Tanja

Mr and Mrs Benson

Kevin

Tanja

4 What have you got in your room?

a) *Ask your partner about his/her room/living room.*

Have you got … ?
Is there … ?
Has it got … ?
Where's the … ?
How many … have you got … ?

b) *Describe your bedroom, your living room or a friend's room.*

There's /There are …
I've got/We've got …

C TV or an evening at the youth club?

a) David, Tanja and Jenny are in the living room.

David: Let's go to the youth club this evening.
Tanja: Good idea.
Jenny: No, I'd like to watch TV.
David: OK. Let's see what's on. Give me the newspaper please, Tanja. There's a good programme on about cities in the USA.
Jenny: Oh no. Look at this: there's a sports programme on in five minutes. Basketball and tennis. I'd like to watch that.
Tanja: I'd like to watch the sports programme, too.
David: There's also a sports programme on the radio, Tanja. Listen to that!

b) *Mr Benson:* Hello, everybody. What's on TV this evening?
Jenny: There's a sports programme …
David: And a programme about the USA.
Mr Benson: Where's the newspaper?
Jenny: Here it is, Dad.
Mr Benson: Let's find a programme for everybody. Oh! There's football on in ten minutes. I'd like to watch football.
David: Football? Oh no! Listen, I've got an idea. Let's go to the youth club and play table-tennis or have a coke.
Tanja: Good idea. Let's go with Kevin.
Jenny: Bye, Dad.
Mr Benson: Bye. Have a nice evening, everybody.
Mrs Benson: *(from upstairs)* Jim, we're late!
Mr Benson: Late?
Mrs Benson: Yes. It's our evening at the club.
Mr Benson: Oh no, not this evening!

1 Let's do something

Put in the verbs and make sentences.

Let's
I'd like to

TV.
what's on TV.
the youth club.
the radio.
football on TV.
a programme for everybody.
table-tennis.
the programme about the USA.
a coke.
the newspaper.

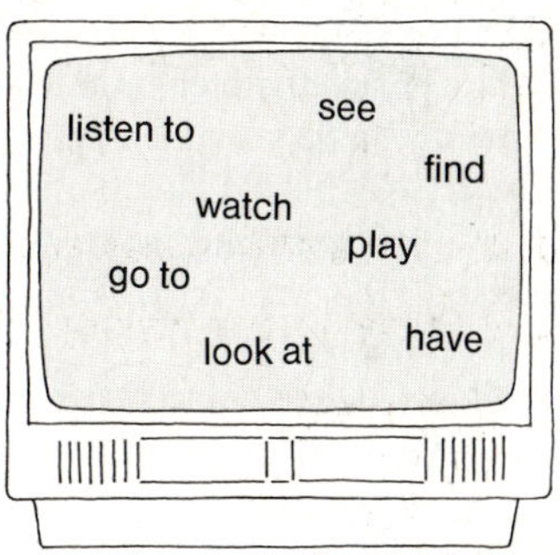

2 I'd like to play basketball *Make dialogues.*

Example: A: I'd like to play basketball.
B: Oh no! Let's go to the youth club.
A: OK./That's a good idea, too.

D Horfield Sports Centre

Tanja, David and Jenny are now in the Browns' living room. Kevin is there, too.

Tanja: I'd like to join a sports club. How many sports clubs are there in Bristol, Kevin?
Kevin: There are two or three sports clubs in the centre of Bristol. But there's also a sports centre in Horfield, only ten minutes from here. It's got two football teams and a basketball group.
Jenny: Yes, and there's volleyball, too. Kevin's dad is the coach there.
Tanja: Your dad, Kevin? Is that his job?
David: Mr Brown hasn't got a job at the moment, Tanja, but he's the coach of the football and the basketball teams at the sports centre.
Kevin: Would you like to play basketball … or football?
Tanja: No, but I'd like to play hockey. I'm the captain of the hockey team at my school in Hanover.
Kevin: I'm sorry, Tanja. There's no hockey at the sports centre.
Tanja: Oh … Is the centre open to everybody?
Kevin: I'm not sure, but there are a lot of boys and girls from Filton schools at the centre. Ask my dad.
Tanja: Good idea.

Kevin**'s** dad
the Browns**'** living room

a suburb **of** a big city
the centre **of** Bristol
the captain **of** the hockey team

1 Is that Jenny's book?

Example: Is that Jenny's book? – No, it isn't.
Is it Tanja's book? – Yes, it is.

2 Make one sentence

Example: This is Kevin. Mr Brown is his dad.
Mr Brown is Kevin**'s** dad.
Westbury is in Bristol. Westbury is a suburb.
Westbury is a suburb **of** Bristol.

1. This is David. And this is his bike.
   This is …
2. Filton is in Bristol. Filton is a suburb.
   Filton is …
3. Kevin has got a dog. Look, here is Red.
   Red is …
4. This is a football team. There are only boys in the team.
   It is a …
5. There are football and basketball teams. Mr Brown is the coach.
   Mr Brown is the …
6. Tanja is in a hockey team. She is the captain.
   Tanja is …
7. The Bensons have got a house. It is in York Road.
   The …
8. This is Mrs Benson. Here is her car.
   This is …

E Filton and Westbury

1 Photos

Put in this, that, these *or* those.

Tanja: Look at … photos here.
Jenny: Hey! … photo there is very nice.
Tanja: Nice?! …'s my brother Thomas. And … boys over there are his friends.
Jenny: Are … girls here in your hockey team?
Tanja: Yes, they are. … two girls are my best friends and … girl over there is the best in our team.
Jenny: Is … your school here?
Tanja: No, it isn't. … is our school over there.

2 This and that

Complete with this, that, these *or* those.

1. … house here is small.
   … house over there is big.

2. … chairs here are in the living room.
   … chairs are in the kitchen.

3. … boys are in the football team and …

4. … shelves …

5. …

3 Numbers

Teacher: What is seven and eight?
Boy: Seven and eight is fifteen.
Teacher: What is two and nine?
Boy: Two and nine is eleven.

You: What is six and ten?
Partner: …

Go on.

4 How many are there?

Example: How many sandwiches are there in picture number one?
There are …

⟨5 Let's sing a song: Ten green bottles⟩

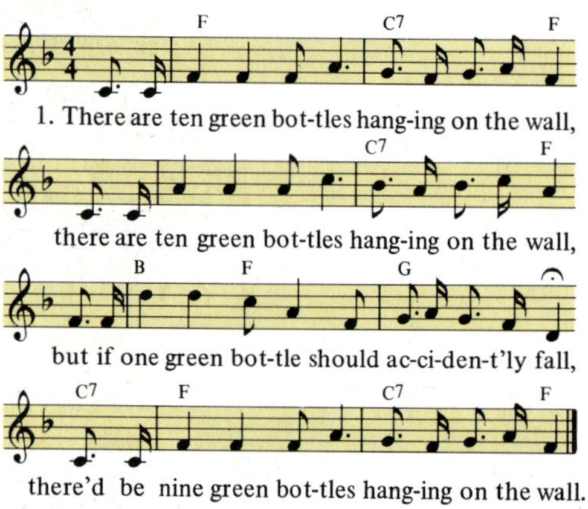

There are nine (eight, …) green bottles …

There is one green bottle hanging on the wall,
There is one green bottle hanging on the wall,
And if that green bottle should accident'ly fall,
There'd be no green bottle hanging on the wall.

6 Look, listen and say

a) [ɪ]	[iː]	b) [eɪ]	[aɪ]
this	these	always	beside
his	he's	newspaper	dining room
it	me	radio	find
…	…	…	…

Find other examples.

F A city with something for everybody

a) Bristol has got something for everybody. For young people there are the best discos in the West of England. There are cinemas, youth clubs, sports clubs, large parks and gardens, and there is even a balloon festival.

b) Are you interested in ships? Go to the City Docks and look at the old ships there.
The old ship in the photo on the left is the 'Great Britain', one of the first steamers from England to the USA.

c) Have you got time for a cup of tea or a coke? Sit with your friends in one of the cafés and have a hamburger or a snack. Watch the people in the streets and listen to the music there.

d) Bristol has got a lot of good shops. The large shops in Broadmead Shopping Centre have got something for everybody.
There are small shops, too, in the old town and at the City Docks – with interesting things for everybody.

1 Right or wrong? (a, b)

Answer with: Yes, that's right. / No, that's wrong. …

1. Bristol has got the best discos in Great Britain.
2. There are only small parks in Bristol.
3. There is something for everybody in Bristol.
4. There are three balloon festivals in Bristol.
5. There are a lot of old ships at the City Docks.
6. The name of the steamer in the photo is the 'Great Bristol'.

2 Something for everybody (c, d)

a) *What is there in Bristol?*

In Bristol At the City Docks In Broadmead Shopping Centre In the old town In the centre of Bristol	there is there are	discos cinemas youth clubs sports clubs parks and gardens a balloon festival small shops …	for young people. for old people. for boys and girls. for everybody.

b) *Ask and answer questions about Bristol.*

3 Your town

a) *What has your town got?*

Has your town got	a shopping centre? cafés for young people? a balloon festival? a lot of small shops? discos? parks and gardens? a cinema? a youth club? docks with old ships? …	Yes, it has. No, it hasn't.

b) *Make a dialogue with your partner.*

You: Is there a youth club in your town?
Partner: No, there isn't. But there *is* a good sports club.
You: Has your town got a cinema?
Partner: Yes, …

Go on.

G A snack with friends

a) Tanja is in the centre of Bristol with Jenny and David. They are in Corn Street, near Broadmead Shopping Centre, and they have got time for a snack.

Jenny: That's enough shopping for today! Let's go into this café for a coke and a snack.
David: Oh no, Jenny! Not *that* café! Let's go to the new café in Ship Street.
Jenny: No. That's not a café, it's a disco!
David: What about the 'Great Britain'? That's a nice café.
Tanja: I've got my book about Bristol here. Let's see .... Cafés for young people .... Here's one! Listen: "'The Black Cat' has got something for everybody: music, tea, coke, good hamburgers, cakes, sandwiches and snacks."
Jenny: Hm! That's a new café. Where is it, Tanja?
Tanja: Let me see .... Here it is: Small Street. Where's that?
David: It's the next street on the right. Come on.

b) Now David, Jenny and Tanja are in 'The Black Cat'. It is a café with glass tables, modern chairs and good music. There are a lot of young people and tourists in the café, and there are only four or five seats free. David's girlfriend Sandra is at one of the tables near the window, but there is only one seat free at her table.

David: Oh! Hello, Sandra. Is this seat free?
Sandra: Hello, David. Yes, sit down. But what about Jenny and her friend?
Jenny: Sit here with Sandra, David. There are two seats free at that table over there. Come on, Tanja. Oh, look! It's Kevin. Hi, Kevin!
Kevin: Oh! Hello, you two.
Jenny: Three. David's with us.
Kevin: Where is he?
Jenny: Behind you! His girlfriend Sandra is here.
Tanja: Are these seats free?
Kevin: Yes. Sit down.
Jenny: Have they got good hamburgers here?
Kevin: Yes, they're the best in Bristol!
Waitress: Yes, please?
Jenny: Two hamburgers and two cokes, please.

1 Questions

a)
1. Where is Tanja?
2. Who is with her?
3. Is there a new café in Ship Street?
4. Where is 'The Black Cat'?
5. Where is Small Street?

b)
1. What have they got at 'The Black Cat'?
2. Are there a lot of old people in the café?
3. How many seats are free?
4. Who is Sandra?
5. Where is she?

2 Dialogues

a) *Is there a good café here?*

Tourist: good café – centre – city?
Jenny: Yes – 'The Old Steamer' – good café – Dock Street
Tourist: young people?
Jenny: No – 'The Black Cat' – modern café – young people and tourists
Tourist: What – for young people?
Jenny: good music – coke – snacks – hamburgers
Tourist: Where?
Jenny: near the shopping centre – Small Street
Tourist: Thanks.

b) *At the café*

Tourist: seats – free?
Young man: Yes – sit down
Tourist: coffee – good here?
Young man: very good – tea – OK, too
Tourist: sandwiches?
Young man: …
Tourist: Thanks.
Waitress: …
Tourist: …

c) *You are in London and you would like to have a cup of coffee in a café. Make up a dialogue.*

3 A city for everybody

Please complete.

Bristol has got something … everybody. Are you interested … ships? Go … the City Docks and look … the 'Great Britain', one … the first steamers … England … the USA. Bristol has got a lot … nice cafés. 'The Black Cat' is a café … good music. It is … Small Street … the shopping centre. There are a lot … young people … the café, but there are some free seats … one corner. Sandra is … one of the tables. David is … Tanja and Jenny.

4 The house in York Road

Look at the pictures on pages 19 and 20.

What	have has	the Bensons Jenny/David/Tanja	got?

What is there … ? – There is … ./There are … .
How many … ?

⟨5 Listening comprehension: In town⟩

Listen to the cassette and answer the questions.

1. Where are Tanja and Kevin?
2. Where is Mr Brown?
3. Have they got sandwiches at the café?
4. The three hamburgers are for … .
5. What has the man at their table got?
6. What is on TV?
7. Would Tanja like to watch TV?
8. Has Mr Brown got the German tennis shoes?

UNIT 3

A All about Horfield Sports Centre

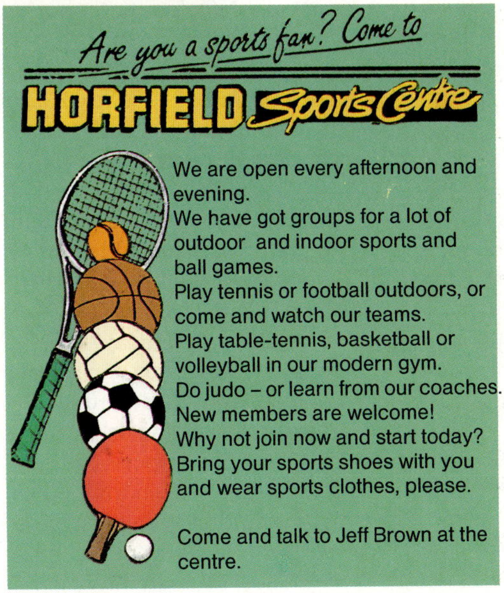

1 Tanja and Jenny *Look at the sentences and make a dialogue.*

Tanja

1. Look at that poster, Jenny! Are you a member of Horfield Sports Centre? → d)
2. Yes, I would. But are they open today?
3. Jeff Brown? Isn't that Kevin's father?
4. But why only watch? Why not play one of the ball games?
5. OK, let's do judo!

Jenny

a) Yes, they're open every afternoon and evening. Let's go and talk to Jeff Brown.
b) Ball games? Listen, I've got an idea. Let's go and learn judo.
c) Great, why not start today?
d) No, Tanja, I'm not. – Would you like to go to the centre with me this evening?
e) That's right, and Kevin is a member, too. Let's go and watch – he's in one of the teams.

2 A poster *Make a poster for a sports club. Here are some words and phrases:*

Are you interested in	football	at the club
There is/are	basketball	at … Sports Centre
Come and watch	…	in our modern gym
We have got	groups for boys/girls	…
Come and play (with)	groups for old people	every afternoon
Why not play/do	…	in the evening
Come and learn (from)	our coaches	
Why not talk to	your friends	

B A new member at Horfield Sports Centre

a) *Tanja:* I'm a sports fan, Mr Brown, and I'd like to join Horfield Sports Centre.
Mr Brown: Good. What games can you play, Tanja?
Tanja: I can play hockey – I'm the captain of our school team – and I can play basketball and volleyball, too.
Mr Brown: Can you play football?
Tanja: Football? No, I can't. That's a game for boys.
Mr Brown: Not only for boys. We've got a good girls' football team at our centre – the best girls' team in Bristol! But you needn't play football. Come and sit here. Let's talk about sports at the centre.

b) *Mr Brown:* Now, what are you interested in, Tanja?
Tanja: I'd like to learn judo. May I join the judo group?
Mr Brown: You may come and watch. Kevin is in the judo group.
Tanja: Oh … Can I start today?
Mr Brown: I'm sorry, Tanja, you can't start today. For judo I must have a note from your mum and dad.
Tanja: OK. What about sports clothes?
Mr Brown: You needn't wear sports clothes this evening, but you must bring sports shoes with you. You mustn't wear street shoes in the gym.
Tanja: OK, Mr Brown.

1 Questions

a)
1. What ball games can Tanja play?
2. Is she the captain of her school volley-ball team?
3. What can't she play?
4. Is football only a game for boys?

b)
1. What is Tanja interested in?
2. Can Tanja start judo today?
3. What must Tanja bring with her?
4. Where mustn't she wear street shoes?

Tanja **can** play basketball,
but she **can't** play football.
Can Tanja join the judo group?
Yes, she **can.**
But she **can't** start judo today.
"**May** I join the judo group?"
"You **may** come and watch.
But you **mustn't** wear street shoes in the gym.
You **needn't** wear sports clothes this evening.
For judo you **must** have a note."

2 Short answers

Answer the questions. Give short answers.

1. Is Tanja a sports fan?
2. Can she play volleyball and basketball?
3. Can she play football?
4. Have they got a girls' football team at Horfield Sports Centre?
5. Can Tanja and Jenny come and watch the judo group?
6. Must Mr Brown have a note from Tanja's mum and dad?
7. Must the girls bring their sports clothes to the gym?
8. Must they bring their sports shoes?
9. May they wear street shoes in the gym?

3 At Horfield Sports Centre

John King is new at Horfield Sports Centre.
He would like to ask Mr Brown
some questions about the sports
at the centre.
He has got some notes
in his notebook.

- Judo/judo clothes?
- A note for judo from my mum and dad?
- Other sports: a note from my mum and dad, too?
- Outdoor sports/indoor sports?
- Coffee, coke, sandwiches at the centre?
- Street shoes on the sports field?
- Everybody welcome at the centre – my dog, too?
  Play with him on the sports fields?

a) *Ask John's questions.*

b) Role Play *Now one of you is John, one of you is Mr Brown. Make up a dialogue.*

4 Sports at your school

Ask your partner questions about sports at your school and in your town.
Your partner can give long or short answers to your questions.

Has your school/town got ... ?
Are you interested in ... ?
Can you play/do ... ?
Must you ... ?

C Rules for the gym

a) New members of Horfield Sports Centre must read the rules on the notice-board. Players and spectators must always bring sports shoes, but spectators need not wear sports clothes, of course. Only members may use the gym. Spectators must not use the gym. Members must keep the gym clean: they must not bring food or drinks into the gym. Teams may book the gym for a match, but they must ask Jeff Brown first.

b) This is on the notice-board at Horfield Sports Centre.

HORFIELD Sports Centre

TEAM MEMBERS:
Teams may book the gym for matches with teams from other clubs or sports centres, but they must ask me first.

Bring gym shoes with you and always wear them in the gym. Please help us in the gym: keep it clean.

BASKETBALL AND VOLLEYBALL:
Sandra Long and Jim Mead are the captains of the teams. Ask her about basketball and him about volleyball.

TABLE-TENNIS AND JUDO:
Tom White is the table-tennis and judo coach. Talk to him. He can help you.

PLEASE ...
Don't be late for matches with other clubs.

Don't ask the other team first.

Don't wear street shoes.

Don't bring food or drinks into the gym with you.

Jeff Brown

1 Right or wrong? (a)

1. Members can find the rules in the Bristol newspapers. – That's wrong, they ... .
2. Players and spectators must wear sports shoes in the gym.
3. Members may bring food and drinks into the gym.
4. Spectators may use the gym.
5. Teams may not book the gym for a match.

I	–	me
you	–	you
he	–	him
she	–	her
it	–	it
we	–	us
you	–	you
they	–	them

2 Rules

1. What must members and teams do at Horfield Sports Centre?
2. What mustn't they do?
3. What must / mustn't / needn't spectators do?

3 At the sports centre

Examples:

1. a) Don't bring food or drinks into the gym.
   b) You mustn't bring … .
2. a) Look at the notice-board.
   b) You … .

4 New members (b)

Complete the dialogue with pronouns.

Tanja and Jenny are now members of Horfield Sports Centre. The next day they are at the centre.

a) *Jenny:* Come over to the notice-board with …, Tanja. Let's look at the rules on … . We must read … .

b) *Kevin:* Hi, Jenny, hi, Tanja. There's a basketball match in ten minutes. Would you like to play in …? Have you two got your sports clothes with …?
Jenny: Tanja and I have got our sports shoes with …, and I've got my sports clothes here.
Tanja: But I haven't got my sports clothes with … .
Kevin: My dad can help … . I can ask … for … . Or I can go to Sandra and talk to … . I'm sure she can help … .

c) *Sandra (at the door):* Come in, you three. Don't be late for the match!
Kevin: Listen, Sandra, Tanja hasn't got her sports clothes here. Can't you help …?
Sandra: Yes, I can, Tanja – I've got some clothes for … in my room. You can wear … . But come in now, we mustn't be late for the match!

5 Look, listen and say

a)

[æ]	[e]
apple	d**e**sk
b**a**ck	b**e**droom
c**a**ptain	fri**e**nd
…	…

b)

[θ]	[ð]
thanks	fa**th**er
thing	bro**th**er
some**th**ing	o**th**er
…	…

D The volleyball match

a) It is seven o'clock on Friday evening. Tanja and Jenny are in the living room.

Jenny: Are you ready, Tanja? Can't you write that letter to your mum and dad later? There's a volleyball match at the sports centre this evening. We must be there at a quarter past seven.

Tanja: What time is it?

Jenny: It's seven o'clock.

Tanja: Just a minute, Jenny. Can you fetch my sports things from my room? They're on the bed.

Jenny: OK, Tanja, but hurry up.

Horfield Sports Centre is not far from the Bensons' house, so Jenny and Tanja need not take a bus. They are not the first in the gym. Mr Brown the coach is there, too. There are six people in each team – three boys and three girls. Tanja and Jenny are very good players, so Tanja is not in Jenny's team. Kevin Brown is one of the boys in Jenny's team, and Sandra, David's girlfriend, is in Tanja's team. She is a good volleyball player, too.

b) It is half past seven now, and the score is 8–7 for Jenny's team. Tanja's team must stop the next ball. Sandra is in front and Tanja is behind her. Sandra cannot stop the ball ... There is an accident. Sandra and Tanja are on the floor.

Sandra: Sorry, Tanja.

Kevin: Are you OK, Tanja?

Tanja: Ouch! ... It's my leg ... .

Mr Brown: What's the matter, Tanja?

Tanja: There's something wrong with my right leg, Mr Brown. I can't move it.

Mr Brown: Well, don't try then, Tanja. Let me look at it. Hm, it isn't broken, but you must see a doctor. Kevin, call an ambulance and then Mr and Mrs Benson, please.

Kevin: Yes, Dad, of course.

Now it is a quarter to eight.

1 Questions (a)

Ask questions.

1. Tanja and Jenny are in the living room. – Where are ... ?
2. They must be at the sports centre at a quarter past seven.
3. There is a volleyball match at the sports centre this evening.
4. Tanja's sports things are on the bed in her room.
5. Twelve people can play in a volleyball match.
6. There are six players in each team.
7. Kevin is in Jenny's team.

2 Complete the sentences (a)

Example:
It is seven o'clock, and the volleyball match is at a quarter past seven, so they must hurry up.

1. Jenny would like to go now, but ...
2. The volleyball match is at a quarter past seven, so ....
3. Not all the players are in the gym, but ....
4. Horfield Sports Centre is not far from the Bensons' house, so ....
5. There are twelve players in the two teams, so ....
6. Tanja and Jenny are very good volleyball players, so ....

3 Right or wrong? (b)

1. It is half past seven, and the score is 14-13.
2. Kevin's team must stop the next ball.
3. Tanja is in front of Sandra.
4. Sandra can stop the ball.
5. There is something wrong with Tanja's right leg.
6. Tanja's right leg is broken.
7. Kevin must call Mrs Brown.

4 What time is it?

Example: It's a quarter to seven.

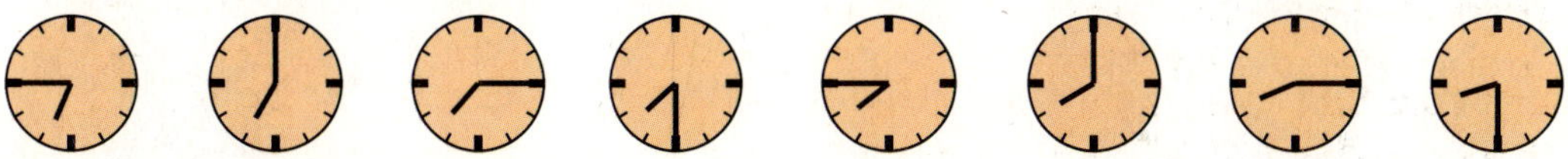

5 Role Play 999

Take Kevin's role in the dialogue.

Man: Hello.
Kevin: An ambulance, please.
Can you come to our sports centre – there's a girl here –
Man: Just a moment. What's your name?
Kevin: ....
Man: OK, Kevin. And where are you?
Kevin: ....
Man: Now, what's the matter with – what's her name?
Kevin: ....
Man: An accident?
Kevin: ....
Man: Is her leg broken?
Kevin: ....
Man: Is there a coach with her at the moment?
Kevin: ....
Man: OK, Kevin. We can be there in ten minutes.

E Southmead Hospital

a) This is Southmead Hospital. There are ten people in the waiting room. Seven of them are patients: two men, two women and three children with their mothers. In one corner there is a woman with a bandage over her left eye. The woman next to the door cannot walk. There is something wrong with her right leg.
Why are the two men in the waiting room? One man has got a sprained ankle. The other man is there because he has got a broken leg.

b) What is the matter with the boy? There is something wrong with his right eye. The girl has got a bandage round her left arm and hand. She cannot use her hand.

The other little child has got a bandage round his hand. His left wrist is sprained, and it is very painful. He must stay at home. He needn't go to school.

man [mæn]	–	men [men]
woman ['wʊmən]	–	women ['wɪmɪn]
child [tʃaɪld]	–	children ['tʃɪldrən]

1 In the waiting room

Put in the right words.

a) This is the waiting room … Bristol Hospital. There are pictures … the walls. … the centre … the room there is a table. There are a lot … newspapers … it. Some … the newspapers are … the floor. Are the patients … the room interested … the newspapers? No, they are not. There are two patients … the waiting room. One is a boy … a bandage … his right eye. There is an old woman … him.

b) *Old woman:* Hello, young man.
What's wrong … your eye?
Boy: An accident … my sports club.
Old woman: So you can't go … school. You can stay … home. Isn't that lovely?
Boy: Yes and no. No school, that's lovely! No sports, that's not so good! And why are you here?
Old woman: Look … the bandage … my leg.
Boy: What's the matter … it?
Old woman: Well, I –
Nurse (at the door): Next patient! Would you come in please, Mrs Black?
Old woman: Yes, nurse. Bye, young man.

2 What's the matter?

Example: What's the matter with the boy? What can't/needn't he do?
He's got a broken leg. He can't play volleyball. He needn't … .

F At the hospital

a) At eight o'clock the ambulance is outside the sports centre. Tanja's ankle is very painful and she cannot walk, so the ambulance men must help her. Kevin and Jenny can go to the hospital with her in the ambulance.

Nurse: What's your name, please?
Tanja: Tanja Schulz.
Nurse: Isn't that a German name? Can you spell it for me?
Tanja: T - a - n ... Hm ... Oh yes - j - a S - c - h - u - l - z.
Nurse: And your address, Tanja?
Tanja: 10 York Road, Filton.
Nurse: What's the matter, Tanja?
Tanja: It's my ankle. It's very painful.
Nurse: OK, Tanja. Take this card and wait in the waiting room.

There are five other people in the waiting room: two men, two women and a boy. So the doctor cannot see Tanja before a quarter past nine.

b) *Doctor:* Can I have your card, please?
Tanja: Here you are, doctor.
Doctor: Thank you. Hm – a sports accident, Tanja?
Tanja: Yes, doctor. Volleyball. It's my ankle.
Doctor: OK. Sit down here, please. Is your ankle painful?
Tanja: Yes, doctor. Very.
Doctor: Let me look at it. ... Well, your ankle isn't broken, it's only sprained. I must put a bandage on it, then you can go home in an ambulance.
Tanja: Must I stay in bed, doctor?
Doctor: No, you needn't, but you mustn't walk far for the first day or two. Come and see me next week, and no sports for a week or two, I'm afraid.
Tanja: Oh dear! No judo for me, then?
Doctor: No, I'm sorry about that, Tanja.

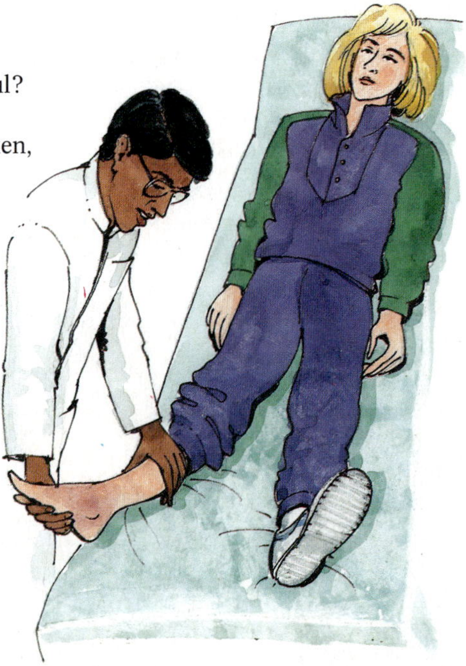

Tanja is back in the waiting room. Mr and Mrs Benson are there, too. They have got the car with them, so Tanja need not wait for an ambulance.

c) At home Tanja cannot walk upstairs to her bedroom. Mr Benson must help her. Her ankle is very painful, so she must lie in bed. She is unhappy because she cannot do judo. Mr Benson must call Mr and Mrs Schulz in Hanover. He cannot speak German, but Tanja's mum can speak English – she *is* English!

Mrs Schulz: Schulz.
Mr Benson: Hello?
Mrs Schulz: Is that you, Mr Benson?
Mr Benson: Yes, I'm sorry, it's very late, Mrs Schulz. It must be eleven o'clock in Germany.
Mrs Schulz: Yes, it is. What's the matter? Is it Tanja?
Mr Benson: Yes. An accident at the sports centre.
Mrs Schulz: Oh dear! What's wrong with her?
Mr Benson: She's got a sprained ankle. It's very painful, but she's OK.
Mrs Schulz: Oh ... Can I talk to her for a minute, Mr Benson?
Mr Benson: I'm afraid she's upstairs in bed at the moment, but she can call you tomorrow. It's Saturday – are you at home all day?
Mrs Schulz: Well, can Tanja call at nine o'clock in the morning, please, because we'd like to go shopping?
Mr Benson: OK. Goodbye, Mrs Schulz.
Mrs Schulz: Goodbye. And thank you for your call.

1 Comprehension (a)

1. When is the ambulance outside the sports centre?
2. What is the matter with Tanja's ankle?
3. What must the ambulance men do, and why?
4. Who is in the ambulance with Tanja?
5. Where must Tanja go?
6. How many people are there in the waiting room?
7. When can the doctor see Tanja?

2 The alphabet (a)

a	**b**	**c**	**d**	**e**	**f**	**g**	**h**	**i**	**j**	**k**	**l**	**m**
[eɪ]	[bi:]	[si:]	[di:]	[i:]	[ef]	[dʒi:]	[eɪtʃ]	[aɪ]	[dʒeɪ]	[keɪ]	[el]	[em]
n	**o**	**p**	**q**	**r**	**s**	**t**	**u**	**v**	**w**	**x**	**y**	**z**
[en]	[əʊ]	[pi:]	[kju:]	[ɑ:]	[es]	[ti:]	[ju:]	[vi:]	['dʌblju:]	[eks]	[waɪ]	[zed]

E is a capital letter; **e** is a small letter.
Can you spell this?
Small Street = capital S – m – a – double l – capital S – t – r – double e – t

3 Patients' cards (a)

a) *Look at these patients' cards on the nurse's desk at Southmead Hospital. Can you read the cards and spell the names, addresses, etc.*

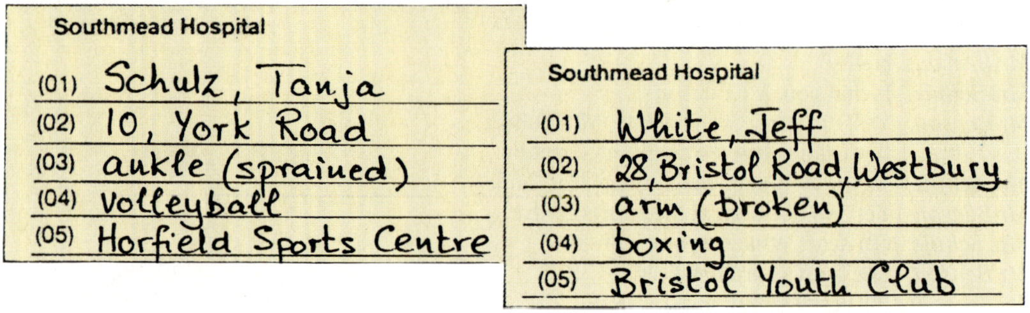
Southmead Hospital
(01) Schulz, Tanja
(02) 10, York Road
(03) ankle (sprained)
(04) volleyball
(05) Horfield Sports Centre

Southmead Hospital
(01) White, Jeff
(02) 28, Bristol Road, Westbury
(03) arm (broken)
(04) boxing
(05) Bristol Youth Club

b) *Now make more cards for other patients.*

4 Nurse and patient (a)

a) *Complete the dialogue.*

Nurse: …
Patient: John Ottaway.
Nurse: …
Patient: Of course.
Capital o – double t – a – w – a – y.
Nurse: …
Patient: 23 Park Street, Westbury.
Nurse: …
Patient: It's my eye. It's very painful.
Nurse: …
Patient: Thank you, nurse.

b) Role Play *Use your patients' cards from exercise 3b).*

Nurse: Next, please. What's your name, please?
Patient: …
Nurse: … *Go on.*

5 Why? (c)

Ask and answer questions with 'Why' and 'because'.

Example: Why must Mr Benson help Tanja?
Mr Benson must help her because she cannot walk upstairs.

1. … because her ankle is very painful.
2. … because she cannot do judo.
3. … because Mrs Schulz can speak English, and Mr Schulz can only speak German.
4. … because she *is* English.
5. … because Tanja is upstairs in bed at the moment.
6. … because Mr and Mrs Schulz would like to go shopping.

6 Look, listen and say

a) [tʃ]	[dʒ]	b) [ɜː]	[əʊ]
coa**ch**	banda**ge**	l**ear**n	cl**o**thes
ea**ch**	**G**erman(y)	f**ir**st	c**oa**ch
…	…	…	…

7 Pairs

Make pairs with the words. Example: mum and dad

a)

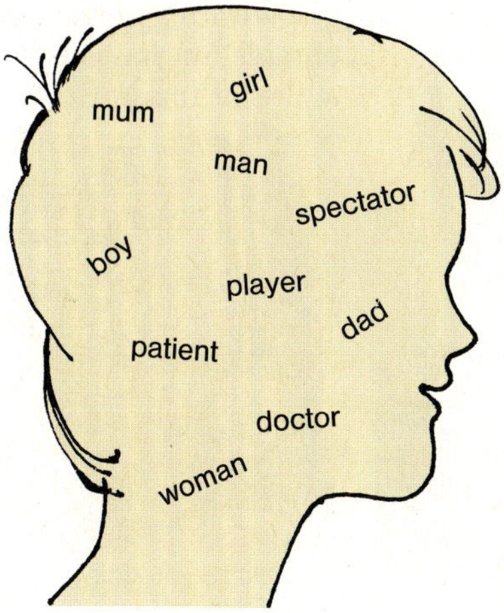

b)

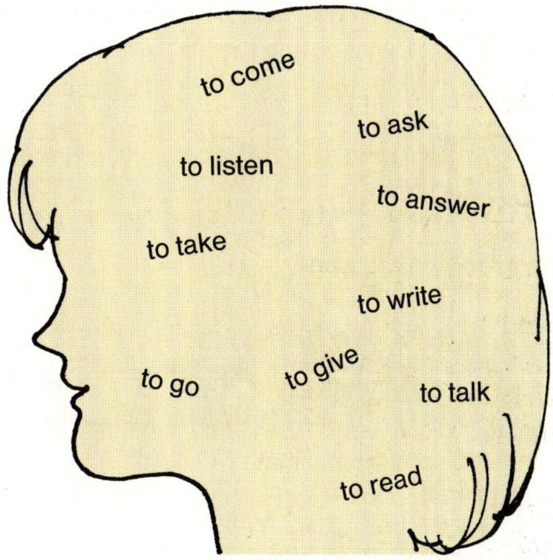

8 Can you find the words?

1. He or she would like to do sports every day.
2. He/She is at a sports centre. You can learn a lot from him/her.
3. Would you like to be one? Then you must join a club.
4. You can find all the sports and games for each day of the week on it.

Explain these words: 1. team 2. gym 3. bandage 4. ambulance

⟨9 Listening comprehension: A sports quiz⟩

Listen to the cassette. Can you find the pairs?

A

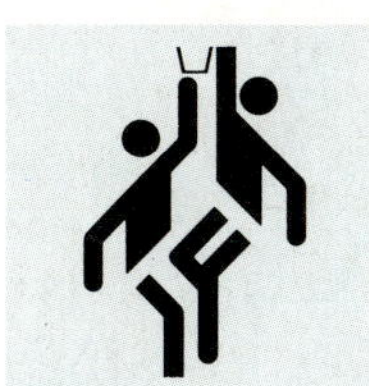
B

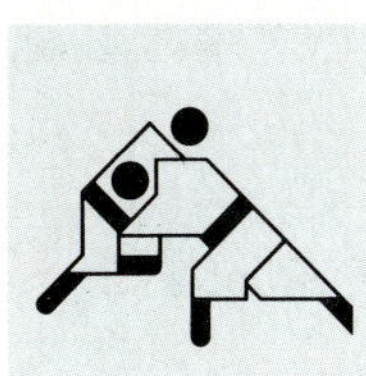
C

D

E

UNIT 4

A Saturday morning in York Road

a) It is Saturday morning in York Road, and at the moment it is lovely outside.

Mr Benson is making a coffee cake in the kitchen. He is putting coffee into the cake, but there is a lot of coffee on the kitchen table, too.

- Pam? Where's the big plate? I can't find it.
- It's in the cupboard, Jim. Why?
- I'm making a coffee cake.
- Jenny can help you.
- No, thanks, Pam. I can do it.

David and Jenny are going into town. Jenny has got some 'Friends of the Earth' posters for shops in the centre of Bristol.

- It's late, Jenny. Hurry up.
- I'm coming, David.

Mrs Benson is sitting at the table in the dining room. She is learning some German phrases. She has got a job at Bristol Tourist Centre.

- What are you doing, Pam?
- I'm learning some German phrases.

Kevin and his mother are talking in the garden. Kevin is playing with Red.

- Kevin! You're wearing your good clothes! Don't play with Red in the garden.
- I'm going to the Bensons' house, Mum.
- What about your homework?
- Oh, Mum! I can do it later.

Tanja is unhappy. She cannot walk, so she is lying on the sofa. She is watching TV.

to learn	–	learning
to make	–	making
to put	–	putting
⚠ to lie	–	lying

b) Tanja's ankle is very painful.

Tanja: Mr Benson? Can you help me, please? … Mr Benson … ?

Mr Benson is not listening. He is in the kitchen, and he has got the radio on. He is not making a cake now, he is making hamburgers.

Mrs Benson is not learning German phrases now, she is reading the newspaper.

Mrs Benson: What's the matter, Tanja? What are you doing? Are you trying to move that armchair?
Tanja: Yes, I am. I'd like to put my leg up.
Mrs Benson: Just a minute. Let me help you. … Is that OK?
Tanja: Yes, thanks.

Kevin is in the Bensons' kitchen. He is talking to Mr Benson.

Kevin: Hello, Mr Benson. Are you making a snack?
Mr Benson: No, I'm not. I'm making hamburgers for this evening.
Kevin: Where's Tanja? Is she lying on the sofa?
Mr Benson: Yes, she is. She's watching TV. Go in and say hello. …
Kevin: Hi, Tanja. I've got something for you.
Tanja: Oh, Kevin, how nice! Thanks a lot.

Kevin has got a cassette for Tanja.

1 Right or wrong? (a)

1. Mr Benson is making sandwiches. – No, that's wrong. He is …
2. Mr Benson is putting chocolate into the cake.
3. Mrs Benson is sitting at the table in the kitchen.
4. Mrs Benson is learning some German phrases.
5. David and Jenny are going to the sports centre.
6. Kevin is playing with Red in the garden.
7. Tanja is watching Kevin.
8. Tanja is lying on her bed upstairs.

2 What are they doing? (b)

1. Is Mr Benson listening to the radio. – Yes, he is.
2. Is he making a cake? – No, he isn't.
3. Is he making hamburgers?
4. Is Mrs Benson learning German phrases?
5. Is she reading the newspaper?
6. Is Tanja trying to move the armchair?
7. Are Kevin and Mr Benson talking in the kitchen?
8. Is Mr Benson making tea?
9. Is Tanja lying on the floor?
10. Are Mr and Mrs Benson watching TV?

3 What are you doing?

Examples: What are you doing, Tanja? – I'm watching TV.
What are you doing, Mr and Mrs Benson? – We're talking about Germany.

4 Mr Gossip at the sports centre

Mr Gossip is the Browns' neighbour in York Road. He is outside the sports centre. He is talking to Mr Brown. He would like to know everything about the people at the centre, so he is asking questions.

Example:
Mr Gossip: What are the girls doing? Are they playing football?
Mr Brown: No, they aren't playing football. They're playing table-tennis.

5 A postcard to an English friend

It is Saturday afternoon. Write a postcard to a friend in England. Say what you and other members of your family are doing at the moment.
Begin like this: Hi, Susan,/Hi, Jeff, It's Saturday afternoon and …

B Later that morning

Mrs Schulz: How's your ankle now, love? Is it painful?

Tanja: Oh, it's not so bad, Mum, but I can't walk very far.

Mrs Schulz: Well, don't worry. You can stay at home for a day or two. … How are Mr and Mrs Benson?

Tanja: They're OK. They've got an invitation to Wales. Mrs Brown next door has got a brother there.

Jenny: *(from upstairs)* Are you still talking on the phone, Tanja? I *must* call Andy about my saxophone, and the band's waiting for me!

Mrs Schulz: Can't you go with them? You'd like Wales. It's nice.

Tanja: But not with this ankle, Mum. And the weather's not so good at the moment. There's a storm on the way. Mum, I must stop now. Can you call me tomorrow, at about 11? Is that all right? Bye, Mum.

Mr Benson: Oh, good, Tanja. I'd like to make a phone call. Now where's that number? Here we are. 625 … 139.

Jenny: Oh, Dad, *I'd* like to use the phone, and I'm late.

Mr Benson: I'm only calling Peter at the Aerospace Club. I've got a list of things for the club evening. Peter's waiting for it. … Oh, dear, he's not there. Jenny! The phone's free! …

(The phone is ringing.)

Mr Benson: Hello. Bristol 317 509. … Pamela! Pam! Telephone! It's your German teacher. … Sorry, Jenny.

Jenny: Oh, Dad! I'm so angry!

Mrs Benson: Pamela Benson speaking. Hello, Susanne … Have you got the name of that German book? … Good. Just a moment. I must find a pencil. 'Riktikes Deutsch' … Can you spell that, please? Yes, I'm writing it … . There. Is that right, Tanja?

Tanja: Ja, das ist richtig, Frau Benson. Sehr gut.

1 Questions

1. Who is on the phone before Mr Benson?
2. Is Tanja's ankle all right?
3. Why would Jenny like to make a phone call?
4. Why is Mr Benson calling Peter?
5. Why can't Jenny use the phone after that?
6. What is the Bensons' telephone number?
7. Why is Jenny angry?
8. Who is Susanne?
9. What is the name of the German book? Spell it in English.
10. Is it a lovely day?

⇄ 2 A phone call to a friend

Sandra: Bristol 672894.
David: Hello, Sandra.
Sandra: Hi, Dave.
David: Are you free this evening?
Sandra: Yes, I am. What can we do?
David: Let's go into Bristol.
Sandra: What about the café in Dock Street?
David: No, the music there isn't very good. There's a good film on at the Broadmead Cinema – 'The Spectator'.
Sandra: OK, that's a good idea. When is it on?
David: At half past seven.
Sandra: Let's say a quarter past seven outside the cinema, OK?
David: All right, a quarter past seven. Bye, Sandra.
Sandra: Bye.

Role Play *Phone a friend and talk about plans for the afternoon/evening. Here are some words and phrases.*

Bristol 188945.
This is … speaking.
… speaking.

→ Hello, … .
Hi, … .

← Hello, … .
Hi, … .

→ Are you free today/this … ?
Have you got a lot of homework … ?

← Yes, I am. What can we do?
No, I haven't. What would you like to do?

→ Let's go …
Let's play …
I'd like to …

← No, … . What about … ?
Not today. The weather's not very good. – There's … .

→ OK, that's a good idea. When is it?
All right. When can you be there?

← At seven o'clock/a quarter past … / half past … / a quarter to …

→ Let's say …
I can be there at …
See you at …

Bye.

← All right./OK./Bye, … .

C Numbers and colours

a)

0 oh	1	2	3	4	5	6	7	8	9
10 ten	11 eleven	12	13	14	15	16	17	18	19
20 twenty	21	22 twenty-two	23	24	25	26	27	28	29
30 thirty	31	32	33 thirty-three	34	35	36	37	38	39
40 forty	41	42	43	44 forty-four	45	46	47	48	49
50 fifty	51	52	53	54	55 fifty-five	56	57	58	59
60 sixty	61	62	63	64	65	66 sixty-six	67	68	69
70 seventy	71	72	73	74	75	76	77 seventy-seven	78	79
80 eighty	81	82	83	84	85	86	87	88 eighty-eight	89
90 ninety	91	92	93	94	95	96	97	98	99 ninety-nine
100 a/one hundred	101								
200 two hundred									
1000 a/one thousand									

b) *Now read these numbers:* 34; 48; 55; 69; 72; 87; 93; 111; 561; 717; 999

1 What colour is it?

What colour is an apple, milk, coffee, a table-tennis ball, Tanja's cat, a Bristol bus ...?
Make lists of red, green, white, brown, ... things.

⟨2 Let's sing a song: I can sing a rainbow⟩

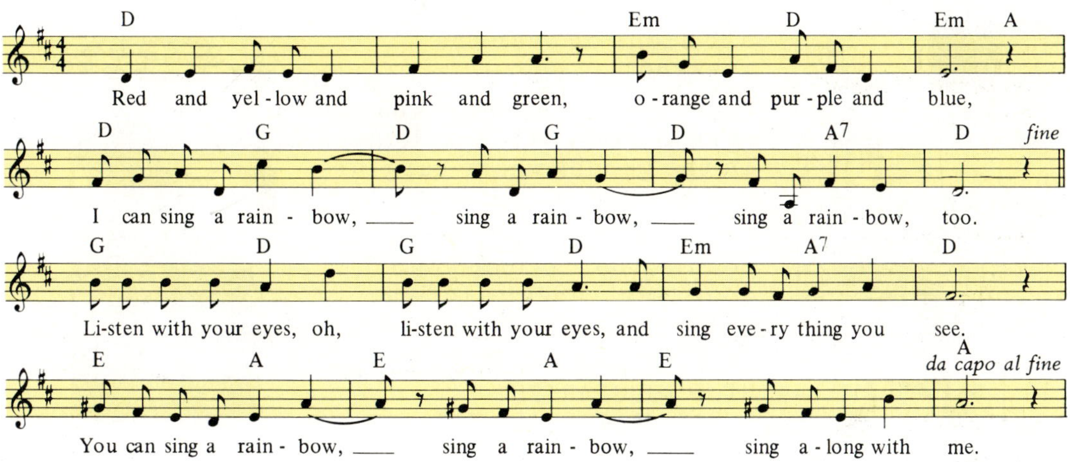

D A message from the police

a) Tanja and Jenny are alone in the house. Mr and Mrs Benson are away in Wales for the weekend and David is out. It is dark and the weather is very bad now. A nasty wind is blowing outside. The window is open and the wind is blowing the evening newspaper round the living room.

"Why are you shutting the window, Tanja?"

"It's the wind. Can't you hear it? – Hey, look at this message from the police in the newspaper. It's about burglars and burglaries in Bristol."

"Shh – I can't look now!"

"What are you doing anyway?"

"I'm writing something special for our school magazine about 'Friends of the Earth'. I can't write *and* read the paper."

"OK, OK."

b)

HELP THE POLICE IN BRISTOL

There are a lot of burglaries in Bristol and its suburbs every month. Please help us:

Lock all outside doors at night.

Don't put your door key where burglars can find it. Leave it with a neighbour.

Away from home this weekend? Tell your neighbours.

Switch the light on in the hall when you are out for the evening and switch it off when you are back, but don't leave lights on all night or over the weekend.

Don't leave bedroom windows open and don't leave ladders in the garden where burglars can see them.

<ins>A special message for old people:</ins> Don't open your door to strangers late at night.

HELP THE POLICE IN BRISTOL –
STOP BURGLARIES.
DON'T WAIT – CALL US.

1 Alone at home (a)

Read the sentences and ask your partner two or three questions about them. Work in pairs.
Example: – Where are Tanja and Jenny?
– They're alone in the house.
– Why are Tanja and Jenny ... ?
– Because .... .

1. Tanja and Jenny are alone in the house.
2. Mr and Mrs Benson are away in Wales.
3. David is out.
4. The wind is blowing the newspaper round the living room.
5. Tanja is shutting the window.
6. There is a police message in the newspaper.
7. Jenny is writing something for her school magazine.

2 Stop burglaries (b)

a) *Remember these things:*

Don't leave Don't put Tell Switch on Lock Switch off	the hall light your doors your neighbours your keys ladders	where when	burglars can see them. you are away from home. you are back. burglars can find them. you are out for the evening.

b) *Now make up a poster/special message for a school or sports centre: 'Stop Burglaries'.*

3 The 'Friends of the Earth' meeting

Jenny has got a 'Friends of the Earth' meeting at school. The members of the group are talking about a new information stand in Broadmead Shopping Centre.

a) *Say what they* can / can't / must / mustn't / needn't *do.*

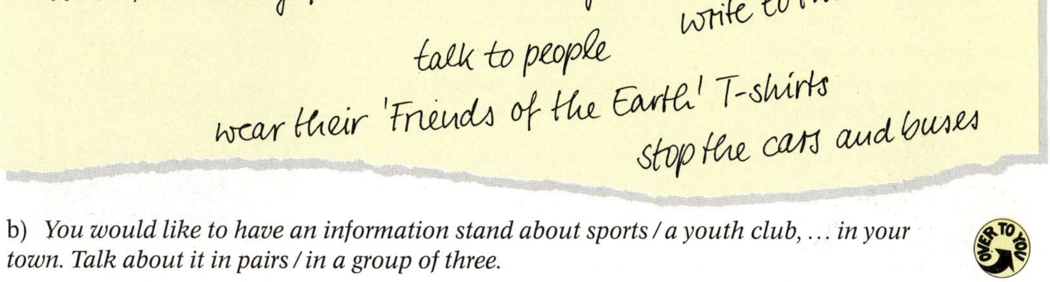

b) *You would like to have an information stand about sports / a youth club, ... in your town. Talk about it in pairs / in a group of three.*

E The storm

a) It is eleven o'clock on Saturday evening and there is a nasty storm outside. Tanja is repairing Jenny's cassette recorder. She is sitting on the sofa, and she has got all the pieces on the coffee table next to her. The TV is on. They are showing a film, but Tanja is not watching it. Jenny is playing the saxophone in the dining room. Red is asleep in front of the TV.

"Jenny? I can't find one of the pieces. Can you come and look?"
"Just a minute, Tanja. I'm practising a difficult phrase …"
Jenny is now in the living room, near the back window.
"Hey, Tanja. There's somebody in the Browns' garden."
"It must be Kevin."
"Quiet, Red! No, Kevin's still at the party."
"He's doing something in their garden shed."
"What's he doing? Let's go into the kitchen and see what's happening. Switch the light off first."
"Tanja, he's taking a ladder out of their shed and he's putting it against the wall of their house."
"It must be a burglar. – Oh, Jenny – that police message:
'Stop Burglaries. Don't Wait – Call the Police.' We must phone the police."
"OK, but then let's go outside and see what's going on. Come on, Tanja. This is exciting!"

b) The two girls are out in the Bensons' back garden. The storm is really nasty now and the wind is very strong.
"Oh, look, Jenny. It *is* Kevin."
"Kevin! What are you doing up there?"
"You needn't look at me like that, Jenny. I'm not a burglar. Can you come and hold the ladder for me? There's a loose chimney pot on our roof. It's dangerous."
"You're crazy, Kevin. Come down again. You mustn't climb the ladder in this wind. Call the firemen. They can look at it. It's their job."

The police – a policewoman and a policeman – and the firemen are there in ten minutes.
"Hello, what's happening here? What about the man with the ladder in your back garden?"
"Oh, that's our ladder and I … ."
"So you're not a burglar. It's a job for the firemen."
"Yes, sorry …"
Tanja, Jenny and Kevin are now watching what the firemen are doing.
"Oh look, Jenny. They're switching on the big lights. There's a fireman on the ladder."
"It's going up now. The fireman's near the chimney pot. It *is* loose, Kevin's right. … The fireman's got the chimney pot and he's coming down with it now."
There are other loose chimney pots in York Road, so the firemen have got a lot of work.

Jenny, Tanja and Kevin are back in the Bensons' living room.
"Woof!"
"Oh, Red! Can't you move?"
"What's the matter, Tanja?"
"It's the piece from your cassette recorder. Red's sitting on it!"

1 Saturday evening (a)

Complete the sentences.

1. It is eleven o'clock and the weather ....
2. Tanja is not watching TV because ....
3. She is looking for one of the pieces but ....
4. Jenny cannot look for the missing piece because ....
5. Now she is near the back window of the living room and ....
6. Red is at the Bensons' house because ....
7. The man has got the Browns' ladder, so he ....
8. Jenny and Tanja would like to stop the burglary, so ....

2 The loose chimney pot (b)

What is right here? Put the sentences together.

1. The storm
2. Kevin is up
3. The chimney pot on the Browns' roof
4. Kevin and the girls must
5. The firemen and the police
6. The police would like to
7. The firemen have got
8. Red is still

a) hear about the burglar.
b) call the firemen.
c) a lot of work in York Road.
d) on the ladder.
e) in the Bensons' living room.
f) is very nasty now.
g) are there in ten minutes.
h) is loose and so it is dangerous.

3 Titles

'The storm' is in five parts. Can you find titles for them?
Example: Late on Saturday evening

4 Wendy and Tanja

Wendy is Sandra's friend at Horfield Sports Centre.
She is talking to Tanja on the phone.
What are they saying?

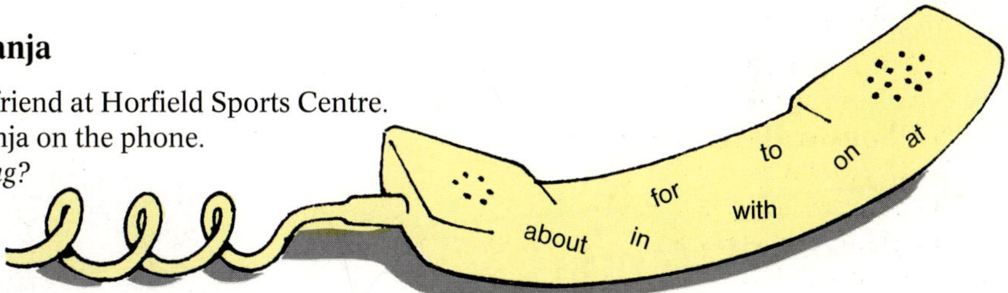

Tanja: Bristol 317 509.
Wendy: Hello, Tanja. This is Wendy speaking.
Tanja: Oh, hello, Wendy.
Wendy: What are you doing ... the moment? Are you watching the film ... TV?
Tanja: No, I'm not. I'm ... the living room. I'm listening ... a sports programme ... the radio.
Wendy: I'm sorry ... your accident.
Tanja: Oh, my ankle's OK now.
Wendy: Is Mrs Benson ... home? I'd like to talk ... her.
Tanja: No, she isn't here today. Mr and Mrs Benson are ... Wales ... the weekend.
Wendy: Oh yes, that's right. They're ... Wales ... the Browns. Well, what ... David? Is he ... home?
Tanja: No, he isn't. He's ... a friend's house. But Jenny is here. She's upstairs. She's listening ... some music.
Wendy: Oh, there's somebody ... the door. I must stop now. Bye.

5 On the farm in Wales

The Bensons and the Browns are in Wales. They are staying with Mrs Brown's brother, Mr Davey, and his family. Everybody is outside in the garden.

What are they doing? Describe the picture.

⟨6 Phone calls in Britain⟩

EMERGENCY SERVICES

FIRE · POLICE · AMBULANCE

CALL THE OPERATOR
DIAL 999

Tell the operator: fire, police or ambulance.
Give your number.
Wait for the answer of the emergency service.
Then give the address and other information.

You are alone at your friend's home in England. You can see a man in the back garden next door. He has got a ladder and he is climbing into a room upstairs. Call the police. Make up the dialogue.

7 Look, listen and say

a) *Read the words and put them in the correct column.*

[w]	[v]	[f]
window	volleyball	family

four / one / what / fifteen / even / Kevin / away / move / far / why / over / verb / woman / have / painful

b) *Read and link.*

This is a message for old people.
Lock all outside doors at night.
Don't open your front door.
And don't talk to a stranger.
There are two messages in the newspapers.

8 Mr Gossip from York Road

Mr Gossip, the Browns' neighbour, is talking to Mrs Morgan in the shop at the corner of York Road. Kevin is in the shop, too.

Mr Gossip: Thank you, Mrs Morgan. Oh, hm – that new girl in York Road. She's from Switzerland. Her name is Sonja Schweizer.
Mrs Morgan: Oh, that's interesting.
Kevin: But that's not right, Mr Gossip. She's from ... and her name is ... .
Mr Gossip: Her father is Swiss and her mother is German. She can't speak English.
Kevin: No, Mr Gossip ... .
Mr Gossip: She's got a broken leg. She's in Southmead Hospital at the moment.
Kevin: That's not right ... .
Mr Gossip: She's staying with the Whites. The Bensons are in London this weekend. They're staying with a friend.
Kevin: Wrong again, Mr Gossip ... .

9 Opposites

a) *Find the opposites. Example:* left – right

in front of	– ?	big	– ?	nasty	– ?	front door	– ?
on	– ?	wrong	– ?	to switch on	– ?	long	– ?
upstairs	– ?	black	– ?	day	– ?	here	– ?
questions	– ?	good	– ?	morning	– ?	indoor	– ?
old	– ?	to open	– ?	away	– ?		

b) *Now take the opposites and make sentences with them.*
Example: In the Bensons' house the kitchen is downstairs, but the toilet is upstairs.

⟨10 Listening comprehension: The shed⟩

1. What time is it?
2. Where is Whisky Bravo going?
3. What is Alpha Fox?
4. Where is Alpha Fox going?
5. What can the policeman see in the shed?
6. What are the children doing?

UNIT 5

A In and around Bristol

a)

Use your local shops and post offices.

THE CORNER SHOP
Your friendly local shop.

COME TO WESTON-SUPER-MARE
Sun – seaside – fine beaches – fun

BEST PRICES IN TOWN
GAMES COMPUTERS, PCs and MONITORS

b) Morgan's Corner Shop in Filton is at the corner of York Road and Horfield Road. It is also a post office. The man at the post office counter is Mr Wilson. He can sell stamps for your postcards and letters from 9 to 5, but not from 1 to 2 o'clock. (There are special rules for small post offices. For example, they are not open on one afternoon a week or on Saturday afternoons.)
Mr and Mrs Morgan's shop is open every day from 8 in the morning to 9 in the evening. On the shelves you can find tea, coffee, bread, fruit and other kinds of food. They have also got milk and butter. There are newspapers, cards, postcards, writing paper and pencils, too. The Morgans can buy all these things at the cash-and-carry.

c) Mrs Morgan is from Wales. In her shop she has also got romantic books, and Jenny is buying some for old Mrs Dale in York Road. She is buying a few things for her mother, too: a bottle of milk, a loaf of brown bread, half a pound of butter, a bar of Swiss chocolate (that's for Tanja) and a packet of tea. Tanja is with her. She is making a cassette shelf for Kevin and she'd like to buy some glue. Mrs Morgan has got everything for them.

Mrs Morgan: That's £4.95.
Jenny: Here's £5.
Mrs Morgan: And here's your change – 5p.

1 In and around your town (a)

Make up slogans for the shops in your town or for your town.

Examples:
Best shop in town for sports shoes and sports clothes.
Come to ... – a town for young people.

2 Shops and post offices (b)

What can you buy/get in a corner shop/ a shopping centre/a computer shop/ a post office?
You can buy ... but you can't buy ... .
You can get ... but you can't get ... .
They've got ... but they haven't got ... .

Compare shops in Britain and Germany.

3 What goes together?

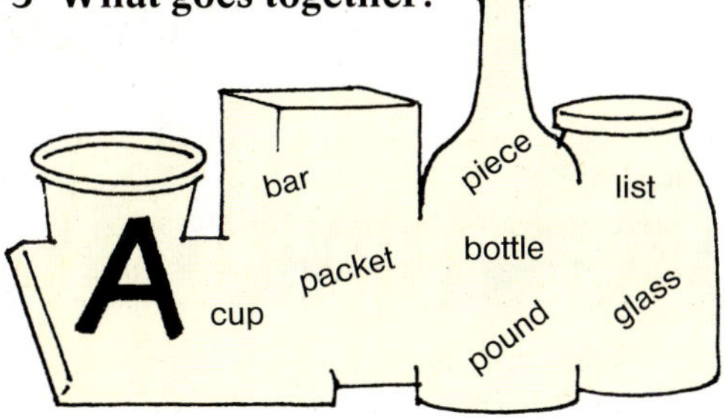

Example: a bottle of milk *How many can you find?*

B Homework for the Morgans and Jenny

a) It is cash-and-carry day for the Corner Shop, and Mr and Mrs Morgan are looking at their shelves. What have they got? What haven't they got?

Mrs Morgan: Hm, where's my list? Apples ... How many Granny Smiths have we got, John? Can you look?

Mr Morgan: Just a minute ... we haven't got many.

Mrs Morgan: Right. Let's buy some Granny Smiths. What about bread?

Mr Morgan: We haven't got any brown bread, but we've got some white loaves ... one big loaf and four small loaves.

Mrs Morgan: That's five white ... Mr Smith can bring some brown loaves in the morning. What about butter? How much butter is there on that shelf, John?

Mr Morgan: We haven't got much English butter, but we've got a few pounds of that butter from the other cash-and-carry.

Mrs Morgan: Some English butter ... .

Mr Morgan: Have we got any Swiss chocolate – for that German girl at Number 10?

Mrs Morgan: We haven't got any bars of Swiss chocolate, but we've got a lot of English chocolate. ... Oh, hello, Mr Fletcher.

Man: Good evening, Mrs Morgan. Hello, Mr Morgan. I've got some nice tourist postcards for you today.

Mrs Morgan: Can I see them? There aren't many tourists in Filton. ... They're very nice. How much are they?

Man: 25p each, or two pounds for a packet of ten.

Mrs Morgan: That's a lot. How many pictures are there in a packet?

Man: Bristol, Weston-super-Mare, Bath, three pictures of each, and one picture of the 'Great Britain'.

Mrs Morgan: Yes, very nice. Can I have two packets, please? Oh, hello, Jenny.

Jenny: Have you got any old newspapers, Mrs Morgan? They're for my homework.

Mrs Morgan: Of course. Look behind that door.

b) Jenny is doing her homework now. It is about roads and traffic in Bristol. She is sitting at her desk, but there is nothing in her exercise book at the moment. Tanja is lying on the floor and is reading old newspapers for her. She cannot find anything about traffic in Bristol, but there is something about London.

"Can't you find anything about roads in Bristol?"

"There's something in the 'Letters' here. Somebody in Horfield has got an idea for special bus roads ... ."

"But nobody's got any really good ideas for my homework .... Look for something on the front page. Isn't anybody doing anything about the traffic in Bristol?"

"Well, I can't find anything. Hey, Jenny, look! Here's a picture of somebody in Broadmead Shopping Centre. She's putting something on a wall – it's a 'Friends of the Earth' poster – and there's a policeman behind her. The girl is like you, Jenny!"

"It *is* me, Tanja! Dad is very angry about that photo!"

There is nothing in the newspapers for Jenny's homework.

1 Mrs Baker (a)

Put in some *or* any.

Mrs Morgan: Hello, Mrs Baker. What would you like?
Mrs Baker: Let me see. I'd like … tea and … milk.
Mrs Morgan: Come over to the other counter. A packet of tea?
Mrs Baker: Yes, please. And a bottle of milk. Have you got … brown bread today?
Mrs Morgan: Oh, yes. There's … special brown bread on that shelf over there.
Mrs Baker: And I'd like … Swiss chocolate for my children. Have you got … ?
Mrs Morgan: I haven't got … Swiss chocolate today, but this English chocolate is very nice. It's new.
Mrs Baker: Well, I'd like to try … of it.
Mrs Morgan: Is that everything?
Mrs Baker: Have you got … postcards with pictures of Filton?
Mrs Morgan: Sorry, there aren't … postcards of Filton. But I've got … of Bristol.
Mrs Baker: Well, give me three then. That's everything now. Thank you very much.

2 In the corner shop (a)

Ask and answer questions about the corner shop with 'How much' and 'How many'. Work in pairs.
Examples: – How many apples have they got?
– They haven't got many.
– How much brown bread is there?
– …

3 Morgan's Corner Shop (a)

Read the text again and look at the picture on page 59. Now describe Morgan's Corner Shop.
Use the words 'some', 'any', 'a lot of' 'much' and 'many'.
You can begin like this: There are a lot of things in the shop. On the left …

4 The traffic in Bristol is awful! (b)

This is part of a letter to a Bristol newspaper.
Complete the letter and put in:

Isn't … doing … about the traffic in Bristol? … must begin to do …! And we must do … about it *now!* But … has got … good ideas. I can't do … – I'm an old man – but I've got … ideas. … must take a bus into town. We mustn't have … big car parks in the city centre. Buses must take … from the car parks into the city centre. Please do … now – because a lot of people are doing … about it!

5 English money

a)

Notes:

£50

£20

£10

£5

Coins:

1p

2p

5p

10p

20p

50p

£1

(Reduced in size)

b) You would like to buy some stamps, books, computer games, Swiss chocolate, saxophone music or postcards.

Make up dialogues and use the words some, any, something, anything, *etc.*

C David's new computer

a) David has got a job with computers at a big bank in Bristol. On two days a week he has got computer classes at their training centre. He has only got a small CompuStar computer at home, but he is a clever young man, and he would like to buy a new computer – a PC. He is very interested in computer graphics. You cannot do any interesting computer graphics on a small computer. He has not got enough money for a PC, so he is trying to sell his CompuStar.

b) David is looking at the evening newspaper. He is interested in one of the ads. It is an interesting offer from a computer shop in the centre of Bristol.

Shop assistant: Lawrence Road Computers.
David: Hello, I'd like to speak to John Wilson, please.
Assistant: Speaking.
David: I've got a second-hand CompuStar and monitor and I'd like to buy a new PC. How much can you offer for my old computer and monitor?
Assistant: Well, I'd like to see your computer. Can you bring it to the shop?
David: Yes, of course.
Assistant: We're open until 6 o'clock, but we're very busy in the afternoons.
David: About 5 o'clock? Is that OK?
Assistant: That's fine. See you later. Goodbye.
David: Bye.

1 Comprehension (a)

1. Where has David got a job?
2. What is he interested in?
3. What would he like to buy?
4. Has he got enough money for a PC?
5. What is he trying to do?

2 Right or wrong? (b)

1. David is looking at the ads on a notice-board.
2. He would like to speak to John Wilson.
3. David would like to buy a second-hand PC.
4. The assistant would like to see David's CompuStar.
5. The shop is open until 8 o'clock in the evening.
6. They are very busy in the mornings.

D At Lawrence Road Computers

a) There are a lot of people in the big computer shop in Lawrence Road and only a few shop assistants. David has not got much time, and the assistants have got very little time for David and his computer. One of the assistants is showing a new computer to a young man.

Young man: Can't you show me any second-hand games computers?
Assistant: Well, we've got a few second-hand computers downstairs. But we've also got some new games computers over there for £150.
Young man: That's too much for me. I've only got about £90.
Assistant: I'm sorry, I can't offer you anything at that price. Try the computer shop in Broadmead Centre.
David: Hello. I've got a second-hand computer and monitor here. How much can you offer me for it?
Assistant: Let's see. Hm ... an old CompuStar. Very few people are interested in these things today. I can't offer you very much. £50.
David: Only £50! The best prices in Bristol?! Can't you give me £100 for it? It's only 15 months old and the monitor is very good.
Assistant: No, I'm sorry.
Young man: Excuse me ... Can you come outside for a moment and bring your computer with you?

b) *Young man:* My name's Rajiv Pratap. I'm interested in your computer and monitor. How much are they?
David: Hello, I'm David Benson. I'd like £100 for them.
Young man: That's too much for me. I can't offer you anything like that. It's an old computer.
David: It's only fifteen months old. What can you give me for it?
Young man: Fifteen months is a long time in computers. A lot of people have got CompuStars at home, but few people are buying them now. I can only give you £80 for it.
David: That's not very much. Why are you interested in a CompuStar computer anyway?
Young man: I'm writing some programs for games computers like the CompuStar. There's very little good software for it.
David: And that's why you're offering me so little for it?
Young man: Well, I can offer you a little more. Let's say £90.
David: OK then.

1 Why? (a)

1. Why is David in the computer shop?
2. Why have the assistants only got very little time for David and his computer?
3. Why can't the young man buy a games computer from Lawrence Road Computers?
4. Why can't the assistants offer David much for his CompuStar?
5. Why would the young man like to talk to David outside?

2 Tony and his computer (b)

Complete the text with few, a few, little, a little.

Tony is interested in computers. He would like to sell his CompuStar and buy a new PC but he has very … money. He has got … money at his bank but it is not enough for a new PC. Tony has got … computer magazines at home but there are … 'Wanted' ads for CompuStars. Lawrence Road Computers have got a special offer. The shop is only … streets from the city centre. Tony has got very … time because he must play football for his sports club at half past six. The assistant can only offer Tony … money for his old computer because very … people are interested in CompuStars. A young man in the shop would like to buy Tony's computer and can offer him … more.

3 In the shopping centre

a) *Look at the pictures and make sentences with 'to sell', 'to give' and 'to offer'.*

Example: The shop assistant is showing Tanja some postcards.

Now you would like to stress the indirect object:
The shop assistant is offering a computer **to a young woman** (not to a young man).
The shop assistant is showing some postcards **to Kevin and his friend**.

b) *Now use pronouns. Example:* The shop assistant is offering **her** a computer.

4 Role Play Your friend's birthday

It is your friend's birthday. You would like to give him/her a present. What can you buy? Have you got enough money? Perhaps you can sell something to somebody at school or to a second-hand shop.

Make up a dialogue and use the verbs 'to give', 'to buy', 'to sell'.

E On Lundy Island

a) It is ten o'clock on Saturday morning. Tanja would like to go to the seaside. Jenny is looking at her 'Friends of the Earth' magazine. There is an interesting article in it about the sea birds of Devon. She would like to go there, but it is a long way from Bristol and they have not got the car. David is only interested in the computer shops in Bristol. Kevin has got a good idea. There are fast trains from Bristol to Weston. Weston is a seaside town and perhaps Jenny can watch sea birds there. There are some good computer shops in Weston, so there is something for David, too.
There are a lot of people on the beach in Weston, but there are not many interesting sea birds. One of the people on the beach is a young man with a 'Friends of the Earth' T-shirt. He has got a camera and binoculars. It is Rajiv Pratap.

Jenny: Hello, Friend of the Earth!
Rajiv: Hello.
David: Oh, it's you – Rajiv! This is my sister Jenny, our German friend Tanja from Hanover, and our next-door neighbour Kevin Brown. Rajiv has got my old CompuStar computer.
Rajiv: Nice to meet you all. But what on earth are you doing here in Weston?
David: Oh, well ....
Jenny: I'm very interested in bird-watching and we ....
Rajiv: Bird-watching? There aren't many interesting birds here in Weston. Look, I've got a good idea. How about Lundy Island? I can show you the sea birds there. It's not too far and it's a wonderful place.
Jenny: Lundy Island? What a great idea!

Tourists on their way to Lundy Island

Lundy Island is famous for its puffins

b) Rajiv is right – Lundy Island *is* a wonderful place for birds. There are no cars on the island and only a few tourists. Lundy is the home of thousands of sea birds and is famous for its puffins. The island has even got a small post office and special stamps with a puffin on them.

Jenny and Rajiv are looking at a map of Lundy Island. What a surprise! There is even a place with the name 'Jenny's Cove' on the island! It is not far, but David, Tanja and Kevin would like to stay near the harbour.

Half an hour later Rajiv and Jenny are at 'Jenny's Cove'. It is a fine place for bird-watching. There are some puffins' nests on the cliffs, and Jenny is looking at one of them through Rajiv's binoculars. Now she can see two men on the cliffs. They have got a bag with them. They are climbing from one nest to the next.

Jenny: Look at those people, Rajiv. I'm sure that they're taking some puffins' eggs!
Rajiv: Let me look. Give me the binoculars. Yes, you're right. That bag must be full of puffins' eggs! We must stop them. Hey – you down there! Put those eggs back!
Jenny: They can't hear anything, Rajiv. They're too far away.
Rajiv: And they're walking down to the beach now. That must be their boat. They're leaving! We can't stop them now.
Jenny: No, but we can show these photos to the police.
Rajiv: Photos?
Jenny: Yes, I've got three good photos of them near the nests on the cliffs, and one of the boat and its number: IL-324.

1 Filton, Weston and Lundy Island (a)

Complete the sentences.

1. Jenny is looking at her 'Friends of the Earth' magazine because … .
2. Jenny is interested in sea birds, so … .
3. David would like to go to the computer shops in Bristol, but … .
4. Weston is a seaside town, so Jenny … .
5. There are a lot of people on the beach, so … .
6. Jenny says, "Hello, Friend of the Earth" because … .
7. Rajiv would like to watch sea birds, so … .

2 The two men on the cliffs (b)

Look at the three pictures and describe what the people ***are doing*** *and what* ***is happening****.*

3 Sandra and David

Sandra and David are in a café in town.
Complete the dialogue with the words on the right.

Sandra: Let's have … tea and … cake.
David: Yes, good idea.
Waitress: Yes, please?
David: Have you got … chocolate cake?
Waitress: Sorry, love, we haven't got … today. But we've got … nice Swiss apple cake.
Sandra: A piece of apple cake and … tea, please.
David: I'd like … apple cake, too, and a glass of milk.
Waitress: OK.
David: What's the matter with you, Sandra?
Sandra: Oh, everything! I've got another year at school. … else has got a Saturday or weekend job, but … can offer me a job. There's … in Filton. I'd like to do … interesting but I haven't got … ideas – or … money.
David: But I've got enough money for us.
Sandra: That's your money, David!
David: OK, OK, there isn't … in Filton, but why not try in Westbury? Perhaps one of the shops in Westbury Road has got … for you. We can go there together.
Sandra: That's an idea.
David: Here's the Swiss apple cake!

⇄ 4 The school notice-board

Jenny and Kevin are looking at the ads on the school notice-board.

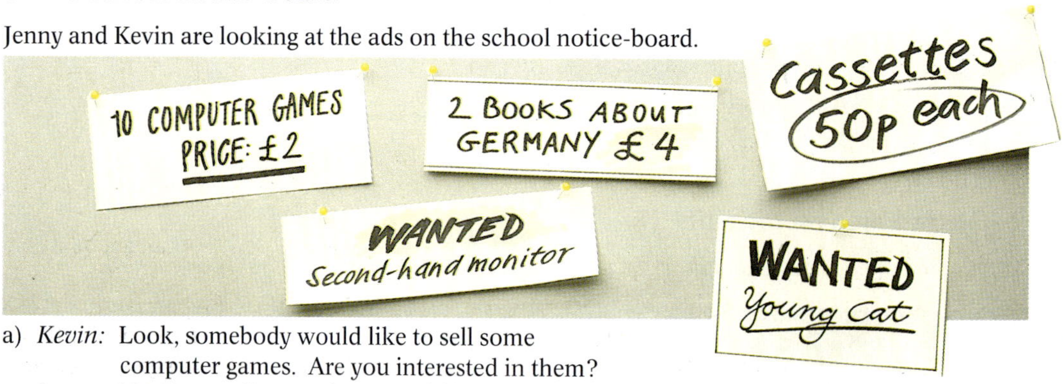

a) *Kevin:* Look, somebody would like to sell some computer games. Are you interested in them?
Jenny: No, I'm not, but I'm interested in …

Go on with their dialogue. You can use the following sentences:

I'd like to buy …	I wouldn't like to buy …
see …	have …
have …	I'm not looking for …
sell …	I'm not interested in …
I'm interested in …	I haven't got much / enough / any money …
I'm looking for …	

b) *You have got some old things at home. You would like to sell them. Write two or three ads for the notice-board.*

5 Look, listen and say

[-t] and [-d]

Fin**d** the righ**t** stree**t**.
Pu**t** the ca**t** on the be**d**.
This secon**d**-han**d** diske**tte** is no**t** goo**d**.
The bes**t** brea**d** is not whi**te**.

[-k] and [-g]

The bi**g** bla**ck** do**g** is having a sna**ck** under the des**k**.
Drin**k** mil**k** and thin**k** bi**g**.
Don't loo**k** at the bi**g** boo**k**.

[-p] and [-b]

Hel**p** to kee**p** the sho**p** in the subur**b** clean.
Don't sto**p** the grou**p** in the clu**b**.

6 Can you find the words?

1. You can buy a lot of things there. It is small and perhaps it is in a suburb.
2. There are a lot of shops in it.
3. He/She can help you when you would like to buy something.
4. They are on the wall and you can put things on them.
5. You can write it on a piece of paper – what you would like to buy, for example.
6. You can put this in the newspaper when you would like to buy or sell something.
7. It is not new but you can still use it.
8. To show something to someone and to say what the price is.

Explain these words: 1. post office 2. training centre 3. beach 4. island 5. harbour

⟨7 Listening comprehension: Mrs Dale's books⟩

There are ten 'scenes' in the story.
Put them in the right order.

(9) 1. They are giving the books to Mrs Dale.
(1) 2. Mrs Morgan is putting the things for Mrs Benson in a bag.
(5) 3. Tanja is reading 'An Invitation for Jenny'.
(8) 4. Jenny is giving Mrs Morgan the money for the books.
(6) 5. Jenny is trying to read 'An Invitation for Jenny'.
(4) 6. Mrs Morgan is telling them about the new books.
(3) 7. Jenny is asking Mrs Morgan about Mrs Dale's books.
(2) 8. Tanja is holding the bag for Jenny.
(7) 9. Tanja is reading 'The House on the Island'.
(10.) Mrs Dale is giving Tanja some chocolate.

UNIT 6

A British schools

a) Most British schools for boys and girls from 11 to 18 are comprehensive schools. Schools in Britain are different from German schools. At German schools pupils can wear jeans and a T-shirt. At some British schools pupils must wear a special school uniform: for example, a blazer with the school badge, a white shirt or blouse, a school tie (sometimes for the girls, too!), grey trousers or a skirt and a school pullover. Other schools are not strict about uniform; pupils may wear trousers, shirts, blouses and skirts of different colours, but normally there is a school tie or a badge. This is not 'school uniform', it is 'school dress'. But at a lot of schools there is no school uniform.

b) Jenny's school is Filton Comprehensive. It has got 1100 pupils. Jenny is normally at school from 8.45 to 3.45. There is a cafeteria at school, so she often has lunch there, or sometimes at a snack bar. She is usually home at 4 o'clock.

Jenny and Tanja are in the Bensons' back garden.

Jenny: How long is *your* school day, Tanja?
Tanja: Well, I have breakfast at seven o'clock. We have lessons every morning, of course, and one afternoon a week, but most afternoons are free.
Jenny: You're lucky! I'd like four free afternoons. And I'd also like a free Saturday this week.
Tanja: But there are never any lessons on Saturdays at British schools.
Jenny: You're right, but we've got a hockey match. It's OK for you, Tanja. Hockey's fun for you. And tomorrow afternoon there's a practice for the school band. It's just too much!
Tanja: But the saxophone's your favourite activity!
Jenny: Yes, it is. Well, I'm lucky I haven't got much work today. Just a French word list!

1 Right or wrong? (a)

1. Not many British schools are comprehensive schools.
2. German and British schools are not different.
3. In Germany pupils may wear jeans at school.
4. At some British schools pupils must wear a blazer and a white shirt or blouse.
5. All British schools are very strict about school uniform.
6. Boys and girls at British schools must normally wear a school tie or badge.
7. School dress is not different from school uniform.

2 What are they wearing? (a)

a) *What are Jenny and her friends wearing? Look at the picture on the right.*
b) *And what are your friends wearing today?*

3 Jenny and her school (b)

Complete the following text.

How is Jenny's school day? It is from 8.45 to 3.45, so she has … in the mornings and afternoons. She has … at about eight o'clock. It is a long day at school, so she often has … in the … at school. She is … home again at 4 o'clock.

She would … a free Saturday this week but she must play hockey. Sometimes there is a … for the band after school. Jenny can play the saxophone – it is her … … . Today Jenny is … because she has not got much … for school. She has only got a list of new … words.

4 Your school (b)

Write a short text about your school.
You can begin like this:
My school is … . It has got … pupils.
Go on.

B At home and at school

a) Jenny's school is not far from home, so she usually walks to school. At 10 York Road, the day normally starts at a quarter past seven. Jenny's dad always sings in the bathroom.

Mr Benson: 'Oh, what a wonderful morning, Oh, what a ....'
Jenny: Not that song again, Dad.
David: Hurry up, Dad. It's twenty past seven. My bus goes in twenty-five minutes!
Mr Benson: 'Oh what a wonderful morning ....'

David always tries to use the bathroom first because Mr Benson's bus goes at eight and his bus goes at a quarter to. But David often stays in bed too long, so Mr Benson uses the bathroom first. Mrs Benson leaves home at a quarter to nine. At the Tourist Information Centre they start work at a quarter past nine.

Everybody has something different for breakfast, and they often leave their plates and cups on the table when they go. The TV is always on at breakfast time but nobody watches it. It just tells them the time.

Every morning at half past eight Jenny hurries down York Road. Sometimes she goes into the corner shop, says 'Hello' to Mrs Morgan and buys something there. She usually meets some friends, and then they walk to Filton Comprehensive.

to walk	–	she walks
to use	–	he uses
to watch	–	she watches
to try	–	he tries
to hurry	–	he hurries
to buy	–	she buys
to have	–	it has
to go	–	it goes [gəʊz]
to say	–	he says [sez]
to do	–	she does [dʌz]

b) A lot of the pupils at Filton Comprehensive go to the school cafeteria for lunch. Sometimes Jenny does not want to have lunch at school, so she takes a bus into Westbury with some friends and they have a snack lunch. They do not stay in the snack bar all lunchtime. On nice days they do not leave Westbury until half past one. They often walk round Westbury or sit in the sun.

Every week, Jenny goes to her 'Friends of the Earth' meeting after school and one day a week the members of the school band meet for a practice. On those days Jenny does not get home until six o'clock.

1 Jenny and the Bensons (a) *Put together the following sentences.*

1. Jenny usually walks to school
2. Mr Benson uses the bathroom first
3. Mr Benson always sings 'Oh, what a wonderful morning!' in the bathroom
4. Mrs Benson always leaves the house at a quarter to nine
5. They often leave their plates and cups on the table
6. Jenny usually meets some friends at the corner of York Road

a) because it is his favourite song.
b) because she starts work at a quarter past.
c) because they have not got much time.
d) because David often stays in bed too long.
e) because she wants to talk to them on the way to school.
f) because Filton Comprehensive is not far from the Bensons' house.

2 Jenny and her friends (b)

Correct these sentences.

1. Jenny always has lunch at school.
2. She takes a bus into the centre of Bristol and has a snack there.
3. Jenny and her friends always stay in the snack bar until half past one.
4. On nice days they go to Horfield Sports Centre.
5. Jenny goes to her 'Friends of the Earth' meeting at lunchtime.
6. The members of the school band meet in Westbury for their practice.
7. On those days Jenny gets home at 5 o'clock.

3 Verbs

Put the verbs from text a) on page 72 in the right columns.

	[s]	[z]	[ɪz]
Example:	she walks	he sings	he uses
	...	...	...

4 Kevin

Say what Kevin does and what he doesn't do.

Examples: Kevin usually has … .

C Tanja's first day at an English school

a) It is Tanja's first day at Jenny's school. They are in the classroom before the first lesson. Jenny's friends have got a lot of questions about school in Germany.

Barbara: Do you like school in Germany, Tanja?
Tanja: Yes, I do. Well, I normally like it. But it's different from school in England.
Melanie: Do you wear school uniform at your school?
Tanja: No, we don't. We wear jeans and T-shirts and things like that.
Peter: Do you go to school every afternoon?
Tanja: No, we don't. We only have lessons in the mornings and one afternoon a week.
Nivruti: Do your teachers usually give you a lot of homework?
Tanja: Yes, they do. We have homework every day, but we don't get any at the weekend.
Patrick: Does your school offer many activities?
Tanja: Well, there's a camera club and ... .
Peter: That's not very much! Does it have many sports teams then?
Tanja: No, it doesn't. I play hockey at school, but we don't have any football teams.
Melanie: Do many girls play football in Germany?
Tanja: I don't really know. Do girls in England play football?
Melanie: Yes, they do. Barbara and I would like to. We want to play at Horfield Sports Centre.

b) *Tanja:* What time do you have lunch?
Barbara: Lunch is at 12.
Tanja: And where do you go?
Barbara: Well, the food at the school cafeteria is not too bad. I usually go there, but not always.
Tanja: What do they have there?
Patrick: Oh, things like hamburgers, sandwiches ... .
Tanja: What else do they sell? Do they have fruit, too?
Patrick: Yes, they do – usually.
Tanja: And when do we start school after lunch?
Melanie: At a quarter to two.
Tanja: Why don't you go home for lunch?
Melanie: My mum and dad are at work all day, that's why.
Patrick: Hey, everyone. Grey's on the way!

1 Tanja and her school (a)

Ask questions with 'to do'. Your partner can answer the questions with short answers. Are all the answers in the text?

1. … Tanja … school in Germany?
2. … she … school uniform?
3. … Tanja and her German friends … lessons only in the mornings?
4. … the teachers … homework every day?
5. … the school … many activities?
6. … it … a school band?
7. … the pupils at Tanja's school … football?
8. … many girls in Germany … football?
9. … the school … a volleyball team?

2 Questions about school (b)

You meet a boy/girl from Britain and ask him/her questions about school there. Use the question words 'What', 'Where', 'What time', 'What else' and 'Why'. You can start like this:

You: Where do you go to school?
Boy/Girl: …

3 Partner work

Example:

- Do you like sports?
- Yes, I do./No, I don't.

like sports/school/English/…
normally wear what you like
sometimes walk to school
go home for lunch
sometimes speak English at home
know London/any English games/…
play football/hockey/…

4 Your day

Tell your friends about your day.
Start like this: I/We normally get up at …

normally get up at
usually go to school at
wear … at school
school normally begins at
normally have … lessons a day/a week
often … after school
sometimes … in the evening
don't … in the evening

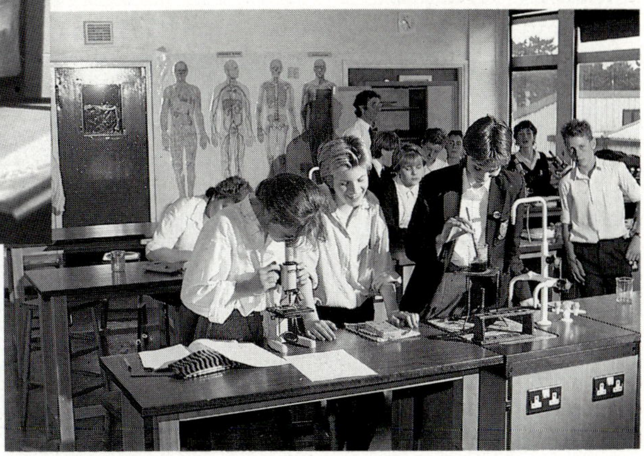

D The new timetable

a) *Mrs Grey:* Good morning, everyone. Listen, please. This is your timetable.
Melanie: Can't you give us copies, Mrs Grey? You usually do.
Mrs Grey: No, I'm sorry I haven't got any today, so listen to me and write everything down in your exercise books. Ready? ... The first lesson on Mondays is Maths with me, then English with Mr Brown, then there's break. Have you all got that?
Patrick: Maths with Ms Mee? But she's our PE teacher, Mrs Grey.
Mrs Grey: Not with Ms Mee – with *me,* Patrick. Please listen!
Peter: Excuse me, Mrs Grey. *Who's* our English teacher?
Mrs Grey: You have English with Mr Brown. After break you have a double Biology lesson with Mr Eliot ...
Jenny: He's great! I love Biology. It's my favourite subject.
Patrick: What do we have after lunch?
Mrs Grey: PE in the old gym with Ms Mee, Geography with Mrs Phillips and History with Mr Hart.
Melanie: Ugh! Mrs Phillips is awful. I hate Geography!
Patrick: Why? I think it's great, and Mrs Phillips is OK.
Peter: But History is so boring. All those dates!
Melanie: You're right!
Barbara: Shh, you three! Excuse me, Mrs Grey. When do we have Art? After Geography?
Mrs Grey: Oh, please listen to me, everyone! You don't have Art on Mondays, Barbara. You have *Mr* Hart. All right Jenny?
Jenny: Maths with Mrs Grey, English with Mr Brown.
Biology with Mr Eliot ... Geography with Mrs Phillips ...
Peter: She's fantastic!

b)

	TIMETABLE				
	Monday	Tuesday	Wednesday	Thursday	Friday
8.45 – 9.15	Assembly				
9.15 – 9.55	MATHS	FRENCH	HISTORY	CHEMISTRY	PHYSICS
9.55 – 10.35	ENGLISH	FRENCH	ENGLISH	CHEMISTRY	PHYSICS
10.35 – 10.50	Break				
10.50 – 11.30	BIOLOGY	ENGLISH	MATHS	FRENCH	HISTORY
11.30 – 12.10	BIOLOGY	ART	RELIGIOUS EDUCATION	GEOGRAPHY	MATHS
12.10 – 1.45	Lunch break				
1.45 – 2.25	PE (PHYSICAL EDUCATION)	CIVICS	GAMES	MATHS	PE (PHYSICAL EDUCATION)
2.25 – 3.05	GEOGRAPHY	MATHS		FRENCH	ENGLISH
3.05 – 3.45	HISTORY	ENGLISH		GEOGRAPHY	HOME ECONOMICS

1 At Jenny's school

Read the sentences and choose the correct statement(s).

1. Mrs Grey
   puts the new timetable on the notice-board in the classroom.
   reads out the new timetable to the boys and girls in Jenny's class.
   gives the pupils in Jenny's class copies of their new timetable.
   cannot give the pupils copies because she has not got any.

2. Their second lesson on Monday is
   after Maths with Ms Mee.
   after English with Mr Brown.
   before Biology with Mr Eliot.
   before Maths with Mrs Grey.

3. PE
   is Physical Education.
   is at 9 o'clock on Fridays.
   is different from RE.
   is on Mondays with Mrs Grey.

4. In the afternoon
   there are no lessons.
   there is Geography with Mrs Phillips on Mondays.
   the boys and girls have got PE with old Jim. He is very strict!
   school finishes at 3 o'clock.

⇆ 2 What's your favourite subject?

a) *What's your favourite subject? Why do you like it?*
What subjects don't you like and why? What about the other subjects?
Use the following words.

	like				nice.
I/We	don't like	English	because	the teacher is (not)	awful.
	love	…		it is (not)	interesting.
	hate			…	boring.
	…				…

b) *Write down* your *timetable in English.*

[3 Playing table-tennis is great]

Melanie: Playing table-tennis is nice/fantastic/… .
Peter: Yes, but doing judo is fun/great/…, too.
Patrick: I don't like/hate playing indoor games.
Climbing/… is my favourite activity.

Now talk about what is fun/interesting/what you like/don't like, etc. Work with a partner.

bird-watching, listening to pop music, doing sports, lying on the beach, playing games, making cakes, going to the seaside, reading, repairing things, taking photos, telephoning, writing letters, learning English, watching TV

E School cafeteria or snack bar?

a)

b) It is lunchtime. After Biology with Mr Eliot, Jenny and Tanja go to the school cafeteria and look at the menu, but the food there is not very exciting.

Tanja: Baked beans with everything. Ugh.
Jenny: But they've got egg, sausage and chips.
Tanja: Not for me, Jenny. I like salads.
Jenny: The snack bar in Station Road has good salads. Let's go there.

The two girls go to the snack bar in Station Road. First they look at the menu outside. It is not very different from the menu at the school cafeteria but they have got sandwiches and salads, and their ice-cream is good.

Jenny and Tanja look in through the window. Patrick, Peter and Melanie are at one of the tables. The girls go in and sit down at their table. First Jenny and Tanja have fruit juice. Then Tanja has a large mixed salad, and Jenny has egg, sausage and chips. After that they all have an ice-cream and talk about Tanja's first morning at Filton Comprehensive. At half past one they leave the snack bar and walk back for afternoon school.

Jenny: Hurry up, all of you. You know Ms Mee is very strict!

1 Two menus (a) *Make up two dialogues.*

a) Patrick, Peter and Melanie look at the menu in the school cafeteria. They talk about what they would like/what they like/don't like. But then they go to the snack bar in Station Road.

b) Jenny and Tanja are outside the snack bar in Station Road.
They talk about the menu and then they go in.

2 Lunch in the snack bar (b)

Look at the pictures and put them into the right order.
Write down what the girls do. Begin like this: First .... Then .... After that ....

3 Lunchtime

Put the words in the right order and write two short texts.

a) Sandra and Pamela

1. at lunchtime / to the cafeteria / to go / Sandra and Pamela
2. to their table / to take / they / first / their food
3. their new teachers / then / to talk about / to have lunch / and / they
4. to go back / after that / to their classroom / they

b) Roger

1. to have lunch / Roger Hall / not / in the school cafeteria / normally
2. usually / to go / he / at lunchtime / home
3. to help / first / he / in the kitchen / his mother
4. lunch / the Halls / together / to have / then
5. Mr Hall / to go / after that / back to work / Roger / back to school / and / in his car / to take

4 A friend from Britain

You meet a boy/girl from Britain. You want to ask him/her a lot of questions about his/her home, sports club or youth club.

a) *Make a list of questions.*
b) *Work with a partner. One of you asks the questions, the other gives the answers and notes them down.*
c) *Tell your class about your friend.*

F A ticket for a pop concert

a) It is Friday afternoon. Jenny and Tanja are in the school playground. They have only got five minutes before afternoon school. The first lesson is PE, one of Tanja's favourite subjects, but her ankle is still not strong enough for PE or games. She waits outside in the playground while Jenny goes to their classroom to get her PE things. Kevin Brown comes into the playground and sees Tanja. She does not see him, so he walks up behind her and puts his hands over her eyes.

Tanja: Hey! Who's that? ... Oh, hello, Kevin!

Kevin: What are your plans for tomorrow evening, Tanja?

Tanja: I haven't got any. Why?

Kevin: There's a pop concert in Bristol tomorrow, and I've got two tickets. Do you want to come?

Tanja: Oh yes, I'd love to come with you, Kevin.

Kevin: It's at eight o'clock. Can you meet me at 'The Black Cat' at seven thirty? I want to go into Bristol in the afternoon but I don't want to come home again.

Tanja: 'The Black Cat'? Where's that?

Kevin: Don't you remember 'The Black Cat'? It's the café in Small Street.

Tanja: That's right, I remember now. Doesn't your girlfriend want to go with you?

Kevin: Girlfriend? I haven't got a girlfriend, Tanja. But don't tell Jenny about the concert. This is our little secret!

Kevin gives Tanja her ticket. At that moment Jenny comes out into the playground and shuts the door. Tanja and Kevin look round.

Jenny: Hello, you two. Haven't you got any lessons this afternoon, Kevin? Come on, Tanja. I know you can't do PE, but we're late, and Ms Mee is very strict.

Tanja: OK, Jenny. Bye, Kevin!

Kevin: Bye!

Jenny: What's the matter, Tanja? Is there anything wrong?

Tanja: No, nothing's wrong. Everything's fine!

When Jenny arrives home after school that afternoon, she sees something red outside the front door.

b) The next day after tea Tanja goes upstairs into the bathroom and takes a shower. Then she goes into her bedroom and puts on her best blouse and jeans. After that she sits down in front of the mirror and puts on some make-up. Next she puts her money in her bag and looks for the ticket for the concert. It is not in her bag, so she looks in the pocket of her jeans. The ticket is not there. It is not on her desk or in her suitcase or under her bed. Tanja is very unhappy.

Five minutes later Jenny comes out of her bedroom and knocks on Tanja's door.

Jenny: Tanja. Are you ready?
Tanja: Ready? Ready for what?
Jenny: Don't you want to go into Bristol?
Tanja: Er – yes ... Why? Do you want to go out this evening, too?
Jenny: Yes. I've got a ticket for a pop concert in Bristol tonight. Look!

Tanja looks at it. It is a big red ticket. She knows it is *her* ticket, but she cannot say anything.

Jenny: What's the matter? Haven't you got a ticket, too?
Tanja: No, I haven't. Hm, Jenny, I've got a date ....
Jenny: Oh yes? A boyfriend? – Kevin wants to go the concert. I know *that.* He wants to be at 'The Black Cat' at seven thirty, so I must hurry. Bye!

Jenny walks to the door and opens it. Tanja is very angry with her.

Tanja: Jenny! Come here! I know that's my ticket. Give it back!
Jenny: I'm sorry, Tanja. Here you are. Don't be angry! Have a good time with Kevin. But remember next time.
I'm your best friend in Bristol.
And I can keep a secret, too!

1 What do you think? (a)

1. Why does Kevin ask Tanja to a pop concert?
2. Why does Tanja want to go to the pop concert with Kevin?
3. Is Tanja a pop music fan? How do you know?
4. Why doesn't Tanja tell Jenny about the concert?
5. Why doesn't Jenny ask any more questions?
6. Jenny finds Tanja's ticket outside the front door. She doesn't give it back to Tanja. Why?

2 What happens the next day? (b)

Complete the sentences.

1. The next day Tanja is upstairs for a long time because ....
2. When she is ready, she ... but ....
3. Where is it? She cannot ask Jenny, of course, because ....
4. Jenny knows that Tanja ....
5. When Tanja sees the red ticket, she ....
6. She is very angry, so Jenny ....
7. Always remember: "Best friends ...."

3 Differences between schools

Describe the differences between British schools and your school. Think of the school uniform, the school day, lessons, the timetable, the breaks, activities and sports, etc.

4 Before the pop concert

What does Kevin do before he meets Tanja at 'The Black Cat'?
Look at the pictures and tell the story.
Start like this: First Kevin goes .... Then .... After that ... Next ....

5 Role Play I'm hungry and thirsty!

You are hungry and thirsty. You go into Horfield Snack Bar with a friend and talk about what you want to have.

What would you like?
What do you want to eat?

→ I'd like ...
I want ...

← And I'd like ...
And after that let's try the ...

→ Yes, let's. I'm hungry.
Oh no. I don't like ... !
I'd like ....

← All right. And let's have a cup of ... / a glass of ...

→ No, let's ....
Good idea.
Not for me. I'm not thirsty.

Horfield Snack Bar

MENU

Eggs on toast
Beans on toast
Sausages and chips
Hamburger and chips

***

Chocolate ice-cream
Chocolate pudding
Fruit salad
Cheese

***

Tea / Coffee / Milk
Hot chocolate / Coke
Fruit juice

6 At home in Hanover

Put the words in the right order. Be careful with the position of the adverbials.

Example: Mrs Schulz sometimes takes Tanja home from school in her car.

1. Tanja / in her car / Mrs Schulz / to take / home / sometimes / from school
2. Tanja and her family / at half past one / normally / to have lunch
3. then / to do her homework / Tanja / usually
4. to go out / in the afternoon / often / she / with her friends
5. sometimes / to see / they / a film / to go to the cinema / for young people / and
6. to go out / Tanja / often / in the evenings? Does . . .
7. no / but / to go to a party / she / at weekends / sometimes
8. sometimes / to play volleyball / she / in her sports club / and
9. she / can / stay / until 9 o'clock / in a café / usually / in the evening?
10. no / cannot / she / must / she / to be / at 8 o'clock / home
11. very angry / she / about that / to be / often

Erst Ortsangabe, dann Zeitangabe

"We're against uniform, sir. We don't all want to look the same."

7 Rhyming words

Example: date – to wait, to hate
Now find more pairs.
to wear; to like; ball; now; make; …

8 Odd one out

Example: blazer – tie – trousers – skirt – [second-hand] – blouse

a) *Think of the meaning.*
black – red – right – blue – green – grey
suitcase – shelf – bed – cupboard – sofa – armchair
football – table-tennis – volleyball – tennis – judo
to look at – to watch – to see – to hear
baked beans – milk – chips – sausages – bread – toast

b) *Look at the forms.*
families – boys – cities – parties – lorries
she plays – she says – she hurries – she stays
women – men – girls – children

c) *Pronounce the words.*
old – only – other – over
go – do – no – so
she sees – he lives – she walks – he joins
paper – game – table – to have – late – to hate

9 ⟨Listening comprehension: What the teachers spend⟩

Listen to the cassette.
How much does each teacher spend in the school cafeteria every week?

1. Mrs Phillips 2. Ms Mee 3. Mr Brown
4. Mr Hart 5. Mr Eliot 6. Mrs Grey

Stopover A ⟨The pond⟩

Jobs or frogs?

Mr Benson is a technician at British Aerospace. Sometimes he works in the mornings, sometimes in the afternoons and evenings.

One afternoon, when Jenny comes home from school, she goes into the living room. Her dad is asleep on the sofa with the local newspaper over his face.

Jenny: Hello, Dad. What are you doing?

Mr Benson: Oh, hello Jenny. Can't you see? … I'm reading the newspaper. There's an article in it about British Aerospace.

Jenny: Oh, what are they doing now?

Mr Benson: British Aerospace want to build some new buildings. Look, there's a photo in the paper.

Jenny: Oh, no! Those fields are not far from our school. There's a pond with a lot of frogs and other animals in it. – You needn't look at me like that, Dad!

Mr Benson: Frogs are interesting, Jenny, but in my opinion these new buildings are important.

Jenny: Animals are important, too.

Mr Benson: I agree. But we're building a lot of new aircraft at British Aerospace, so we need more buildings.

Jenny: I'm sorry, I don't agree. Why do we need more aircraft?

Mr Benson: Well, more people want to fly. And remember, 75,000 people work for British Aerospace. We help to build the Airbus, so think about the jobs in France, Germany and Spain, too.

Jenny: Everybody says 'Jobs, jobs, jobs!'. Somebody must think about the environment. That's why I'm in 'Friends of the Earth'.

Mr Benson: 'Friends of the Earth' is a very good idea, but we must have jobs. No jobs, no money – and the environment needs money too, Jenny.

Jenny: Hm … perhaps, but aircraft make a lot of noise.

Mr Benson: Yes, but we also build quiet aircraft. The BAe 146 is a quiet aircraft, you know.

Jenny: That's good, but I still think too many people want to fly.

Mr Benson: Well then, think about our holidays in Spain. We can fly there in two hours … or do you want to stay at home?

Jenny: Hm … perhaps.

High-tech in Filton

This is an Airbus. It is a European aircraft. British Aerospace build the wings of the Airbus A320 and parts for other aircraft in the Airbus family in Filton. Other companies build parts in Germany, France and Spain. A lot of Airbuses have British engines, too.

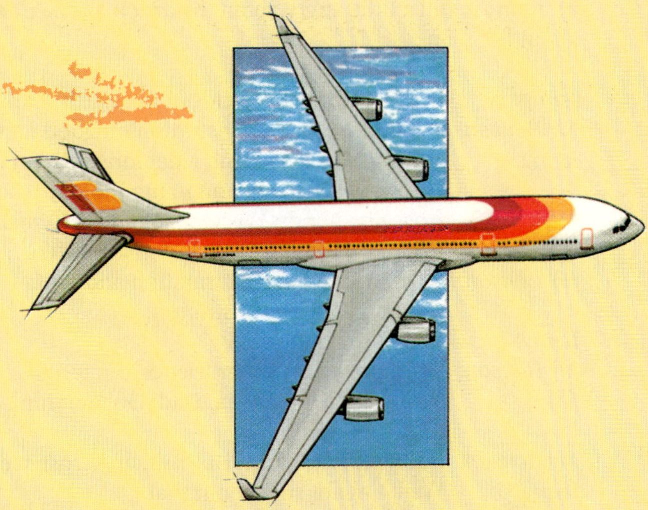

All aircraft make a noise, but the BAe 146 is a 'quiet' aircraft. It can fly into airports in or near the centres of cities with very little noise.

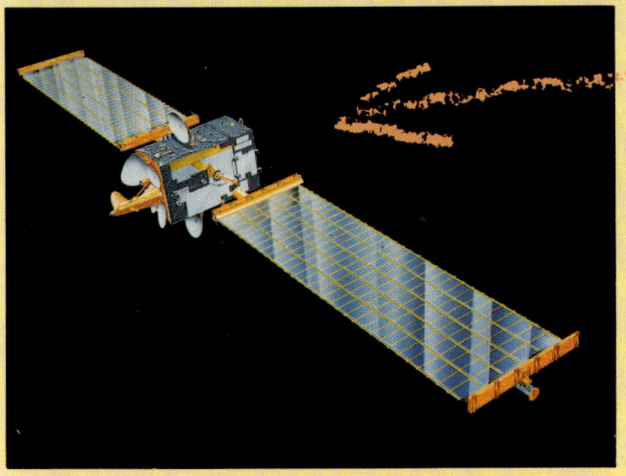

Perhaps your TV programme comes from a satellite. Satellites can also carry telephone calls and tell aircraft and ships where they are. And they can help to make maps and do lots of other jobs.

Jenny and her plans

a) Jenny is still a little angry about the article in the newspaper, but now she is talking to her dad about her plans.

Jenny: We must plan a 'Friends of the Earth' information stand and a demonstration.
Mr Benson: I don't think a demonstration's a good idea, Jenny.
Jenny: Why not, Dad? *I* think a demonstration's important, too. I want to talk to all my friends at school ... and to my Biology teacher. And I'd like to read something about frogs and ponds. We need a lot of information first. For example, what do frogs need? What do they like? What don't they like? Then we can explain it to British Aerospace.
Mr Benson: Of course, get the information and write it down. But I'm not sure you can change things with a demonstration.
Jenny: Well, *I* think we can.
Mr Benson: Perhaps you and your friends can write a letter to British Aerospace.
Jenny: Yes, that's a good idea, Dad. Do you think they can build the buildings in another place?
Mr Benson: I don't know, Jenny. But British Aerospace are interested in the environment, too.
Jenny: Well, I'm not sure about that.

Jenny talks to her friends and her Biology teacher, and also goes to the local library for more information. Together they write a letter to British Aerospace. About ten days later they get an invitation to BAe. Jenny and a small group of 'Friends of the Earth' go there and talk to a woman about BAe's plans, the pond, the frogs and the other animals.

b) One day after school, Jenny goes into Morgan's Corner Shop. There are newspapers in the shop and Jenny sees a headline about British Aerospace. She begins to read the article:

New BAe Buildings in Wales
British Aerospace now want to build their new buildings near Cardiff and not in Filton. Local politicians in Bristol are against the plan. Other groups, including the 'Friends of the Earth' are against the buildings because

1 The discussion at BAe

Make up and act the discussion between the woman from BAe and Jenny and her friends. Use the words and phrases in the box on page 87.

2 For and against

I think … .	I don't think … .
I agree.	I don't agree.
That's right.	That's wrong.
You're right.	You're wrong.
That's a good idea.	That's not a good idea.
That's very interesting.	That's not very interesting.
OK./All right.	Perhaps, but … .
Well, … .	I'm sorry but … .
What a great idea.	You're crazy!
The question is: … .	But the answer is difficult.
Let's talk about … .	That's not important.
In my opinion, … .	But remember: … .
Can't you see … ?	But you must think about … .
Don't you think … ?	…, you know.
That's why … .	

3 Environmental questions

Talk about the pros and cons of the following:

a) bikes, cars and buses in big cities;
b) large supermarkets outside towns;
c) holidays at home or abroad.

4 A poster for 'Friends of the Earth'

Work in groups and make a poster for 'Friends of the Earth'. You can deal with one environmental problem or a number of questions on your poster. Write slogans and short texts and use pictures and articles from newspapers and magazines.

There's a happy ending. The whale wins.

UNIT 7

A Croeso i Gymru – Welcome to Wales

a) This is the first page of a brochure about Wales. The first three words are in Welsh.

Croeso i Gymru
Welcome to Wales

Wales is wonderful!
There is something for all the family in Wales. You can enjoy the beautiful scenery of the Welsh mountains.
You can visit our old castles, for example in Cardiff, the capital of Wales.

You must visit one of our National Parks. And young people love our sandy beaches. You can find some of the best beaches in Britain around the coasts of Wales.
Wales is a great place!

But please remember:

Welsh is not English with a funny accent.
All Welsh people can speak English, but most of them have a Welsh accent. In some places a lot of them also speak Welsh – an old and beautiful Celtic language. The Celtic languages are very different from English.

Wales is not a part of England.
England, Wales and Scotland are the three countries in Great Britain. Each country is different.

b)

Carmarthen Castle

Brecon Beacons

The coast near Pembroke

Newport Docks

One of the interesting museums in Bristol

1 Wales is wonderful (a)

Now you know something about Wales. *Put the following sentences together.*

1. Most Welsh people
2. Cardiff has got
3. There are mountains
4. You can enjoy
5. Young people love
6. Wales has something
7. Croeso i Gymru

a) is Welsh for 'Welcome to Wales'.
b) for all the family.
c) the sandy beaches around the Welsh coast.
d) in Wales.
e) speak English with a Welsh accent.
f) an old castle.
g) the beautiful scenery.

2 Questions about South Wales and Bristol (b)

a) *Ask and answer questions about the map and the photos on page 89. Work with a partner.*

What can you see / find / look at in Cardiff/... ? – Well, Cardiff has got ... .
Where can you find sandy beaches /... ?
...

b) *Describe the photos and find other captions for them.*

B Plans for a trip to South Wales

Mrs Benson has a job at the Tourist Information Centre, so she knows quite a lot about trips from Bristol.

Tanja: I'd like to go on a trip to Wales next weekend. Is that OK, Mrs Benson?
Mrs Benson: Well, who wants to go with you?
Tanja: David and Kevin, but Jenny can't go because she's got a concert with the school band. David and Kevin want to take their bikes with them.
Mrs Benson: David's old enough, so that's fine with me, Tanja. But whose bike can you borrow?
Tanja: I can have Sandra's bike, I think. – You know a lot about Wales, Mrs Benson. Where can we go on our bikes? And where can we go by train from Bristol?
Mrs Benson: Well, you can go to Abergavenny and the Black Mountains, for example.
Tanja: How do we get there?
Mrs Benson: You catch a train from Bristol to Newport and change there for Abergavenny. And then you can ride on your bikes.
Tanja: The Black Mountains – that's a romantic name.
Mrs Benson: Yes, it is. They're very beautiful. But you can have a look at Abergavenny first. It's a nice little town with a market.
Tanja: Is there a youth hostel?
Mrs Benson: I don't know, Tanja.
Tanja: Well, who can I ask?
Mrs Benson: Wait a minute. I've got a good idea. Kevin's aunt and uncle live on a farm near Llanthony – that's in the Black Mountains – and I'm sure you can all stay there.
Tanja: That's a super idea, Mrs Benson. I can ask Kevin this afternoon. Thanks.

1 Tanja and Kevin

That afternoon Kevin phones from the sports centre. He wants to talk to Tanja about a party on Friday. She tells him about Mrs Benson's idea. Kevin wants to stay at a youth hostel because it is more fun there. Tanja would like to stay at his aunt's farm because there are a lot of animals there.
Make up the telephone call.

2 Oh, Mum!

Jenny is putting the tea things on the dining room table. She is talking to her mother, but Mrs Benson can't hear everything because she is making the tea in the kitchen.
Ask questions with 'who' and 'whose'.

Jenny: **Kevin** wants to have a party on Friday.
Mrs B.: Sorry, dear. **Who wants** to have a party?
Jenny: Kevin. He wants to ask all the people in our class. But **Mrs Brown** says that's too many.
Mrs B.: … ?
Jenny: Mrs Brown! Do you know **Mrs Brown's** brother lives near Llanthony in Wales?
Mrs B.: … ?
Jenny: Mrs Brown's. Oh, I must buy a present. It's **Sandra's** birthday tomorrow.
Mrs B.: … ?
Jenny: Sandra's. – Listen, Dad and Tanja are back. I can hear **them** outside.
Mrs B.: … ?
Jenny: Dad and Tanja! Oh, Mum!
Mrs B.: Oh, are they back? That's good. We can have tea now.

3 Jenny's friend

Jenny's friend Melanie lives at 22 York Road. She is thirteen, and her brother Tony is twelve. She has got a sister, too; her name is Barbara. Melanie is awful. When she cannot find her pen, she puts Tony's pen in her schoolbag and takes it to school. And sometimes she wears her sister's blouses and pullovers. But Jenny likes her. Melanie often meets Jenny in the mornings, and the two girls go to school together.
Now ask questions with 'who' and 'whose'. How many questions can you ask?
Examples: Who lives at 22 York Road? Whose friend lives in York Road?

4 How they get to school or to work

to go to school / work by car / bus / train
to go / ride to school / work on a / my bike
to walk to school / work

a)

David (always) | Mrs Benson (usually) | Jenny (always) | Kevin (sometimes) | Rajiv (often) | Mr Brown (always)

b) And how do *you* usually / sometimes get to school?

C Tanja's letter to her aunt in London

10 York Road
Filton
Bristol BS12 2PE

8th August

Dear Aunt Carol,

Thanks for your letter and the funny postcards.
I like them very much.

It is Friday today, and on Fridays I usually go to the sports centre here, but this evening I am staying at home because I want to write some letters.

Yes, my ankle is OK now. Tomorrow I want to go on a trip to South Wales with David and our neighbour, Kevin Brown. Jenny cannot go because she has got a concert on Saturday evening. She is practising the saxophone at the moment. She sometimes even plays it late in the evening when I am in bed!!

David is upstairs in his room. He is not working with his computer today. He is making plans for our trip to Wales. He always makes plans for everything! I think that is awful! My friend Kevin is quite different. He never makes plans - like me. He has not got very much money - just enough for the trip to Wales. His father is very unhappy because he has not got a job at the moment, but in the afternoons and evenings he works as a coach at the sports centre.

The wind is blowing again today. It blows quite a lot here in Bristol, but the weather is not too bad. How about that? Am I English enough after six weeks in England? I talk about the weather to everybody, and now I am even writing about the weather!

Love,
Tanja

usually / always / sometimes / never

On Fridays I **usually** go to the sports centre.

Jenny **sometimes** plays her saxophone late in the evening.

at the moment / now / this evening / today

This evening I am staying at home.

She is playing her saxophone **at the moment**.

1 Comprehension

a) 1. What is Tanja doing this evening?
2. What is Jenny doing at the moment?
3. What is David doing?
What isn't he doing today?
4. And what about the weather today?

b) 1. What does Tanja usually do on Fridays?
2. What does Jenny sometimes do late in the evening?
3. What does David always do?
4. And what about Kevin and Tanja?
5. What does Kevin's father do?
6. What does Tanja talk about to everybody?

2 A letter to an English friend

Write a letter to your English friend. Tell him / her what you do on a normal day. You can write about when you usually have breakfast / normally go to school / get home; what you often / never / sometimes do in the afternoons / evenings. Ask him / her what he / she usually does after school.

3 On the way home from school

School is over, and Jenny and Melanie are going home from school together. They see Kevin.

1. (to go)
Jenny: Where … Kevin … ?
Melanie: He … to the corner shop.
He often … there after school.

Kevin comes out.

2. (to eat)
Melanie: Hey, Kevin! Give us some sweets!
Kevin: I haven't got any sweets.
I never … sweets.
Jenny: But you … a sweet now!
Kevin: No, I (not) … a sweet, I … a piece of chocolate. Bye-bye!

3. (to walk)
Jenny: Look, there's Sharon on a bike.
She usually … home from school.
Melanie: Yes, I know. But she (not) … today because her sister has got a sprained ankle and so she's got her bike.

They arrive at the Morgans' shop.

4. (to repair)
Jenny: Let's go and see Mr Morgan.
I want to ask him about my cassette recorder. He … it for me.
Melanie: He sometimes … things for me, too.

They go into the Morgans' shop.

5. (to write)
Jenny: Hello, Mrs Morgan.
Is Mr Morgan in?
Mrs Morgan: Yes, he is, dear, but he … a letter upstairs at the moment.
He (not) usually … letters in the afternoon, but he has got a lot to write today.
Jenny: I can come back this evening, Mrs Morgan. Bye-bye.

4 The Bensons

What do you know about the Bensons – Jenny, David, Mrs Benson and Mr Benson?
What do they sometimes / usually / often do? Describe their day at home / at school / at work.

D On time

What time is it? Example: It's twenty-five past two.

Look at the clock again. What's the exact time?

It's eight minutes past five.

It's twenty-four minutes past seven.

It's twenty-one minutes to four.

It's seventeen minutes to five.

Say what time it is.

1 Timetables

a) In timetables you often see:

6.47	9.09	5.15
6.27	8.30	7.59

Then you can say: 'six forty-seven' 'nine oh nine' …

b) Here is the timetable for morning trains from Bristol to Abergavenny.

What time do they arrive and leave?

Bristol	arrives	7.40	8.38	9.38
	leaves	7.43	8.40	9.40
Newport	arrives	8.11	9.08	10.06
	leaves	8.18	9.15	10.55
Abergavenny	arrives	8.41	9.41	11.29

2 Early, late, on time

a) *Look at the* **pictures**.
It is ten to eight.
(or: It is seven fifty.)
A train **is arriving** in Bristol.
(A train is leaving Bristol.) …

b) *Now look at the* **timetable** again.
The train (in picture 1) usually **arrives** in Bristol at twenty to eight (or: seven forty).
(It usually leaves …)
It is early / late / on time.

E (Mr Benson's cake)

Mr Benson is in the kitchen. He wants to make another cake.

Mr Benson: Jenny! You're upstairs, aren't you?
Jenny: Yes, Dad. I'm in my room. Why?
Mr Benson: You aren't doing your homework, are you?
Jenny: No, I'm reading a magazine.
Mr Benson: Well, you've got ten minutes, haven't you? Come and help me in the kitchen, please. You can read your magazine later, can't you?
Jenny: Oh, Dad! You want to make another cake, don't you?
Mr Benson: Well, mum and Tanja are out. I can't ask them, can I?
Jenny: ... Let me see. Oh dear! You never learn, do you, Dad?
Mr Benson: No, I know. So we must start again, mustn't we?
Jenny: We?? Why not *you,* Dad?

[1 A lonely job?]

Mrs Benson and Tanja are out in Bristol. They meet Kevin. Mrs Benson must get back to the Tourist Information Centre, so Tanja and Kevin go and have a look at the ships in the docks.
Complete the dialogue with question tags.

Tanja: I wouldn't like to work on a ship.
Kevin: Oh, I don't know. Work on a ship is quite exciting, **isn't it**?
Tanja: For the first few days, but then it would be boring, ...? You can't visit your friends, ...?
Kevin: No, but you don't have to take a bus or train to work!
Tanja: The men are often lonely, ...?
Kevin: Well, they don't have much time to be lonely, ...?
Tanja: They sometimes work for 16 hours a day, ...?
Kevin: Yes, but they can watch videos or play cards after work, ...?
Tanja: But that's boring after a time, ...?
Kevin: Sometimes they're away from home for two or three months, ...?
Tanja: Yes, but then they have two or three weeks at home, ...? But they don't get much money, ...?
Kevin: That's right. But a job is a job.
Tanja: Yes, your dad would like to find a job, ...?
Kevin: Hm ... very much!

Bristol Docks

F The farm near Llanthony

a) On Saturday morning Tanja and David wake up before everybody else. They get up and have breakfast. Jenny comes downstairs at twenty to eight. She cannot go to Wales with them because she is in the school band and there is a concert that evening.

Tanja: We're going now, Jenny. Bye!
Jenny: Bye, Tanja. Bye, David. Have a nice time.

Kevin is waiting for them outside with his bike. They get on their bikes and ride to the station. They must catch the 8.40 train from Bristol. They buy their tickets at the station.

David: How much is a ticket to Abergavenny, please?
Man: Single or return?
David: Return.
Man: £9.50.
David: I'd like three returns. And how much is a bike ticket?
Man: £3 for a bike, so that's £37.50 altogether. Platform six, change at Newport.
David: Thanks.

They arrive at Abergavenny Station on time, at 9.41. The weather is not very good, but it is not raining. They cycle into town and have a look at the old castle on the hill. After that they go down to the market. It is market day, so they sit on the wall and watch.
After lunch they cycle to the Prichards' farm near Llanthony. Kevin's aunt and uncle are very pleased to see them. Mr Prichard shows them the farm. They have got a lot of animals. Most of them are sheep, and they have also got two lovely sheepdogs.

A street in Abergavenny

b) There are five bedrooms in the house, but Tanja would like to sleep in the barn with the sheep-dogs. She has got her sleeping bag with her, but Mrs Prichard is not very happy about this.

Mrs Prichard: Oh dear! It's not very comfortable in there, Tanja, and it's dirty!
Tanja: But it's only for one night.
Mrs Prichard: All right, then. And you've got the dogs with you, so nothing can happen.

Before they all go to bed, Kevin takes Tanja into the hall and tells her why his aunt and uncle are not very happy. The barn is haunted! But Tanja only laughs. She does not believe in ghosts, and anyway she has got the two dogs with her.

At about two o'clock in the morning Tanja wakes up. A strong wind is blowing, and the dogs are barking. They can hear someone – or something – outside. Tanja is still very sleepy. She looks out of the window, but she cannot see anything. It is very dark outside. Then Tanja sees something … a figure in white. She does not believe in ghosts, but can it be the ghost? It is standing at the corner of the house. Now it is moving … it is walking up to the door of the barn … it is opening the door … the wind is blowing in … the dogs are still barking. The figure in white is coming into the barn …

Mrs Prichard: Quiet! What's the matter with you dogs? Are you all right, Tanja?
Tanja: Y-y-yes … So you're the 'ghost' – the ghost in the white nightdress!
Mrs Prichard: Ghost? You don't believe in ghosts? There are no ghosts here!
Tanja: And the barn isn't haunted?
Mrs Prichard: Haunted? Ghosts? No, Tanja! What are you talking about?
Tanja: Well, Kevin …
Mrs Prichard: Kevin? Oh, he often tells stories like that. Don't listen to him! Do you still want to stay in the barn, Tanja?
Tanja: Yes, I do. I'm not afraid now.
Mrs Prichard: OK then. Good night, dear, and sleep well.

1 The journey to Llanthony (a)

What do David, Tanja and Kevin do on Saturday morning? How do they get from Bristol to Llanthony? Describe the journey in your own words.
Start like this: David and Tanja get up at 7 o'clock. Then …. After that ….

2 Why? (b)

1. Why does Tanja want to sleep in the barn?
2. Why is Mrs Prichard not very happy about this?
3. Why does Kevin take Tanja into the hall?
4. Why does Tanja laugh?
5. Why does she wake up at two o'clock in the morning?
6. Why can't Tanja see anything?
7. Why is she afraid?
8. Why does Mrs Prichard come out to the barn?

3 Tanja's photos

A few days later Tanja shows Jenny the pictures of her trip to Wales. *Describe the photos for her.*

4 Tanja's afternoon

Fill in the missing prepositions.

Some days … her trip to Wales, Tanja writes another letter. She sits down … the desk … her room. She has got the photos … Wales … her … the desk. Red is … her. He is lying … her. … her letter Tanja writes … the farm … Llanthony.

Kevin comes … the room and talks … Tanja … the trip and looks … the photos. Then he goes out again, and Tanja can go on … her letter. … that, she goes downstairs … the living room and reads a sports magazine … half an hour.

5 Now – and usually

Put the verbs in the right form.

Example: It is nine o'clock. A Number 71 bus **is going** to the city centre.
The bus **goes** to the city centre at nine o'clock every day.

1. (to play) It is a summer evening. Patrick and Barbara … football against Kevin and Melanie. They often … football against Kevin and Melanie.
2. (to take) It is five o'clock. Kevin … Red's food into the garden. He always … Red's food into the garden in the afternoon.
3. (to have) The Bensons usually … breakfast in the kitchen. But today is Sunday, and they … it in the dining room.
4. (to go) It is Thursday. A coach full of children … to Cardiff. The children at Jenny's school … on a trip every summer.
5. (to use) Kevin always … his new pen for his homework. But he cannot find it, so he … Tanja's pen now.

6 At the Tourist Information Centre

Jochen, a boy from Stuttgart, is staying with a family in Bristol. He wants to visit Wales, so he goes to the Tourist Information Centre. He talks to Mrs Benson about a trip to Wales.
Make up their dialogue.

7 A brochure

Write a brochure for tourists about your home town. It can be a brochure for young people or for all the family. Describe interesting places, castles, parks, sports centres, youth clubs, shops, etc.

8 Practise your vocabulary

a) Hospital: doctor, nurse, bandage, ambulance, …
Can you find other 'hospital' words?

b) *Now make other word groups:* at school; at a station; at a sports centre; what tourists can do

9 Look, listen and say

a)

[-ə]

-er remem**ber**, let**ter**,

-re cent**re**

-ar burgl**ar**

-our col**our**

-ure broch**ure**

-or spectat**or**

Find other examples.

b)

[ʃ] **sh**eepdog, sta**t**ion, Engli**sh**

[tʃ] **ch**ild, ki**tch**en, lun**ch**

[dʒ] **G**erman, dan**g**erous, bri**dge**

She is going to the **sh**opping centre where the **sh**op assistant sells Engli**sh** **sh**oes.
They are buying **ch**ocolate and **ch**ips for lun**ch** on the bea**ch**.
The **ch**ildren are fe**tch**ing **ch**airs from the ki**tch**en.
Join the **g**ym club and do **j**udo.
Just a minute, I must get my **j**eans for this **j**ob on the bri**dge**.

⟨10 Listening comprehension: By train to Abergavenny⟩

Listen to the cassette. What happens at these times?

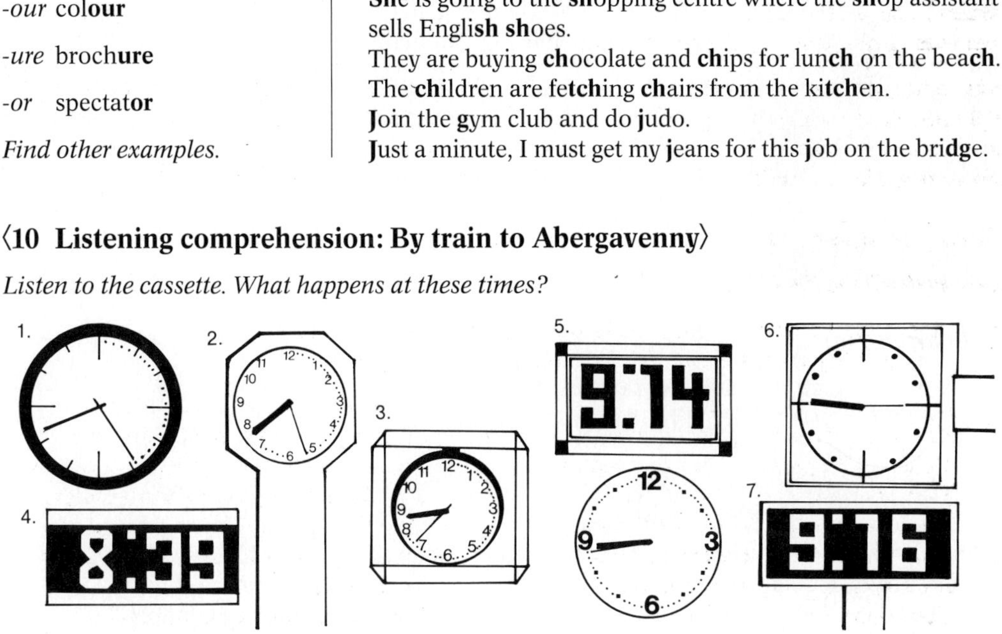

UNIT 8

A A visit to Radio Bristol

a) Mrs Benson is with a group of German tourists from Hanover, the twin town of Bristol. Mrs Benson is their guide. At the moment they are standing outside the Radio Bristol building, and Mrs Benson is telling them about this local radio station.

"A lot of people – twenty-eight per cent of people in the Bristol area – listen to Radio Bristol every week because it broadcasts the local news every hour. It also has a lot of programmes about local events.

Your twin town Bristol is an important tourist centre, and every month a lot of interesting things take place here: sports events, competitions where you can win prizes, exhibitions at the Exhibition Centre and open-air concerts.

Jack Wilkinson of Radio Bristol is waiting for us inside the building, so come with me, please."

b) Jack Wilkinson welcomes the tourists. He talks to them about his work at the local radio station and the most important events of the year. He gives each tourist a copy of the 'Radio Bristol Wall Calendar'.

"In winter there are a lot of indoor events. The first big outdoor event takes place in early spring: the Avon Schools Football Cup Final at the Bristol Rovers football stadium.

The Radio Bristol Swimming Championships are indoors, but in summer and autumn you can see lots of interesting things outdoors: the British Powerboat Championships, the Balloon Festival in Ashton Park and the Radio Bristol Open-air Concert.

And in October Radio Bristol has its Open Day."

1 Questions (a)

Ask your partner questions about Radio Bristol.
Use the question words 'what', 'why', 'how many', 'who', etc.

2 Sports and events (b) OVER TO YOU

a) What are the events in winter, spring, summer and autumn?
b) Describe some indoor and outdoor games, sports and events in the Bristol area.
c) Have you got a local radio station in your town/area? Do you sometimes listen to it? Why or why not? Are there any interesting events in your town/area? Describe them.

c) Have a look at the events on the 'Radio Bristol Wall Calendar':

What's on in Bristol?

JANUARY 1st – 8th
'Environmental and Pollution Problems in Bristol' – Exhibition at Broadmead Shopping Centre

FEBRUARY 2nd and 3rd
West of England Volleyball Championships, Avon Indoor Sports Centre

MARCH 23rd and 24th
Avon Schools Football Cup Final, Bristol Rovers Football Stadium

APRIL 6th and 7th
Fifth Radio Bristol Swimming Championships, Bristol Swimming Baths

MAY 10th and 11th
Boat Show, Bristol Docks

JUNE 9th – 12th
British Powerboat Championships, River Avon

JULY 20th
Balloon Festival, Ashton Park

AUGUST 13th – 16th
Computer Show, Bristol Exhibition Centre
Big Competition! Big Prizes!

AUGUST 31st
Radio Bristol Open-air Concert, Clifton Downs

SEPTEMBER 11th – 17th
'Summer in Bristol' Photo Competition for Children and Young People

OCTOBER 14th
Come to our Open Day at Radio Bristol!

NOVEMBER 15th – 22nd
Bristol Cinema Festival

DECEMBER 18th – 23rd
Winter Sports Exhibition, Bristol Exhibition Centre

first	sixth	eleventh	sixteenth	twenty-first	twenty-sixth	thirty-first
1st	6th	11th	16th	21st	26th	31st
second	seventh	**twelfth**	seventeenth	twenty-second	twenty-seventh	
2nd	7th	12th	17th	22nd	27th	*Go on.*
third	**eighth**	thirteenth	eighteenth	twenty-third	twenty-eighth	
3rd	8th	13th	18th	23rd	28th	
fourth	**ninth**	fourteenth	nineteenth	twenty-fourth	twenty-ninth	
4th	9th	14th	19th	24th	29th	
fifth	tenth	fifteenth	**twentieth**	twenty-fifth	thirtieth	
5th	10th	15th	20th	25th	30th	

⇄ 1 A phone call to the Tourist Information Centre (c)

a)

Mr Finch:	Hello, David Finch speaking. I'd like to come to Bristol in spring/August/… . What's on?
Mrs Benson:	Good morning, Mr Finch. What are you interested in?
Mr Finch:	I'm interested in … .
Mrs Benson:	Well then, you can go to … .
Mr Finch:	… is not really my favourite …/ not so interesting for me.
Mrs Benson:	What about … ?
Mr Finch:	Oh yes, that's a good idea.
Mrs Benson:	It takes place on … .
Mr Finch:	Thank you very much. Goodbye.
Mrs Benson:	Bye, Mr Finch.

Complete the dialogue.

b) *Now phone Mrs Benson. Ask her about events in spring, summer, autumn or winter. You are interested in environmental problems, films, music, computers, etc.*

What is interesting? What is boring?

My favourite activity/sport/event is …
I like/enjoy/always enjoy/love/hate …
That's really nice/interesting/lovely/very exciting/fine/fantastic/great … because …
I'm a … fan.
I'd like to try something new/something special.
I want to watch …
That's a good/great/lovely idea.

I don't like/don't enjoy/hate …
That's not very interesting/boring/difficult/ dangerous/awful.
That's OK/all right, but …
I'm afraid …

2 Jenny's birthday calendar

When is Jenny's birthday?
a) It is in February.
b) It is on the twenty-eighth of February.

When is her father's birthday?
When is your birthday?

3 Happy birthday

Example:
"How old is Mrs Dale?"
"She's seventy.
It's her seventieth birthday today."

B The nine o'clock news

a) "Hello and good morning everybody. It's nine o'clock, and this is Radio Bristol with the local news.

Today is Earth Day, and there is a big meeting of the 'Friends of the Earth' in the centre of Bristol. There are still as many environmental problems in Bristol as in other places. Few people would call our city really clean, but Bristol is cleaner – and greener – than many other large towns in England. The greenest – and cleanest – suburb of Bristol is Westbury. The environmental problems in some suburbs are still as bad as in many other big cities, but they are not worse. The worst areas for pollution are still in the North of England.

Earth Day is also the birthday of the oldest member of 'Friends of the Earth' in Bristol. Mr William Ottaway of 14 West Road, Horfield, is 85 today. You can hear Mr Ottaway on our next programme about environmental problems in the Bristol and Avon area – after the news, here on Radio Bristol."

b) "Today is the last day of the Computer Show, and because the last day is a Saturday it is the busiest day of the show. This year the show is bigger, a day longer and even more interesting. With over fifty stands it's the biggest show in the history of the Exhibition Centre.

Saturday is also the most important day for visitors to the Computer Show because the big computer competition takes place today, and the prizes this year are even better and more fantastic than last year: the first prize is a trip to the USA, the home of the most exciting computers. The second and third prizes are new computers and there are many more prizes, too: from the best colour monitors to very good programs.

But please remember this message from the police:
It's easier – and cleverer – to take a bus than to take your car.
It's the simplest way!

That's all for now. More national and local news at ten o'clock."

clean – cleaner – cleanest
big – bigger – biggest
busy – busier – busiest
interesting – more interesting – most interesting

good – better – best
bad – worse – worst

1 The Bensons and the Browns

Mr Brown	Mr Benson	Mrs Brown	Mrs Benson	David	Kevin	Jenny
45	44	42	40	18	15	13

Mr Benson is **older than** Mrs Benson. He is the **oldest** in the Benson family.
But Mr Benson is not **as old as** Mr Brown. He is **younger.** *Go on.*

2 Clothes at a sale

old / new

short / long

dirty / clean

small / big

Look at all the clothes at this 'Friends of the Earth' sale.

Example: The brown pullover is very old.
The green pullover is newer than the brown pullover.
But the red pullover is the newest (of the three).

Or you can say: The red pullover is new … *Go on.*

3 Compare these things

BOOKS	FOOTBALL	ROMANTIC FILMS	A COMPUTER SHOW
MAGAZINES	VOLLEYBALL	FILMS ABOUT HISTORY	AN ART EXHIBITION
NEWSPAPERS	TABLE-TENNIS	FILMS ABOUT BIRDS	A BALLOON FESTIVAL

Kevin, Tanja and David do not agree.

Kevin: I think football is more exciting than volleyball.
Tanja: Oh no! Football is not as exciting as volleyball.
David: Well, I think volleyball is just as exciting as football.

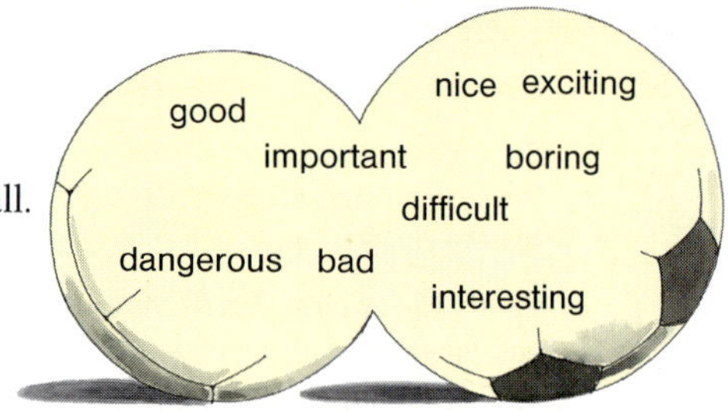

What do you think? Can you make up some more dialogues with two partners?

4 Titles

Find a title for each paragraph on page 103.

⇄ 5 Why don't you come?

a) *David tells Tanja about the Computer Show but Tanja is not very interested. What can he say to her? Here are some ideas:*

It's really great/interesting/exciting.
There are lots of stands/interesting people/things to do.
You can try to win a prize/try new computer games/learn a lot there.
It's the biggest/most fantastic/most important Computer Show in the West of England.
You really must come./Come with us./Why don't you come with us?

David: Tanja, we want to go to the Computer Show. Why don't you come with us?
Tanja: Thanks, David, but I'm not really interested in computers.
David: …

b) *Look at the 'Radio Bristol Wall Calendar'. You want to go to one of the other events but your friend does not want to go. What can you say?*

C From the station to the Exhibition Centre

Sandra's friend Wendy is standing at a bus stop near the station. A young man wants to know the way to the Computer Show.

Young man: Excuse me, how do I get from here to the Exhibition Centre?

Wendy: Do you want to walk or take a bus?

Young man: I've got my car round the corner.

Wendy: Well, leave it there and walk. It's not far – only about ten minutes – and anyway, the car park at the Exhibition Centre is usually full. Turn left into Redcliffe Way here. Go straight on to the crossroads past the big church on your left and then cross Redcliffe Bridge. Go across Queen Square and straight on to the traffic lights. Don't turn right there into the city centre, turn left past the statue of Neptune. The Exhibition Centre's down the road on your left. You can't miss it.

Young man: I'm not so sure! Turn right, straight on to the crossroads ....

Wendy: No, turn left and straight on to the crossroads ....

Young man: ... then past the big church, over the bridge, across Queen Square ....

Wendy: Or you can catch the Number 17 bus. It's quicker by bus.

Young man: No, I think I can find it. Thank you.

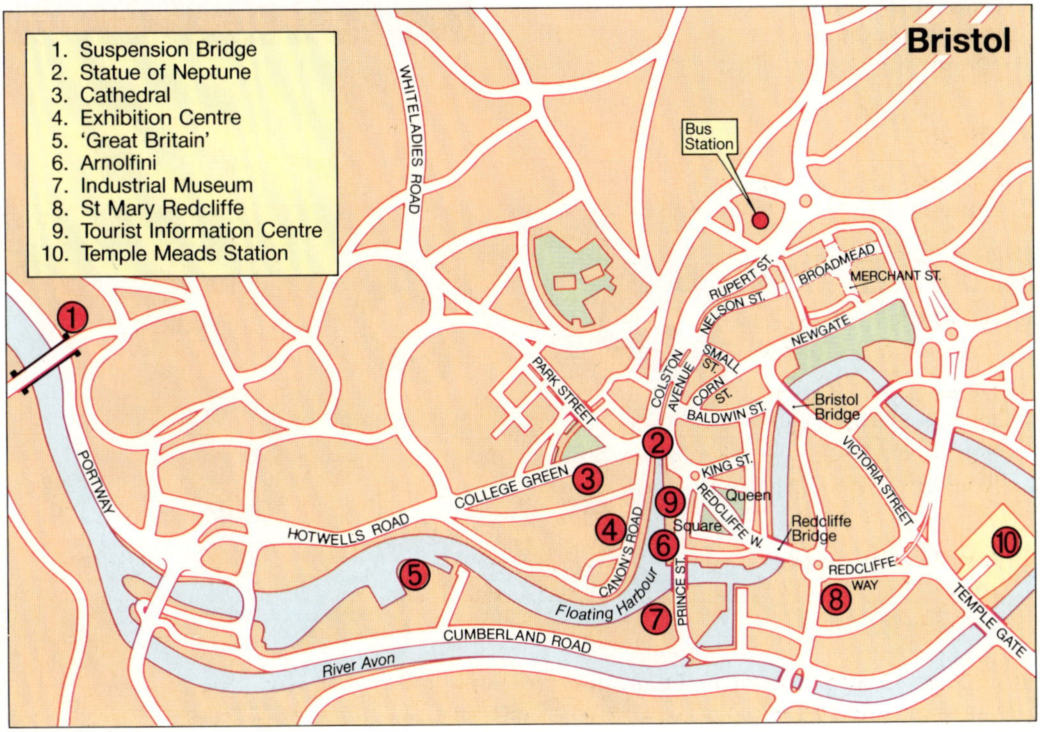

The young man does not want to walk to the Exhibition Centre. He goes round the corner, gets into his car, puts on his seat belt and drives off. But there is a lot of traffic, and he cannot find his way to the Exhibition Centre. Five minutes later he is back at the bus stop again. Wendy is still waiting for her bus. She is surprised to see him.

Wendy: Oh! It's you again. What are you doing here?
Young man: Er ... well ... perhaps it *is* quicker by bus. What's the number of the bus again?
Wendy: The Number 17. Look, I'm going to the Exhibition Centre, too. I can show you the way from the bus stop.
Young man: Well, perhaps that's the best idea.

1 Can you tell me the way?

a) A tourist in Bristol asks you the way to the Exhibition Centre. Give him/her the information. You are waiting at a bus stop near the station.

b) You are at Broadmead Shopping Centre. Someone asks you the way to
- the Tourist Information Centre
- the station
- the Exhibition Centre
- the 'Great Britain'

c) Now tell your partner how you get to school
- from home
- from the bus stop
- from the station

2 Road signs

What must/mustn't/ can/can't/needn't you do here?

Example:
1. I must stop here. I must stop first, then I can go on.

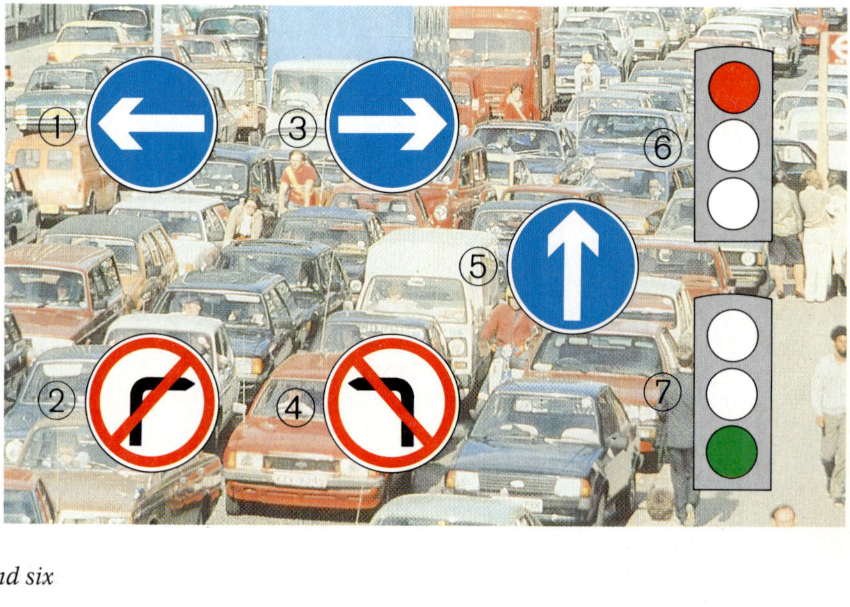

D Saturday afternoon at the Computer Show

There are a lot of people at the Exhibition Centre. David is there with his girlfriend Sandra. They are going to meet Wendy at the snack bar later, but first David and Sandra are going to try the big computer competition.

David: Look, Sandra. There's the stand with the computer competition!

Sandra: Yes, we must hurry. It's nearly five o'clock, and we're going to meet Wendy at half past.

David: Well, I'm not going to hurry with the competition!

Sandra: I'm going to look at the Radio Bristol stand over there first. I want some posters for my bedroom. Are you going to come with me?

David: No, I'm not. I'm going to start the questions now.

At the Radio Bristol stand a young woman wants to ask Sandra some questions about the Computer Show for the local news programme.

Young woman: Excuse me, I'm from Radio Bristol. May I ask you a few questions for our local news programme? Just one or two questions? OK?

Sandra: On local radio? Well, why not?

Young woman: Good afternoon, everybody. I'm at the Computer Show in Bristol and I'm going to ask some people here what they think about it. First a young lady. Please tell us your name. Where are you from?

Sandra: My name's Sandra Long, and I'm from Filton.

Young woman: And are you enjoying the Computer Show, Sandra?

Sandra: Yes, very much. I'm in the computer group at our youth club, and I'm going to try to win a prize in the competition.

Young woman: Good! Thank you, Sandra. ...

Sandra: What time are you going to broadcast your programme?

Young woman: At 7 o'clock this evening. Are you going to listen to it?

Sandra: Yes, of course I am.

1 Comprehension

1. Where are David and Sandra going to meet Wendy?
2. What are David and Sandra going to do?
3. What time are they going to meet Wendy?
4. What is Sandra going to do first?
5. Why isn't David going to look at the posters with her?
6. What is the young woman going to do?
7. What time are they going to broadcast the local news programme?
8. Is Sandra going to listen to it?

2 Melanie's interview

Melanie, Jenny's friend, is at the Computer Show and the young woman is talking to her. Can you think of her questions? Here are Melanie's answers.

1. ...? – My name is Melanie King.
2. ...? – Yes I do, I live in Filton.
3. ...? – I think the Computer Show is great – it's fantastic!
4. ...? – Well, my brother and I have got a computer together.
5. ...? – Yes, he's here today. We want to buy a bigger computer.
6. ...? – Yes, we do. We have a special computer room at school.
7. ...? – I go to school in Filton – Filton Comprehensive.
8. ...? – Yes, I know about the competition. I'm going to try to win a prize.

3 Wendy's plans for next week

What is Wendy going to do next week?

Saturday	16th	5.30. Meet David	and Sandra. Snack bar. Computer Show.
Sunday	17th	3.00. Table-tennis.	7.30 pm, cinema with Andy.
Monday	18th	7.00. Volleyball-	sports centre.
Tuesday	19th	8.15. Good film	on TV.
Wednesday	20th	Buy birthday	present for mum - book?
Thursday	21st	'Friends of	the Earth' meeting at 4.30.
Friday	22nd	Meet Andy	in 'The Black Cat' at 7.00.
Saturday	23rd	Pop concert	in Bristol at 8.00.

4 Plans

a) What are you going to do?
b) And your friends? What are they going to do?

This evening
Tomorrow (morning ...)
On Tuesday/Wednesday ...
At the weekend/Next weekend
On Monday 18th ...
At 10 o'clock tomorrow
...

play tennis/football
clean my room
listen to some music
get up early/late
have a party
learn some English
buy a birthday present for ...
...

E (The world of the future)

"Today we are going to show you how computers will probably change the world in the next twenty years.

There will not be many jobs without computers in the world of the future, so what are *you* going to do after your last year at school? Are you going to work with computers?

Do you want to be a train driver? There are already trains without drivers in London, so there won't be many train drivers in the future. Computers will control the trains.

The world will be a better place with computers. We will have more time for interesting work because computers will do most of the boring work. Computers will help us, for example, at home, in hospitals, in biology and physics and with our environmental problems.

And what about the young people of the future? What will they do at school? They won't write with pens or pencils – they will have PCs in their schoolbags – or in their pockets. And will there be a computer to do their homework? Of course there will. – Now let's have a look at our first film. It's about schools of the future. ..."

will not = won't

[1 Questions]

1. Will there be train drivers in the future?
2. Will we have more interesting work? What do you think?
3. How will computers help us?
4. Will the young people of the future write a lot at school?
5. Will all young people have their own computer?
6. Do *you* want to work with computers?

[2 What do you think?]

What do you think about the future? What do you think will happen?
Do you think

- young people will learn with TVs and computers at home?
- there will still be teachers? Or just computers?
- computers will drive cars for us?
- computers will just do boring jobs or will they think, too?

[3 Computers and jobs]

Put in the correct form of 'will' or 'going to'.

1. Computers ... help to do boring jobs.
2. There ... be a lot of jobs with computers.
3. There ... be trains without drivers.
4. Do you think computers ... drive buses and cars, too?
5. David ... learn more about computers.
6. Then he ... look for a better job.
7. Jenny ... take some computer lessons at school.
8. She is not so interested in computers as David but she ... probably use a computer when she is older.

F After the Computer Show

a) After her interview for Radio Bristol, Sandra answers the questions in the computer competition. Then she and David go to the Exhibition Centre snack bar where Wendy is already waiting for them. Ben, the young man from the bus stop, is still with her. Sandra tells them about the interview.

The Computer Show is over now, and they are just leaving the snack bar when it starts to rain. They have not got raincoats or umbrellas with them, so they sit down again. Ben and David start to talk about their jobs. Ben works in a bank like David, but he is not very happy about his job.

Ben: My job at the bank's boring. I'd like to work with computers, too.
David: Well, what are you going to do about it?
Ben: I'm going to look for a better job. And I'm going to move around a bit – to London, perhaps – or even to the USA. That's where things are really happening in the computer world.
David: Yes, it would be great to visit Silicon Valley. Just imagine – a trip to the USA!
Sandra: That would be really exciting. Oh well, let's wait and see. – What time is it, David?
David: Twenty past six. Why?
Sandra: They're going to broadcast that programme at seven – the local news programme with the interviews at the Computer Show. I'd like to listen to my interview.
David: And I'd like to hear the results of the competition, but it's still raining.
Sandra: Never mind! I'm not going to miss my interview!
Wendy: I've got a better idea. It's not so far to our flat. You can all come home with me and listen to the programme there.
Ben: Me too?
Wendy: Of course. Come on, let's run!

b) Wendy and her family live in a flat in Clifton, one of the oldest suburbs of Bristol. It is not as far as Filton, but they are wet when they get there, so they go into the kitchen and make some hot chocolate.

A street in Clifton

At seven o'clock Wendy switches on Radio Bristol. The news programme is just starting. There are one or two short interviews before they hear Sandra's voice.

Sandra: Isn't my voice funny on the radio!
Ben: There's nothing wrong with it.
Wendy: You're famous now, Sandra! What are you going to do? Be a local radio star?
Sandra: No, I'm going to ....
David: Listen! They're going to give the names of the competition winners next!

The announcer starts with the names of the winners of the twenty-five small prizes, but David and Sandra are not among them. Then they hear the name of the winner of the fifth prize – a colour monitor. But David is not so happy. No prize for him!

Announcer:
And now the name of the lucky winner of the first prize: ten days in the USA. Two days in New York and then a week in California with a visit to Silicon Valley, the home of the most exciting computer technology in the world.
The winner is 18 years old and he lives in Bristol. Are you listening, David Benson of 10 York Road, Filton? Yes, *you* are the winner of the fantastic first prize! Congratulations!

1 At the snack bar (a)

Complete the sentences.

1. Wendy is already waiting in the snack bar when ....
2. They are just going to leave the snack bar when ....
3. They sit down again in the snack bar because ....
4. Ben thinks his job is boring, so ....
5. He would like to go to the USA where ....
6. David would like to go home, but ....
7. Sandra wants to listen to the news programme because ....
8. They all go to Wendy's flat and ....

2 Right or wrong? (b)

1. Wendy lives in one of the newest parts of Bristol.
2. The friends drink milk because it is so hot.
3. Wendy switches on the TV at 6 o'clock.
4. There is some music on the radio.
5. Sandra thinks her voice is funny when she hears it.
6. The announcer starts with the winner of the first prize.
7. Sandra is happy when she wins one of the prizes.
8. The first prize is ten days in New York.
9. Bristol is a centre of computer technology.
10. David wins a fantastic prize.

⇄ 3 Congratulations!

Ben: What a surprise, David. Congratulations! I'm so pleased that you're the winner.
David: Yes, I can't believe it. It's really great – it's fantastic!
Ben: New York and California – how exciting! You're really lucky!

Good news	**Bad news**
That's great/fantastic/ super/nice.	I'm sorry ...
I'm pleased.	I'm afraid ...
Congratulations!	Never mind!
How exciting!	Oh dear!
You're really lucky!	I'm very unhappy about ...
What a surprise!	

Make up three short dialogues.

- Mrs Phillips is the winner of the second prize, a new PC. What does her husband say to her?
- Sandra is unhappy because she has not got a prize. What does David say to her?
- Ben is unhappy about his job at the bank. What does David say to him?

4 David's interview

David is at Radio Bristol for an interview. *Look at the announcer's questions and give David's answers.*

Announcer: Congratulations, David Benson. In a minute we're going to give you an envelope with your prize – the tickets and everything for your trip. Now, are you still at school?
David: (bank)
Announcer: So you work a lot with computers, then?
David: (Yes/learn more)
Announcer: Is this your first trip to the USA?
David: (Yes)
Announcer: OK, open the envelope, please. In it there's a card with the information about your trip. Read it, please. ... Now, tell us about the trip.
David: (two days/New York)
Announcer: And after that?
David: (Silicon Valley/California)
Announcer: Tell us about your plans for the next two or three days. What are you going to do?
David: (tell family/tell bank/buy book about the USA)
Announcer: Well, David, congratulations again, and have a good time in New York and California.

5 Before and after the competition

Look at the pictures and tell the story. First David and Sandra ... Then ... After that ...

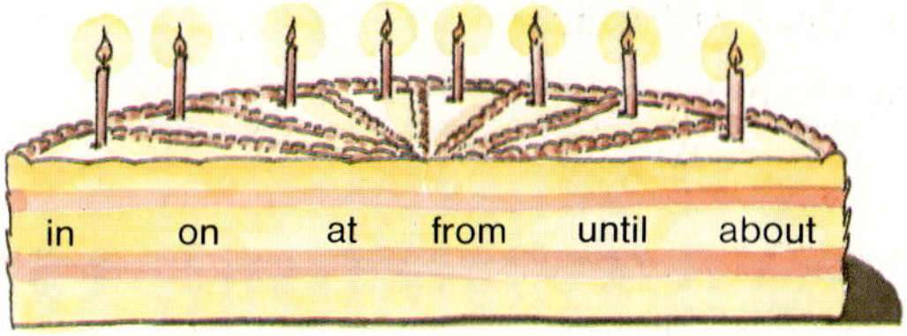

6 Sandra

Put in the correct prepositions.

Sandra is 18 years old. Her birthday is … spring. It is … 5th March. This year her birthday is … a Saturday. She is going to have a party … half past seven … the evening.
Sandra is still at school, so she must get up early … the morning: … seven o'clock. Her bus leaves … ten past eight. She is at school … half past eight … a quarter to four. She usually gets home …… half past four. … the evening she does her homework, reads an interesting book or goes out with David.

7 What is it?

1. It's bigger than a pencil case, but it isn't as big as a car. You can put things in it.
2. It isn't as fast as a car, but it's faster in busy traffic.

Can you find other examples?

8 Word pairs

Find the pairs. Example: Saturday afternoon

1. ~~Saturday~~	11. Silicon	a) news	k) problems
2. Radio	12. balloon	b) Valley	l) lights
3. New	13. Computer	c) concert	m) stop
4. twin	14. Earth	d) Centre	n) town
5. first	15. birthday	e) York	o) chocolate
6. local	16. environmental	f) calendar	p) ~~afternoon~~
7. lucky	17. bus	g) party	q) park
8. open-air	18. traffic	h) festival	r) prize
9. hot	19. Exhibition	i) Bristol	s) Day
10. wall	20. car	j) Show	t) winner

9 A brochure

Make up a brochure or a calendar of the events in your town or area. Say what is best, most important or most exciting about the events.

⟨10 Listening comprehension: Tourists in Bristol⟩

Look at the map of Bristol on page 105 and listen to the cassette.
a) Follow their route.
b) Say what they visit.
c) Say what they see but do not visit.

UNIT 9

A A few more days in Bristol

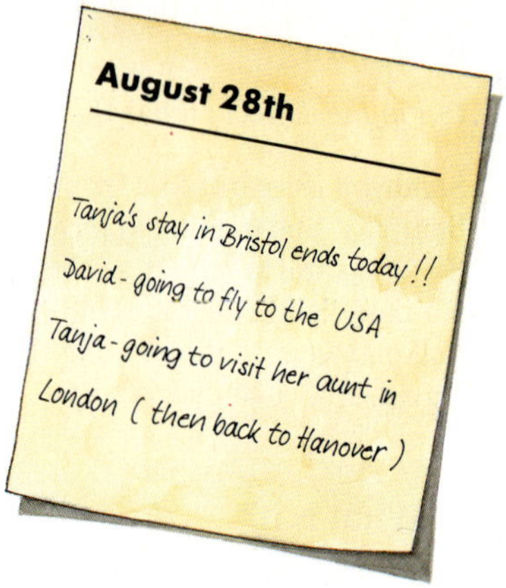

Tanja has only got a few more days in Bristol, and Jenny is very unhappy about it. Tanja would love to stay another week but she has got school again in Germany. Her stay in Britain is over on August 30th. Mrs Benson is going to take Tanja to her aunt in London and David to Heathrow Airport for his flight to the USA. Jenny wants to do something for Tanja and David before they leave. Something exciting ... but what? Then Jenny has a good idea!

Jenny and Kevin are going to organize a farewell party for Tanja and David together on Friday evening. It is a secret but Jenny tells her parents about it, of course. But where can they have the party? Parties are usually very noisy.

Jenny rings Patrick. Patrick's mother answers the phone.
"Can I talk to Patrick, please?"
"He's in the barn, Jenny. Just a minute ... ."
A barn? That's it. Patrick's parents have got a barn – just the place for a party! Jenny is very excited. Patrick thinks the party is a very good idea.

Jenny begins to discuss everything with Patrick. Where can they borrow things for the party? Can they have a barbecue?

That evening Tanja is out at the sports centre, so Jenny and Kevin go to Patrick's house.

"Come on, you two, help me in the barn," Patrick says. "It's a mess but we can tidy it up." It is hard work but it is fun, too. At ten o'clock they finish work in the barn.

1 Plans

What are Tanja, Jenny, David, Kevin and Mrs Benson going to do? Use the verbs on the right.

leave fly visit
give take do ...
meet stay

2 Wednesday 25th August

Tell the story. Use the following phrases and link your sentences with words like 'because', 'so', 'and', 'but', 'first', 'then', 'after that'.

Wednesday / August 25th – Jenny and Kevin / to organize / a party – barn / a good place / parties / noisy – Patrick's parents / barn / tell / plan – Patrick / great idea – Jenny and Patrick / discuss – make / list – borrow – a lot of work – Jenny and Kevin / help / tidy up / a mess – late in the evening – barn / almost ready

Start like this: It is Wednesday, August 25th ...

B A party at the Aerospace Club?

a) It is Thursday, the day before the party. Kevin has started to organize things at home. Jenny and Patrick are in the barn again. They are talking about the party.

Work has ended for the day, and so they go into the kitchen in Patrick's house. "Oh, Mum, you've remembered the sausages. Great!"

b) On Friday afternoon everyone is busy. Jenny, Patrick and Kevin have invited their friends, but Tanja does not know about the party yet.

At the Bensons' house, Tanja and Jenny have just started to make sandwiches. There is a party at the Aerospace Club, and Tanja thinks the sandwiches are for that. Jenny goes round to Kevin's house.

Jenny: Have you looked for those cassettes yet, Kevin?
Kevin: Yes, I have. They're over there. Have you and Patrick fetched Peter's new cassette recorder?
Jenny: No, we haven't. We're going to do that just before the party. Has Patrick called?
Kevin: No, he hasn't. I can call him in a few minutes.

It is already five o'clock but Patrick and his father have not finished the work yet. Patrick has not moved the chairs into the barn and David has not finished the lights. He needs another hour.

1 Pronunciation (a)

	[d]	[t]	[ɪd]
Examples:	we have organiz**ed**	she has ask**ed**	they have start**ed**
	…	…	…

a) *Put the present perfect forms from the text into the right columns.*

b) *Now give the past participle of the following verbs and put them into the right columns:*

to arrive; to play; to climb; to clean; to practise; to hurry; to knock; to visit; to describe; to look at; to end; to tidy up; to wait; to help; to use

2 Work for the party (a) *Complete the text.*

1. It is eight o'clock. Patrick and Jenny **have finished** work. "We … everything, I think," Patrick says. "You … me a lot, Jenny. Let's go in." They are tired but happy. (finish; organize; help)
2. Patrick … some garden tables from the family next door. They are in the garden now. Jenny … to call Rajiv but he is always out. The party is still a secret to Tanja; she does not know about the barbecue. Patrick's parents … her to supper on Friday. (borrow; try; invite)
3. They need some special lights for the barn, so Jenny … her brother David. And what about Kevin? Kevin … to organize things at home, so everybody is busy. (ask; start)

3 Work, work, work! (b)

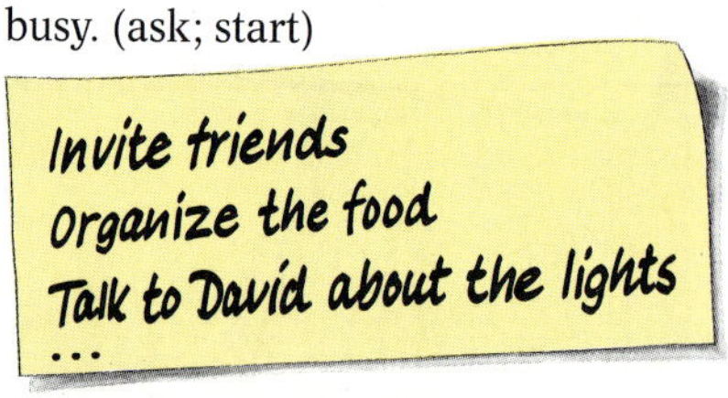

a) *Make a list of the jobs for the party and say who does them.*

b) *Patrick's mum and dad know him very well. He has got a lot of ideas but he often forgets to organize things and to do the work, so they ask his friends some questions before the party.*

Mrs Fox: Have you invited your friends yet?
Kevin: Yes, we have.
Mrs Fox: Fine.

Mr Fox: Have you tidied up the garden yet?
Jenny: No, we haven't, but …
Mr Fox: Well, hurry up, then. You haven't got much time. *Go on.*

4 Before the party

Examples: 1. Don't sit on that chair, Wendy, I haven't cleaned it yet. 2. Please fetch …

C At the barn

a) It is half past six. Mr Benson has taken Tanja and Jenny to Patrick's house. The food is in the back of the car. Nobody has told Tanja about the party yet, so Patrick takes Tanja upstairs and shows her some photos of his holiday in the South of Germany.

"Come on, Jenny," Mr Benson says. "Let's take the food into the barn. The hamburgers are in this box. I've left the sandwiches in the car. Can you fetch them, please?"

Kevin has brought a lot of cassettes. He has made a poster for the party, and he has just put it up on the wall.

b) David has not finished all the lights yet, so Mr Benson has gone up the ladder and is helping him. In the house, Patrick has found a computer game about hockey and is showing it to Tanja on his computer. Tanja must not go to the barn yet. Jenny is in the house, too, but all the others have gone to the barn. Now Tanja is alone in Patrick's room. She is playing hockey on the computer.

"Have you seen my present for Tanja, Patrick?"
"Yes, I've put it on the table over there, Jenny."

"We've forgotten the glasses."
"No, we haven't. I've left them in the box in the kitchen. We must take them into the barn."
"Where are the crisps? Haven't you bought any?"
"Oh no, I haven't!"

At that moment the lights go on in the barn.
"Look, I've done it," David says.
The barn is full of colours from the lights.
"David, that's fantastic. Let's go and get Tanja now."
Jenny hurries out. People are already arriving for the party.
"Come and look, Tanja."
"What is it? … Oh, Jenny, that's fantastic. But why are so many people here?"
"We're having a party for you and David. Come into the barn!"

1 What have they done? (a)

Put the words in the right order and complete the sentences.

1. to Patrick's house / Jenny / Mr Benson / and her German friend / taken
2. made / a lot of / the Bensons / sandwiches and hamburgers
3. yet / Mr Benson / not / taken / into the barn / all the food
4. left / with the sandwiches / the box / in the car / he
5. with pop music / brought / Kevin / his cassettes ?
6. Yes, … .
7. made / a poster / too / he / and / put / on the wall / up / he / just / it
8. Jenny and Patrick / their names / written / yet / on it ?
9. No, … .
10. Tanja / told / nobody / why / yet / about the party ?

2 Just before the party (b)

Complete the sentences.

1. Only Tanja, Jenny and Patrick are in the house, all … (the others / to the barn).
2. Jenny is a bit excited and cannot find her present for Tanja, so she asks: "… (my present)?"
3. Patrick can help her because … (on the table).
4. The glasses are not in the barn yet, so Jenny thinks … (forget them). But … (in the kitchen).
5. But where is Mr Benson? … (to the barn).
6. David is still busy. His father is helping him because … (not / all the lights yet).
7. It is not eight o'clock yet and the people … (not arrive).
8. A few minutes later the barn is full of lights and colours; … (finish / the lights).
9. When the people arrive, they ask: "… (Who / lights)?"

3 Before Tanja and David leave

Mr and Mrs Benson are quite excited because David and Tanja are going to leave Bristol.
Ask Mr and Mrs Benson's questions. Your partner answers the questions.
Example: Have you called Sandra yet? – Yes, I have. / No, I haven't because I haven't had time.

D The farewell present

Tanja and David are leaving Bristol, and Kevin has come round to the Bensons' house. He has got a present for Tanja. It is a small book – and all Tanja's friends have written their names and a poem, a riddle or joke in it. He gives her the book.
"Oh Kevin, what a lovely present. Thanks very much. It's been wonderful here in Bristol."
"Bye, Tanja. It's been great with you here. Come again soon. And drop us a line."
She gives him a big kiss and says, "Why don't you come to Hanover?"
Kevin goes red in the face and says, "Yes, I'd love to."

Here are some of the jokes, poems and riddles:

The town child

I live in the town
in a street;
it is crowded with traffic
and feet;
there are buses and motors
and trams;
I wish there were meadows
and lambs.

The houses all wait
in a row,
there is smoke everywhere
that I go.
I don't like the noises
I hear –
I wish there were woods
very near.

There is only one thing
that I love,
and that is the sky
far above,
there is plenty of room
in the blue
for castles of clouds
and me, too!

Irene Thompson

Jenny

Mice

I think mice
Are rather nice.

Their tails are long,
Their faces small,
They haven't any
Chins at all.
Their ears are pink,
Their teeth are white,
They run about
The house at night.
They nibble things
They shouldn't touch
And no one seems
To like them much.

But I think mice
Are nice.

Rose Fyleman (1877–1957)

Patrick

Roses are red
Violets are blue
Sugar is sweet
And so are you.
Kevin

Rajiv

Why do birds fly south in the winter?
Because it's too far to walk.

This is the end of your stay –
We're sad you are going away.
The time with you has been great,
And all your new friends cannot wait
To see you again.
The question is: When?
Perhaps next year
In Hanover or here?
Let's wait and see!

Love,
Pamela and
Jim Benson

First man: Have you seen a policeman anywhere near here?
Second man: No, I haven't.
First man: Do you know where the nearest police station is?
Second man: Sorry, I don't.
First man: All right then. Hands up!

David

Teacher: Melanie, you've got 20p. You ask your mum for 50p and your dad for 50p. How much have you got?
Melanie: 20p.
Teacher: That's wrong.
Melanie: No, that's right. You don't know my mum and dad.

Melanie

1 Tanja's farewell present

a) *Do you like the poems, riddles and jokes for Tanja. Why? / Why not?*

I think … … because it's funny.
It helps Tanja to remember …
… because I like … I'm interested in …
… because it's beautiful.
… because it's about …

b) *There is an English boy/girl at your school and he/she is leaving for home. You want to write a farewell note. You can use the following words and expressions:*

Remember, … Don't forget, …
Super to have you here. …
Hope to see you again. …
Don't worry – be happy!
Lots of love from …

OVER TO YOU

2 A friend's dog and bird

You are looking after a friend's dog Rex and bird Polly for a few days. Here is your list.

1 Play with Rex ✓
2 Take him to the park
3 Open the Doggofood for him
4 Give him some water ✓
5 Talk to Polly ✓
6 Give her new food
7 Change her water ✓
8 Fetch the neighbour's bird

a) You have already done some of the things when your friend calls.

Friend: Is everything OK?
You: Oh yes, everything's fine.
Friend: Have you played with Rex yet?
You: Yes, I have.
Friend: Have you … yet?
You: No, I haven't. I'm going to do that later.
Friend: Have you …?
Go on.

b) Can you remember everything without the list? *Shut your book and say how you are going to look after Rex and Polly* **tomorrow**. (I'm going to …)

c) You are looking after Kitty, a friend's cat. *What are you going to do?*

OVER TO YOU

⇆ 3 Role Play Have you seen it?

Read the dialogues and act one of the scenes.

Have you taken my cassette/glass …?
Hey – where's my …? Have you seen it?
…

→

No, I haven't. No, I haven't taken your … .
No, I don't know where your … is.
Sorry, I don't know. No, I haven't seen it.
…

→

Well – can you help me look for it?
Where can … be?
Where have I put it?

→

Yes, I can. Let's look over here. Have you put it in … ?
Have you looked for it in the hall/ … ?
Isn't it in your … ?
…

→

OK, thanks. Let's see now. Ah – here it is!
Hm. Yes, perhaps I've put it in … . Thank you.
No, I haven't. That's a good idea.
Yes – it is! Thanks very much.
…

4 Word flowers

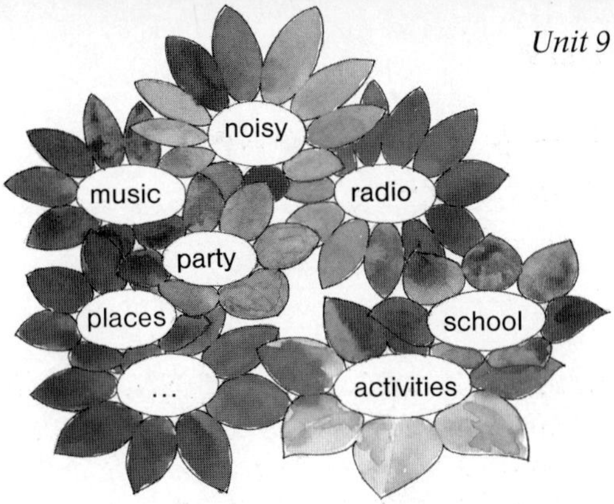

Complete the word flowers. Start with the word 'party'. What do you think of when you hear the word 'party'? What places can you use for a party? For example, your school. Go on. What do you think of when you hear the word 'school', etc.?

5 Vocabulary

a) Some English nouns and verbs have got the same form, for example: 'an answer' – 'to answer'; 'a (telephone) call' – 'to call' *Find other examples.*

b) *Find other words of the same word family. Examples:* 'to meet' – 'meeting'; 'exciting' – 'excited'

to play; to fly; different; interesting; to win; to practise

c) *Find other words/phrases. Examples:* car – car park; every – everything. *Go on.*
every; girl; police; to cross; news; information; shop; class; time; note; week; down

⟨6 Let's sing a song: Octopus's garden⟩

Kevin has also got a cassette for Tanja. This is the song on it:

I'd like to be under the sea
In an octopus's garden, in the shade.

He'd let us in, know where we've been
In his octopus's garden, in the shade.

I'd ask my friends to come and see
All of octopus's garden with me.

I'd like to be under the sea
In an octopus's garden, in the shade.

We would be warm below the storm
In our little hideaway beneath the waves.

Resting a head on the seabed
In an octopus's garden, near a cave.

We would sing and dance around
Because we know we can't be found.

I'd like to be under the sea
In an octopus's garden, in the shade.

We would shout and swim about
The coral that lies beneath the waves.

Oh, what joy, for every girl and boy
Knowing they're happy and they're safe.

We would be so happy, you and me
No one there to tell us what to do.

I'd like to be under the sea
In an octopus's garden with you.

John Lennon

⟨7 Listening comprehension: After the party⟩

Listen to the text. What is wrong with these sentences?

1. Patrick has started to tidy up.
2. Jenny has just come out of the house.
3. There are no cups on the floor of the barn.
4. Someone has put all the plates on the table at the end of the barn.
5. David's lights are still in the barn.
6. The cassettes are beside the cassette recorder.
7. The light in the barn is not on.
8. The bird has just flown into the barn.
9. The girl's shoe is under the table.
10. There are five plates in front of the barbecue.

Stopover B ⟨London⟩

Mrs Benson is in a coach with a group of language students. She is showing them London.

"London is really two cities, the old City of London and the newer City of Westminster. We are going to drive through Westminster first and then the City of London."

"We are now driving down Oxford Street, the most famous shopping street in London. There are over forty shoe shops in this street, and we are just driving past the biggest record shop in Britain. Only buses and taxis can drive along Oxford Street – and tourist coaches, of course."

"Now you can see Buckingham Palace, the Queen's London home. But she isn't at home today. How do we know? Because you can't see the Queen's flag. Buckingham Palace has got 600 rooms, 1000 windows and even its own post office. The park on the left is St James's Park, the oldest of the parks in London."

"Now we are in Trafalgar Square. Everybody knows Nelson's Column, but can you see the smallest police station in Britain? It's over there. – That big church has an interesting name: St Martin-in-the-Fields, but there are no green fields here now!"

"We are now driving out of Westminster and into the old City of London. When the Queen arrives here she must stop and ask permission before she can drive into the City, but we can drive straight on to St Paul's Cathedral. The dome of St Paul's is one of the biggest in the world."

"The Tower of London is 900 years old and those men in red and yellow uniforms are the Beefeaters. They guard the Tower and the Tower Ravens, those big black birds over there, because – people say – when there are ravens in the Tower nothing bad can happen to Britain."

"Here we are on Westminster Bridge. You all know the Houses of Parliament with its famous tower Big Ben. Big Ben is really only the name of the Great Bell. To make Big Ben more accurate they put pennies on the pendulum or take them off. Each penny makes Big Ben almost half a second slower or faster."

"Tower Bridge is one of the most famous places in London, but the bridge is only about 100 years old. It doesn't often open now, but you can see almost everything in the Cities of London and Westminster from the towers, so come with me, please!"

UNIT 10

A David's ticket to the USA

David has won the first prize in the computer competition but he cannot believe it. Plane tickets, hotels, restaurants, sightseeing tours – they have paid for everything. First he is going to fly to New York City and then across the country to San Francisco. He looks at his plane ticket again. BA 179 takes off … and then David believes it!

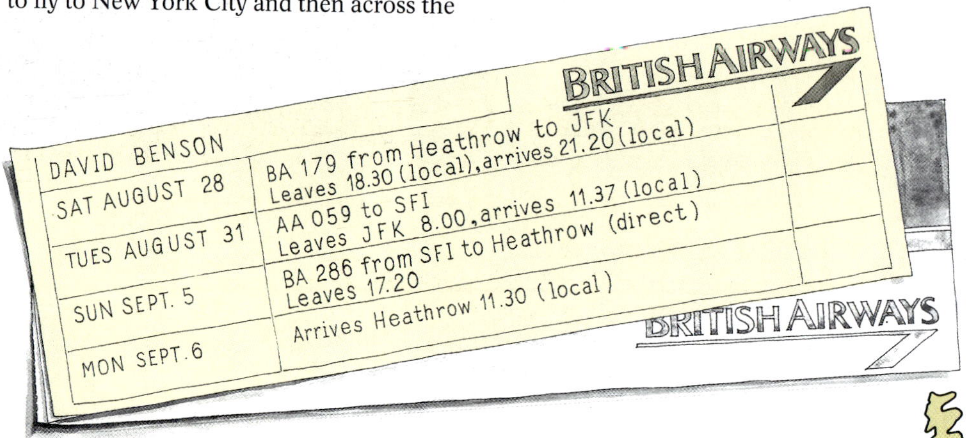

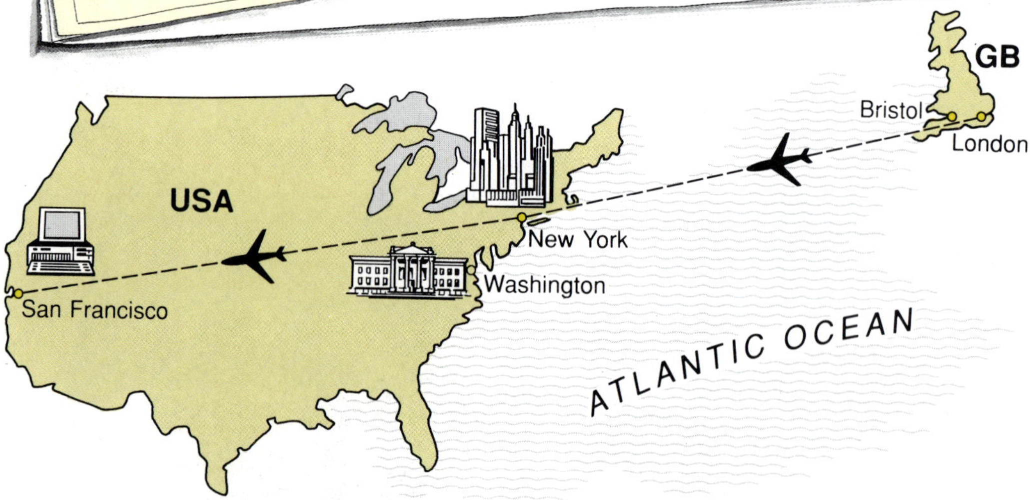

1 David's trip

1. What can't David believe? (Give two or three answers.)
2. How long is David going to stay in New York, in California, in the USA?
3. What is David going to do in the USA?
4. How much money does he need?

2 What do you know?

What do you already know about New York City, San Francisco and California?

B Henry Benson

a) On David's last day in Bristol he and his father talked about the trip to America. And there were a few surprises for David.

Mr Benson: We have 'family' in America!
David: Really? Where?
Mr Benson: We don't know. It's an old family story. It happened many years ago. I remembered it last week.
David: Well, what's the story?
Mr Benson: Around 1850, a Benson sailed from Bristol to New York City. He worked on a ship. His name was Harold. No, it was Henry. That's right: Henry Benson!

b) *David:* And how long did he stay there?
Mr Benson: As far as I know, he didn't stay there long because he dropped our family a line: "I'm on my way to California."
David: What did he want to do there?
Mr Benson: No one knows! Perhaps he didn't make enough money in New York and so he travelled to California and tried to find gold there.
David: Didn't he write again from California?
Mr Benson: No, he didn't. Just that one letter arrived and nothing else.
David: So, in New York and San Francisco …
Mr Benson: … ask about Henry Benson. He's a very old man – about 160 years old – and he doesn't …
David: … write very often!

to be – was/were
to talk – talked
to drop – dropped
to try – tried

1 Henry Benson's story

be try travel work drop be happen arrive arrive start want

Put in the verbs on the right.

It … around 1850. A member of the Benson family … to the USA. It … Henry Benson. He … his trip in Bristol. On his way to America he … on a ship because trips like that … very expensive. When he … in New York, he … his family a line. After a short stay there he … to get to California. Perhaps he … to find gold in the West but the Bensons do not know because no other letter … .

2 How, where, what, why …?

Ask about the underlined part of the sentence.
Example: Where did Henry Benson …?

1. …? Henry Benson started his trip in Bristol.
2. …? He travelled by ship.
3. …? He arrived in New York in September, 1850.
4. …? He did not stay there long.
5. …? He did not like New York because he did not make enough money.
6. …? From there he travelled to San Francisco.
7. …? He wanted to find gold there.

3 What do you do in your free time?

1. Do you play football?
   Did you play football last week?
2. Do you sometimes visit your friends at the weekends?
   … you visit a friend last weekend?
3. … usually stay at home in the summer holidays?
   … stay at home last summer holidays?
4. … watch TV every day?
   … watch TV yesterday evening?
5. …

Yes, I do.
No, I don't. I …

Yes, I did.
No, I didn't. I …

C New York City

Statue of Liberty

a) David woke up. Where was he? Then he knew. He was in a hotel ... in New York City! He went to the window and looked down at the streets. It was Sunday morning, and there were only a few people in the streets. It was a beautiful morning!

He stood by the window for a minute. Then he ran to the bathroom. On Sunday morning he had a sightseeing tour around Manhattan! It started at nine, and it was already 8.30! He put his clothes on, went downstairs, had breakfast and was outside the hotel at 9.01. The tour bus drove up and David got on.

Manhattan at night

That evening, David ate at the restaurant 'Windows on the World' in the World Trade Center. Manhattan at night – fantastic! New York wasn't the capital of the U.S., David knew. That was Washington, D.C. But now he knew why so many people called New York City 'the capital of the world.'

World Trade Centre

b) On Monday morning David took a boat trip around Manhattan. In the afternoon he bought some postcards. He found a quiet place in Central Park. He sat down, took out a postcard and began to write.

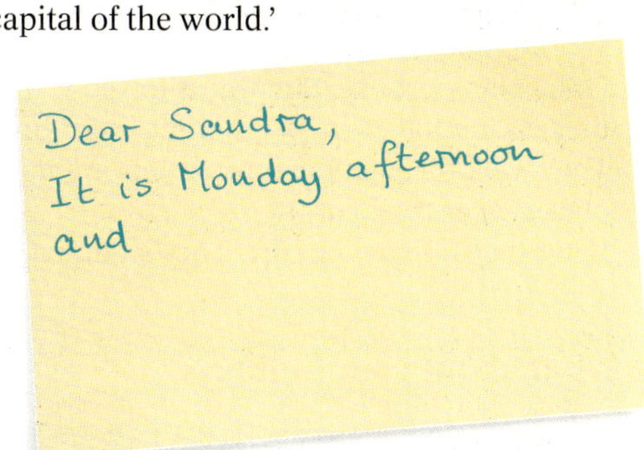

◁ *Central Park*

On his way back from Central Park to his hotel, David had a quick look in the Manhattan phone book. There were 173 Bensons. He counted them. There were four Davids but *no* Henry.

1 David in New York (a)

Look at the pictures and say what David did on his first day in New York.

2 David's postcard (b)

Write David's postcard about the sightseeing tour, the boat trip and his feelings.

3 Tanja in London

Say what **happened** *on 28th August. Put the verbs into the simple past.*

1. On 28th August Mrs Benson takes Tanja and David to London.
2. First they go to Heathrow Airport and say goodbye to David.
3. Then they drive to Victoria Station.
4. Tanja is not very happy and does not talk much. She tries to think about London, not about Kevin, the Bensons and all her other friends in Bristol.
5. Her aunt does not ask any questions, but she knows about Tanja's feelings because she starts to make plans at once. She wants to show Tanja around the City of London in the afternoon, so they do not have lunch at home but get on the bus to the Tower of London.
6. They walk through the busy streets in the City, look at the little shops and listen to a saxophone player on a street corner.
7. Later they find a nice café. They sit down at a small table and have two big ice-creams.

⇆ 4 What about your holidays

What did you *do last year?*

Where did you go?	We went to …
Did you go by car?	Yes, we did./No, we didn't. We …
Where did you stay?	We stayed at …
How long did you stay there?	We …
What did you do there?	We …
What was the weather like?	It was …

D Silicon Valley

The hotel bus picked up David at the San Francisco airport. After a quick lunch he walked around downtown. New York City, then San Francisco – it was almost too much! But tomorrow and the next day looked like hard work!

On Wednesday, a tour of Silicon Valley.
On Thursday, guest at ProNet, a large computer company.
On Friday, the computer department of a bank.
And on Sunday, computers again!

David liked computers, but there was no time to see the city. Oh well. He went back to his hotel room; on his desk there was an article about Silicon Valley. He started to read it.

Silicon Valley is the popular name for an area – about 10 miles wide and 30 miles long – between San Francisco and San Jose. There were a few electronics companies in the area before World War II. Hewlett-Packard, one of the world's largest computer companies today, started in a garage in Palo Alto in 1938. But Silicon Valley really grew after 1955 when William Shockley, one of the inventors of the transistor and a Nobel Prize winner, started a company there. By 1982, there were over 3,000 microelectronics companies in the Valley. Today, over 8,000 high-tech companies are at home there. Silicon Valley is the world's center of communication technology.

David spent all Wednesday on the tour of Silicon Valley. On Thursday, Mr Kramer took him around ProNet. It was all very interesting and everyone was nice to him. They explained everything to him and he even understood some of it. But after two days of computers and programs and chips ... he was tired!
Then, at lunch in the ProNet cafeteria, he met Jan.

Silicon Valley

1 California and Silicon Valley

Are these statements true, false or not in the text?

1. David's stay in San Francisco looked like hard work, but there was still enough time to see the city.
2. David had lunch in the cafeteria of a computer company and later walked around downtown.
3. In the evening, before his tour of Silicon Valley, he started to read an article about the world's centre of communication technology.
4. Silicon Valley is a small area near San Francisco. It is about 10 miles long and 13 miles wide.
5. Its history began after World War II when Hewlett-Packard started a computer company in Palo Alto.
6. After 1955 Silicon Valley really grew, and today there are 8,000 microelectronics companies.
7. More than 50,000 people work there and a lot of computer fans visit the high-tech companies every year.
8. David was a guest of ProNet on Thursday.
9. People were very interested in him because they knew that he was the winner of a computer competition; he explained lots of things to them.
10. After two days of computers, chips and programs, he met Jan in the ProNet cafeteria.

2 Computers

How many 'computer' words do you know? Make three lists:

a) hardware
...

b) software
...

c) other words
...

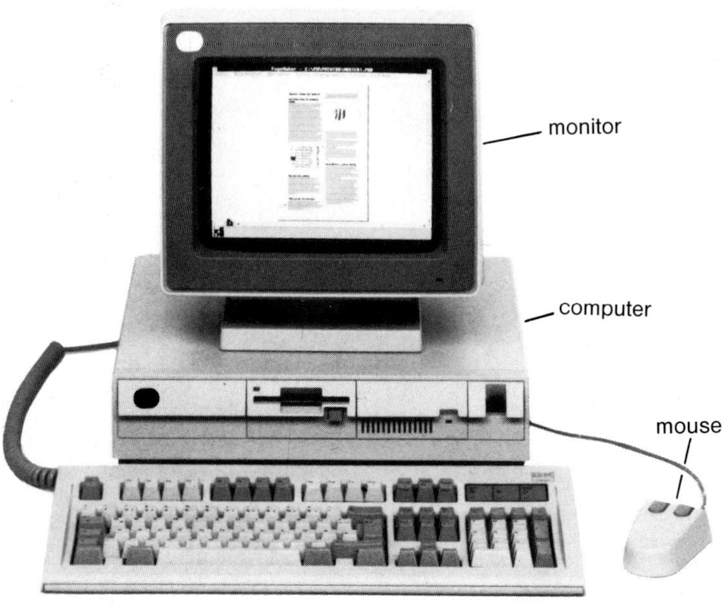

3 Your town, valley or area

Write an article about your town, valley or area. Think of famous buildings, famous people and companies, and the sights there. Write about their history or about interesting events today.

E Jan Benson

a) *Mr Kramer:* David, this is Jan, an old friend. Well, she's not old, but we were at school together, years ago. Jan, this is David Benson from Bristol in England. He won a trip to the U.S. at a computer show there. And we have an office over there.

David: I'm happy to meet you Ms ... uh, I'm sorry, I didn't hear your name.

Jan: That's because my old friend here didn't say it! He has a good sense of humor. You see, my name is Jan Benson.

Mr Kramer: And she's president of the Benson Corporation! Jan, I have a meeting .... Perhaps you can tell David about the family business for an hour or so?

Jan: Sure!

David: Are you *really* president of a computer company?

Jan: Yep! I'm the president. And the only employee! I write programs for small companies and I also train their people. It's hard work with long hours. But I'm the boss and that's nice.

David: I'm sure you do it very well. That's what I really want, my own business! I also work hard at my bank in Bristol but I'm not allowed to write programs.

Jan: Very boring for a Benson!

David: Right!

b) David told Jan about the competition and his two days in New York. He showed her his schedule. "That's awful!" she said angrily. "You aren't able to see the city. What's the name of that bank? I'll phone them. Don't go away!" Jan came back in a few minutes with a happy smile on her face. "I told them you're a member of our family from England. Tomorrow I'm going to visit customers all over San Francisco and the Valley. You're able to come along and see 'the world's favorite city', aren't you?" "Yes," David said happily. And then David told her the story about Henry Benson. "As far as I know, the Bensons came from Britain about then," Jan said. "My grandmother knows the history of the Bensons very well. I'll call her this evening. Perhaps you are a member of our family – you're clever enough!"

1 Jan Benson (a)

Describe Jan Benson. Who is she? What does she do? Find the information about her in the text.

2 Questions about David

a) *Terry Chang, also at ProNet, wants to find out more about David and his family. Ask Terry's questions.*

1. ...? I'm from Bristol. I live in Filton, that's a suburb of Bristol.
2. ...? Yes, I've got a sister. Her name's Jenny.
3. ...? My father works at British Aerospace and my mother works in a tourist information office.
4. ...? I'm 19.
5. ...? I work at a bank.
6. ...? My favourite hobby is computers.
7. ...? I won the trip at a computer show.
8. ...? No, the competition was quite difficult.
9. ...? Before I came here, I visited New York.
10. ...? Of course, I saw the Statue of Liberty. And I took a boat trip around Manhattan.

b) Role Play *Now answer Terry's questions.*

1. How do like your job, David?
2. Would you like to live in New York City?
3. What did you like best in New York? And why?
4. What are you going to do in San Francisco?
5. How long are you going to stay here?

beautiful
hard
well
really
good
large
happily
differently
difficult

3 Mr Kramer – the president (b)

Complete the text with the words on the right.

Mr Kramer is the president of a ... computer company in the ... area around San Francisco. Today he is speaking to his employees. "Last year we all worked very ... ." He smiled ... when he said this. But then he went on: "You all know our business is ... . You can see that the other companies are working ..., too. So let's try to work a bit ... next year. We make very ... programs, but that is not enough. We must be better than the others. Our service and our programs must be ... fantastic!"

4 What did you do?

What did you do yesterday/last week/two weeks ago/...? Work with a partner.

	to travel	yesterday
	to do	in September
Where	to see	the day before yesterday
When	to get up	on your birthday
Why	to go	on your last holidays
What	to play	last week/month
How	to meet your friends	on Monday
How much	to finish your homework	two weeks ago
	to spend	...
	...	

F The party on the beach

a) On Friday night David got a phone call from Jan.

Jan: Do you know the way to Monterey?
David: No, I don't.
Jan: It's down the coast. My grandparents live there. And my grandfather wants to meet you. He's sure you're one of 'our' Bensons.
David: Oh, that's very nice, but … .
Jan: It's his birthday tomorrow. The whole family will be there.
David: But if the whole family is there, I won't be really welcome.
Jan: Yes, you will. They want to have a picnic on the beach. It's beautiful there! And my niece and nephew want to take you to a rock concert tomorrow night. If you go with them, they'll save you from grandfather.
David: Well, okay! And thank you.
Jan: Oh. Did I tell you grandfather's first name?
David: It's not Henry, is it?
Jan: No, it's William. Good night, David.

The birthday picnic was fun. There were 40 or 50 Bensons there, young and old. Then there was the rock concert with Carrie and Scott, Jan's niece and nephew. And after that there was another party on the beach. "You can sleep on the plane," Carrie told him.

b) David turned on the light over his seat. Where were they? Still over Canada? Over the Atlantic? He shut his eyes and tried to sleep. That letter from Jan – where was it? He turned on the light again and found the letter.

Saturday night

Dear David,

Grandfather was very happy – thank you! He said: "David is a nice young man, a real Benson!" I think so, too.

I talked to grandmother about Henry Benson on Thursday night. Well, our Benson's name was George. And he came from Liverpool, in '52. Grandmother said: "It isn't important. We can't choose our family but we can choose our friends!"

Have a good trip home (and say hello to the Bensons of Bristol). If you quit your job at the bank, don't forget the Benson Corporation. I know the president very well!

Jan

Monterey Beach

1 Questions on the text

1. Why did Jan ask David to go to Monterey in the afternoon?
2. What were her plans for the evening?
3. Why did Jan's grandfather want to meet David?
4. What did David find out about the Bensons' family history?
5. Do you think that David was happy about Jan's letter? Say why or why not.

2 The trip to Monterey

Look at the pictures and tell the story of David's trip to Monterey. Start like this:
Jan invited David to Monterey on his last …

⟨3 Let's sing a song: This land is your land⟩

As I went walking that ribbon of highway,
I saw above me that endless skyway.
I saw below me that golden valley,
This land was made for you and me

(Translation Practice)

Was man beim Übersetzen und beim Dolmetschen beachten muß:

Einige Schüler machen manchmal Fehler beim Übersetzen, indem sie versuchen, jedes Wort einzeln in die andere Sprache zu übertragen. Das geht aber nicht, denn zwei Sprachen drücken gleiche Inhalte selten gleich aus. Schaut Euch die folgenden Beispiele an:

1. Thank you.
   Danke schön.
2. What is your name?
   Wie heißt du?
3. Let's go home together.
   Laßt uns zusammen nach Hause gehen.

Mal ist der Satzbau anders, mal werden ganz andere Wörter gebraucht, mal ist die Reihenfolge ganz anders. Denkt also jedesmal beim Übersetzen – wie hätten Jenny und David, Kevin und Tanja es ausgedrückt?

1 Oben in Jennys Zimmer — Unit 1 Step F

Übersetze ins Englische.

Tanja und Jenny sind in Jennys Zimmer.

Jenny: Sieh dir mal dieses Foto an. Das sind Mama, Papa und ich vor unserem Auto. – Und das ist mein großer Bruder David.
Tanja: Und wer ist das in eurem Garten?
Jenny: Das ist natürlich Kevin Brown, unser Nachbar.
Tanja: Und was ist das hier hinter seinem Fahrrad?
Jenny: Das ist Kevins Hund. Er heißt Red.
Tanja: Er ist ein schöner Hund! Wie alt ist er?
Jenny: Er ist drei.
Mr Benson: Jenny, wo bist du?
Jenny: Wir sind oben in meinem Zimmer!
Mr Benson: Kommt runter, es gibt Abendessen.

2 Tanjas Brief — Unit 2 Step B

Tanja schreibt ihren Eltern einen Brief. Eigentlich wollte sie ihn auf deutsch schreiben. Dann entscheidet sie sich doch für das Englische.

Hallo,
die Bensons sind sehr nett. Sie haben ein großes Haus in Filton, einem Vorort von Bristol. Hinter dem Haus ist ein Garten. Ich habe oben ein Zimmer. Es ist nicht sehr groß, aber sehr ruhig. Es gibt keinen Kleiderschrank in meinem Zimmer. Meine Kleidung ist in einem kleinen Schrank. Meine Bücher und die anderen Sachen stehen auf einem Regal. Einige Poster hängen an den Wänden. Der Nachbar von Jenny ist sehr nett. Er heißt Kevin. Sein Hund Red ist wunderschön.

Tschüß
Tanja

3 Bristol

Unit 2 Step F

Tanja zeigt Jenny eine Broschüre mit einem Artikel über Bristol. Da Jenny nur wenig Deutsch versteht, muß ihn Tanja für Jenny übersetzen. Hilf ihr dabei.

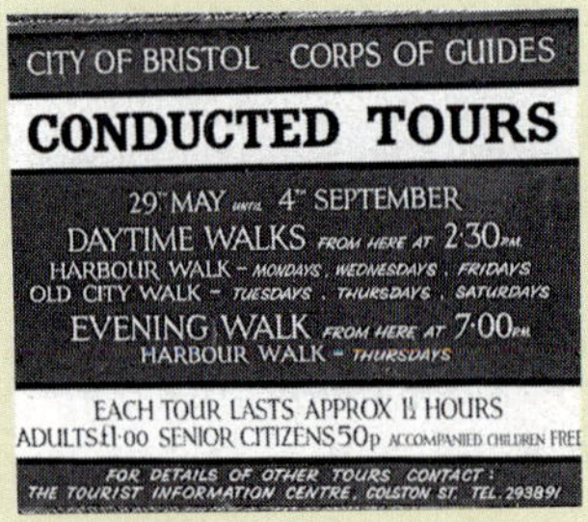

Bristol liegt im Westen von England. Es ist eine interessante Stadt für junge und alte Leute. Es gibt einige Jugendklubs, gute Discos und Kinos. Die Stadt hat auch nette Cafés in der Altstadt. Trinken Sie (doch einfach) eine Tasse Kaffee oder Tee und beobachten Sie die interessanten Leute im Stadtzentrum. Interessieren Sie sich für Sport? Bristol hat zwei gute Fußballmannschaften und viele Sportvereine. Es findet auch ein Ballonfestival statt. Oder gehen Sie zu den Docks und schauen Sie sich die großen alten Schiffe an. Bristol hat für jeden etwas.

4 Sport

Unit 3 Step C

Tanja und Jenny sind Sportfans. Tanja kann Hockey, Volleyball und Basketball spielen und würde auch gern Judo lernen.

Jenny: Komm mit mir. Jeder kann im Sportzentrum in Horfield mitmachen. Sie haben Trainer für viele Sportarten, in der Halle und im Freien. Für welchen Sport interessierst du dich?
Tanja: Ich würde gerne Volleyball spielen. Ist Kevin in der Volleyball-Mannschaft?
Jenny: Ja, aber heute ist er in der Judogruppe. Bring deine Turnschuhe mit. Du darfst keine Straßenschuhe in der Turnhalle tragen.

5 Im Krankenhaus

Unit 3 Step F

Tanjas Knöchel tut sehr weh.
Die Sanitäter müssen ihr helfen, weil sie nicht gehen kann. Sie muß mit ihren Freunden warten. Es sind viele Leute im Wartezimmer.

Es ist Viertel nach neun. Der Arzt hat jetzt Zeit für sie.

Arzt: Du mußt nicht im Bett bleiben, Tanja, aber leider darfst du ein oder zwei Wochen keinen Sport treiben. Dein Knöchel ist verstaucht. Es tut mir sehr leid.

6 Kevins Besuch

Unit 4 Step B

Kevin besucht Tanja. Entwirf einen Dialog nach folgenden Vorgaben.

Kevin begrüßt Tanja und fragt nach ihrem Fußknöchel. Tanja sagt, daß es ihr gut geht, ihr Knöchel aber noch weh tut. Kevin will wissen, was sie momentan macht und ob sie im Bett bleiben muß. Tanja erzählt ihm, daß sie nicht im Bett bleiben muß, sie ein Buch über Bristol liest und sich Musik im Radio anhört. Kevin fragt, wo denn die Eltern von Jenny sind. Tanja antwortet, daß Frau Benson heute im Verkehrsverein ist und Herr Benson etwas im Laden an der Ecke holt. Kevin möchte gerne wissen, ob Tanja zu einer Party kommen kann. Tanja bedauert und sagt, daß es diese Woche nicht geht. Kevin muß wieder gehen und verabschiedet sich.

7 Ein Einbrecher im Garten — Unit 4 Step E

Jenny und ihre Freundin Tanja sind allein zu Hause. Tanja sieht fern und Jenny liest ein interessantes Buch. Aber was ist das? Sie hören etwas im Garten [können ... hören]. Sind Jennys Mutter und Vater (schon) zurück? Nein, es muß ein Einbrecher sein. Oder ist es Kitty, die Katze der Nachbarn? Ja, sie können sie sehen. Sie spielt mit einem Ball. Die beiden [zwei] Mädchen müssen die Polizei nicht rufen.

8 Eine kleine Gartenparty — Unit 5 Step B

Kevin plant eine Party zusammen mit seinen Freunden und Nachbarn. Jeder muß etwas mitbringen. Sie möchten belegte Brote essen. Dafür haben sie alles. Tanja möchte einen Obstkuchen machen. Dazu muß sie noch zwei Pfund Äpfel und ein halbes Pfund Orangen kaufen.

Tanja: Wo kann ich sie kaufen?
Kevin: Natürlich im Laden von Frau Morgan an der Ecke.
Tanja: Aber die Preise dort!
Kevin: Stimmt. Aber wir können dorthin gehen und müssen nicht mit dem Bus zum Einkaufszentrum fahren.
Jenny: Laßt uns (doch) auch ein paar Flaschen Cola kaufen.
Tanja: Na gut.
Wendy: Was können wir später tun? Habt ihr Ideen?
Kevin: Nun, Musik und einige Spiele ....
Jenny: Ja, warum nicht? Ich kann ein paar sehr gute Cassetten mitbringen.
Tanja: Und ich kann einige interessante Spiele [spielen].

9 Ein Computer – Dein neuer Freund — Step D Unit 5

Im Computergeschäft sah David auf einem der Bildschirme einen Werbetext für einen Computer, der bei Hausaufgaben hilft, auch im Fach Deutsch. Momentan erfolgt die Ausgabe auf deutsch.
Hilf David beim Verstehen des Textes.

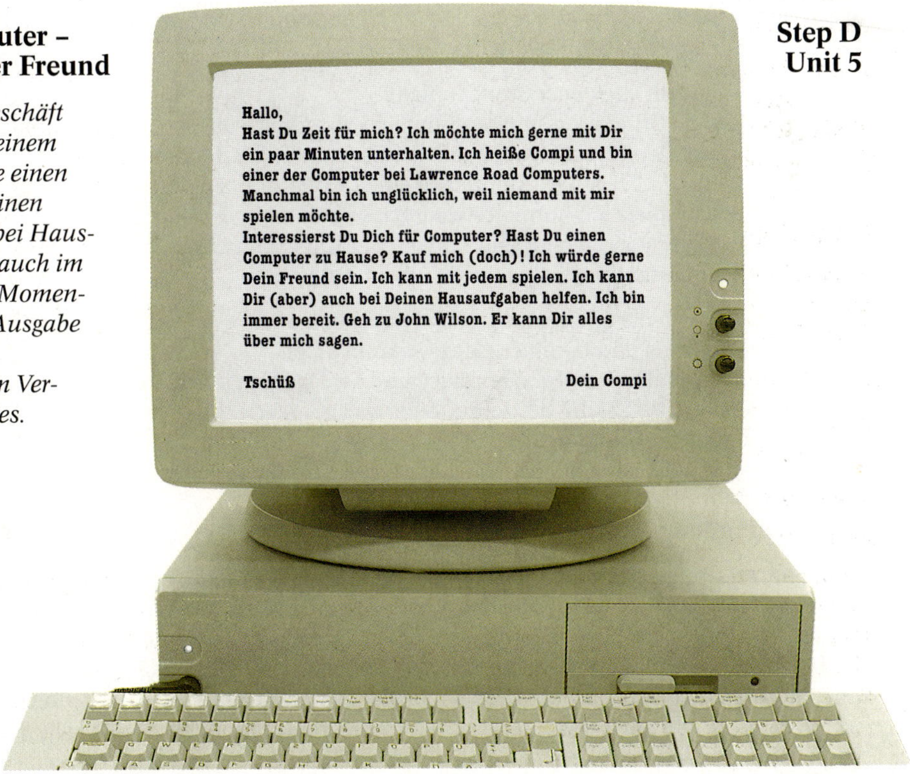

10 Ein Brief — Unit 6 Step D

Tanja schreibt einen Brief an ihre Freundin in Hannover. Jenny kommt ins Zimmer und möchte wissen, was Tanja schreibt. Kannst Du ihr Tanjas Brief übersetzen?

Hallo Julia,
heute kann ich Dir etwas über britische Schulen erzählen. Sie sind sehr verschieden von unseren [Schulen]. Weißt du, daß die meisten Schüler hier nicht tragen dürfen, was sie wollen? Sie tragen normalerweise Schuluniform mit Schulabzeichen – oder Hosen, Hemden, Röcke und Blusen in den Schulfarben. Ich gehe mit Jenny in die Filton Comprehensive School. Gewöhnlich gehen wir zu Fuß. Wir müssen uns immer beeilen, weil wir jeden Morgen spät (dran) sind. Jenny ißt mittags oft in der Schulkantine, aber manchmal nehmen wir den Bus nach Westbury und gehen mit ein paar Freunden in ein Café. Natürlich müssen wir uns dann wieder beeilen, weil der Nachmittagsunterricht um Viertel vor zwei beginnt. Ein Nachmittag ist für Mannschaftspiele, meine Lieblingsbeschäftigung, aber normalerweise gibt es Arbeit, Arbeit, Arbeit ... . Jenny mag Volleyball nicht, aber sie spielt Saxophon in der Schulband und geht abends oft zu ihren 'Friends of the Earth'. Du siehst, wir sind immer beschäftigt, und es ist nicht alles Schule. Möchtest Du wissen, was ich hier normalerweise abends mache? – Dann warte auf meinen nächsten Brief!

Tschüß
Tanja

11 Pause — Unit 6 Step E

In der Mittagspause treffen sich Tanja, Jenny, Melanie und Kevin auf dem Schulhof. Zuerst unterhalten sie sich über ihre Stundenpläne.

Kevin: Wie gefällt euch euer Stundenplan?
Jenny: Zu viele Unterrichtsstunden für mich. Mrs Grey ist unsere Mathematiklehrerin. Sie gibt immer viele Hausaufgaben auf. Wer ist euer Englischlehrer?
Kevin: Mr Brown. Er ist OK. Wir haben eine Doppelstunde Sport am Montag nachmittag. Und danach spiele ich normalerweise Basketball im Sportzentrum. Das ist dann genug Sport!
Tanja: Sport ist mein Lieblingsfach, aber mein Knöchel tut immer noch weh.
Melanie: Kommt, laßt uns jetzt in die Schulkantine gehen.

Dann sehen sie sich die Speisekarte an und Tanja liest vor:
Tanja: Würstchen und Pommes frites – warum nicht!
Ugh! – Bohnen in Tomatensauce und Ei! Das mag ich nicht.
Gemischter Salat – hey Jenny, hörst du zu?
Jenny: ... und ein Hamburger.
Kevin: Nicht schlecht. Und danach gibt es Schokoladenpudding. Pause ist *mein* Lieblingsfach.

12 Wochenende — Unit 7 Step C

Für Jenny und Tanja sind die Wochenenden immer etwas Besonderes. Sie genießen sie immer. Jenny spielt manchmal Saxophon oder geht in Bristol einkaufen. Dort trifft sie sich auch mit ihren Freunden in einem Café. Tanja treibt gewöhnlich Sport; sie spielt Volleyball. Manchmal schaut sie auch Fußballspiele im Fernsehen an. Heute ist Samstag, und die beiden [zwei] Mädchen wachen früh auf. Sie möchten nach Bath fahren und wollen den Zug um 8.15 Uhr nehmen. Bath ist eine wunderschöne, alte Stadt mit einer sehr schönen Kirche. Es gibt aber auch viele Geschäfte dort. Es ist aufregend, weil sie allein fahren können.

13 Am Bahnhof — Unit 7 Step F

Am Bahnhof treffen Jenny und Tanja zwei deutsche Touristen, die nur wenig Englisch können. Sie haben am Schalter Verständigungsschwierigkeiten. Tanja ist hilfsbereit und erweist sich als gute Dolmetscherin. Hilf ihr dabei.

Tourist: Wir möchten nach Cardiff fahren. Wann geht der nächste Zug?
Tanja: …
Schalterbeamte: It leaves at 8.09, but perhaps it's not on time.
Tanja: …
Tourist: Gut, dann haben wir noch ein paar Minuten. Wieviel kostet eine Fahrkarte nach Cardiff?
Tanja: …
Schalterbeamte: Single or return?
Tanja: …
Tourist: Hin und zurück. Zweimal [Zwei Fahrkarten].
Tanja: …
Schalterbeamte: £7 each. Here you are.
Tanja: …
Tourist: Und der Bahnsteig, bitte? Müssen wir umsteigen?
Tanja: …
Schalterbeamte: Platform 5 and you needn't change trains.
Tanja: …
Tourist: Vielen Dank und auf Wiedersehen.

14 Veranstaltungen in Filton — Unit 8 Step B

Es ist Freitag nachmittag. Das Telefon klingelt.

Wendy: Hallo Jenny, ich bin's. Ich würde gerne mit dir und Tanja ausgehen. Was ist diese Woche in Filton los?
Jenny: Laß mich (mal) in meinen Kalender schauen. … Wir können am 3. August zum 'Open-air Jazz Festival' gehen. Es ist die größte Musikveranstaltung in diesem Sommer. Und am 4. August finden die Volleyball-Meisterschaften im Jugendclub statt. Wofür interessierst du dich?
Wendy: Hm, Jazz ist interessanter, aber an *dem* Abend gibt es einen Film über Umweltprobleme in Großbritannien. Ich brauche (noch) mehr Informationen für unsere Ausstellung im Herbst.
Jenny: OK, dann laß uns zu der Sportveranstaltung gehen. Das ist (außerdem) nicht so spät wie das Jazz Festival. Tschüß.

15 Wie komme ich zum Museum? — Unit 8 Step D

In München stehen zwei ratlose japanische Touristen auf dem Marienplatz. Sie wollen zum Stadtmuseum und fragen zwei Damen nach dem Weg. Saskia spricht gut Englisch, aber sie ist selbst nur zu Besuch in München. Deshalb erklärt ihre Freundin Susanne den Weg und Saskia dolmetscht. Was sagt sie?

Tourist: Excuse me, can you tell us the way to the Munich City Museum?
Saskia: …
Susanne: Nehmen Sie den Bus?
Saskia: …
Tourist: How far is it on foot?
Saskia: …
Susanne: Nur etwa 10 Minuten. Biegen Sie rechts in diese Straße dort ein, und gehen Sie an der großen Kirche vorbei.
Saskia: …
Susanne: Gehen Sie (immer) geradeaus bis zur nächsten Kreuzung. Dort überqueren Sie die Straße und zu Ihrer Linken können Sie dann (schon) das Stadtmuseum sehen.
Saskia: …
Susanne: Gehen Sie weiter die Straße entlang und biegen Sie dann links ein. Dort ist der … Moment mal! Wir haben (sowieso) vor, dort um die Ecke einzukaufen. Wir können mit Ihnen gehen.
Saskia: …
Tourist: Thank you very much.

16 Vor und nach der Party — Unit 9 Step D

a) Es ist 7 Uhr am Abend der Party. Tanja ist oben in Patricks Haus. Patrick hat ein Hockeyspiel auf dem Computer gefunden, aber alle anderen sind zur Scheune gegangen. David ist mit den Lampen in der Scheune fertig, und jetzt ist sie voller Farben von den Lichtern. Einige Leute sind schon angekommen. Jenny eilt ins Haus und holt Tanja. Tanja ist überrascht, daß dort so viele Leute sind, weil ihre Freunde ihr noch nichts über die Party gesagt haben.

b) Es ist 8 Uhr am folgenden Abend. Die Freunde haben die Scheune aufgeräumt. David hat die Lichter abgemacht, und Kevin hat seine Cassetten in eine Tasche getan. Das Gras um den Grill herum ist schwarz, aber alles andere ist sauber. David, Jenny und Kevin sind (schon) weggegangen, und Patrick ist nach oben in sein Zimmer gegangen.

17 Davids Reise in die USA — Unit 10 Step F

David machte viele Fotos, als er in den USA war. Wieder in Bristol, zeigte er sie seiner Familie und erzählte etwas über die Bilder:

Grammatik Grammar

Unit 1

§1 Englische Substantive und Personalpronomen
English nouns and personal pronouns

David	is from Bristol.	**He**	is English.
Jenny	is from Bristol, too.	**She**	is English, too.
The bag	is in the car.	**It**	is here.

He steht für eine männliche Person.
She steht für eine weibliche Person.
Im Gegensatz zum Deutschen steht für eine Sache immer *it*.

Auch für Tiere verwendet man gewöhnlich *it*. Für Tiere, die man gut kennt und beim Eigennamen nennt, verwendet man *he* bzw. *she*:
z. B. Where is the cat? – **It**'s in the car.
Red is a dog. – **He**'s nice.

⚠ Alle Substantive werden im Englischen klein geschrieben, außer wenn sie am Satzanfang stehen oder Eigennamen sind.

§2 Das Personalpronomen als Subjekt Personal pronouns as subjects

SINGULAR	This is **David**. This is **Jenny**. This is my **bag**.	**I** **You** **He** **She** **It**	am Jenny. are Tanja. is from Bristol. is English. is here.
PLURAL	**Mr and Mrs Benson** are from Bristol. **The suitcase** and **the bag** are here.	**We** **You** **They** **They**	are in England. are English. are English. are in the car.

- *I* (ich) wird im Englischen immer groß geschrieben.
- *You* kann im Englischen sowohl Singular als auch Plural sein.
- Zugleich wird *you* für Singular und Plural der Höflichkeitsform gebraucht.

You are late, David.	du bist
You are late, David and Jenny.	ihr seid
You are late, Mr Benson.	Sie sind
You are late, Mr and Mrs Benson.	Sie sind

§3 Das Präsens von ‚sein' The present tense of 'to be'

1. **Positive forms**

short forms (Kurzformen) | **long forms** (Langformen)

Singular	**I'm**	German.	**I am**	German.
	You're	English.	**You are**	English.
	He's	from Bristol.	**He is**	from Bristol.
	She's	late.	**She is**	late.
	It's	in the car.	**It is**	in the car.
Plural	**We're**	downstairs.	**We are**	downstairs.
	You're	upstairs.	**You are**	upstairs.
	They're	in Bristol.	**They are**	in Bristol.

2. **Negative forms**

Singular	**I'm not**	German.	**I am not**	German.
	You aren't	English.	**You are not**	English.
	He isn't	German	**He is not**	German.
	She isn't	late.	**She is not**	late.
	It isn't	in the car.	**It is not**	in the car.
Plural	**We aren't**	downstairs.	**We are not**	downstairs.
	You aren't	late.	**You are not**	late.
	They aren't	here.	**They are not**	here.

- Beim Sprechen wird meistens die Kurzform verwendet, beim Schreiben dagegen meist die Langform. Diese Grundregel wird im heutigen schriftlichen Sprachgebrauch allerdings gelegentlich durchbrochen. (Wenn man ein Gespräch aufschreibt, verwendet man meistens die Kurzform.)
- In den bejahten Formen steht der Apostroph für den ausgefallenen Vokal in *am, are, is*, in den verneinten Formen für das ausgefallene *o* in *not*.

⚠ Bei *this is* ist aus Aussprachegründen eine Kurzform nicht möglich.

§4 Fragen und Kurzantworten mit ‚to be' Questions and short answers with 'to be'

a)	**Are**	**you**	German, Tanja?	**Yes, I am.**
	Are	**you**	German, too?	**No, I'm not.**
	Is	**David**	English?	**Yes, he is.**
	Is	**he**	from London?	**No, he isn't.**
	Are	**you**	upstairs, Jenny and Tanja?	**Yes, we are.** / **No, we aren't.**
	Are	**the Bensons**	English?	**Yes, they are.**
	Are	**they**	from London?	**No, they aren't.**
	Aren't	**you**	Tanja?	**Yes, I am.**

- Wie im Deutschen werden bei einer Frage mit *to be* Subjekt und Verb umgestellt (sog. Inversion):
  z. B. Ist Jenny aus Bristol?
  Is Jenny from Bristol?
- *Yes* oder *No* allein kommt als Antwort im Englischen kaum vor. Man antwortet meistens mit einem verkürzten Satz, einer sogenannten Kurzantwort.

⚠ **Yes,** / **No,** + Subjekt (Pronomen) + Langform / Kurzform — (positive Form): **Yes,** she **is.** (negative Form): **No ,** she **isn't.**

b) Is **this**	Tanja?	Yes, **it** is.
Is **this**	her room?	No, **it** isn't.
Is **there**	a desk in her room?	Yes, **there** is.
Is **there**	a cat in her room?	No, **there** isn't.

- Bei Fragen mit *Is this ...?* ist es für die Antwort gleichgültig, ob nach Sachen oder Personen gefragt wird. Die Antwort lautet immer: *Yes, **it** is./No, **it** isn't.*

§5 Fragen mit ‚wer, was, wo' Questions with 'who, what, where'

Who's this?	It's Tanja.	**Who** fragt nach Personen, während **what** nach Sachen fragt.
What's this?	It's a book.	

Where's Tanja?	She's in her room.	**Where** fragt nach einem Ort (wo?), **Where ... from** nach einer Richtung (woher?).
Where is Red?	He's in the garden.	
Where are you **from**?	**I'm from Bristol.**	

⚠ Verwechsle nicht: **where** = wo
who = wer

§6 Der Imperativ The imperative

Der Imperativ wird benutzt, um Anweisungen zu geben oder Aufforderungen auszudrücken.

Put the bag in the car.	Leg / Legt / Legen Sie } die Tasche ins Auto!
Come in.	Komm / Kommt / Kommen Sie } herein!

- Der Imperativ hat die gleiche Form wie der Infinitiv (ohne *to*).
- Der Imperativ unterscheidet nicht zwischen einer oder mehreren angesprochenen Personen. Die Formen sind immer gleich.

§7 Der s-Genitiv, Singular The s-genitive, singular

David is Jenny	**'s**	brother	David ist Jennys	Bruder.
Mrs Benson is Jenny	**'s**	mum.	Frau Benson ist Jennys	Mutti.
Is that Mr Brown	**'s**	car?	Ist das Herrn Browns	Auto?
No, it is Mrs Benson	**'s**	car.	Nein, es ist Frau Bensons	Auto.

- Der s-Genitiv zeigt an, zu wem jemand oder etwas gehört. Im Gegensatz zum Deutschen steht ein Apostroph (') vor dem Genitiv-*s* im Singular.

§8 Der bestimmte und unbestimmte Artikel The definite and indefinite article

The definite article	The indefinite article
the book **the c**ar **the s**mall car	**a b**ook **a c**ar **a s**mall car
[ðə] + consonant	[ə] + consonant
the apple **the o**ld book **the E**nglish car	**an a**pple **an o**ld book **an E**nglish car
[ðɪ] + vowel (Vokal)	[ən] + vowel (Vokal)

- Im Englischen macht der bestimmte Artikel keinen Unterschied zwischen männlich, weiblich und sächlich oder zwischen Singular und Plural. Er wird immer *the* geschrieben.
- Die Aussprache von *the* richtet sich nach dem Anlaut des folgenden Wortes: vor einem Konsonant wird er [ðə] ausgesprochen, vor einem Vokal [ðɪ].

⚠ Ausschlaggebend ist die **Aussprache**, nicht die Schreibung des folgenden Wortes. So sagt man: the unit [ðə ˈjuːnɪt]

Der unbestimmte Artikel hat im Englischen zwei Formen: *a* und *an*.

- Beginnt das folgende Wort mit einem Konsonanten, dann lautet der unbestimmte Artikel *a* [ə], beginnt es aber mit einem Vokal, lautet er *an* [ən].

⚠ Der unbestimmte Artikel richtet sich nach der **Aussprache**, nicht nach der Schreibung des folgenden Worts. Vor einem **u**, das [juː] ausgesprochen wird, lautet er *a* (nicht *an*!): a unit

§9 Die Possessivbegleiter The possessive determiners

Die Possesivpronomen " " pronouns

I'm Tanja.	This is	**my**	room.
	Is this	**your**	room, Jenny?
This is David's room.		**His**	room is upstairs.
This is Jenny's room.		**Her**	room is upstairs, too.
We are in the car.		**Our**	car is an English car.
	Is	**your**	car an English car, too?
This is Mr and Mrs Benson's house.		**Their**	house is nice.
This is Tanja's cat.		**Her**	name is Kitty.

- Durch die Possessivbegleiter kann man ausdrücken, zu wem jemand oder etwas gehört.
- Wie *you* (vgl. §2) hat auch *your* im Englischen mehrere Bedeutungen:

Is that **your** bag, Tanja?	deine
Is that **your** room, Tanja and Jenny?	euer
Is that **your** car, Mr Benson?	Ihr
Is that **your** cat, Mr and Mrs Benson?	Ihre

⚠ Die Formen *your* (dein, euer, Ihr) und *you're* (du bist, ihr seid, Sie sind) sind leicht zu verwechseln, weil sie fast gleich ausgesprochen werden. Beim Schreiben muß man genau aufpassen, welche Form gemeint ist.

Unit 2

§10 Der Plural von Substantiven The plural of nouns

Der regelmäßige Plural wird im Englischen dadurch gebildet, daß man an die Singularform des Substantivs ein *-s* (in bestimmten Fällen auch *-es*) anhängt. Dieses *-s* wird unterschiedlich ausgesprochen:

three book**s** two bike**s** four street**s** ten cup**s** [s]	two chair**s** three sofa**s** five room**s** four table**s** [z]	two piec**es** two bus**es** six sandwich**es** five glass**es** [ɪz]
Nach stimmlosen Konsonanten wie [p, t, k, θ] wird das auslautende *-s* stimmlos (scharf) ausgesprochen.	Nach Vokalen und stimmhaften Konsonanten wie [b, d, g, n, m, v] wird das *-s* stimmhaft (weich) ausgesprochen.	Nach den Zischlauten [s, z, dʒ, ʃ, tʃ] wird das *-es* [ɪz] ausgesprochen. Ist kein stummes End-*e* im Singular vorhanden, so ist die Pluralendung *-es*: *a glass – two glasses*

⚠
- Auslautendes *-y* wird **nach einem Konsonanten** zu *-ies*: a family – famil**ies**, a city – cit**ies**
- Auslautendes *-lf* wird im Plural zu *-ves*: a she**lf** – shel**ves**
- Beachte die unregelmäßige Aussprache von: a house – houses [haʊs] – ['haʊzɪz]

§11 There is/there are

There is	a wardrobe in Jenny's room.	
There's	a sofa in her room, too.	
There are	two chairs in her room.	
Is there	a table in her room?	**Yes, there is.**
Are there	armchairs in her room?	**No, there aren't.**

- *There is* (Kurzform: *there's*) und *there are* entsprechen dem Deutschen *es gibt, es sind*. Nach *there is* folgt ein Substantiv im Singular, nach *there are* steht das Substantiv im Plural.
- Für die Fragebildung und für die Kurzantworten gelten die bereits bekannten Regeln (vgl. § 4).

§12 Das Präsens von ‚have got' The present tense of 'have got'

1. **Positive forms**

short forms			**long forms**		
I've	got	a bike.	I have	got	a bike.
You've	got	a nice car.	You have	got	a nice car.
He's	got	a brother.	He **has**	got	a brother.
She's	got	a friend.	She **has**	got	a friend.
It's	got	a garden.	It **has**	got	a garden.
We've	got	a radio.	We have	got	a radio.
You've	got	a nice house.	You have	got	a nice house.
They've	got	a TV.	They have	got	a TV.

- Man gebraucht *have got/has got* im Sinne von *etwas haben/besitzen*.

2. **Negative forms**

short forms			**long forms**		
I haven't	got	a bike.	I have	not got	a bike.
You haven't	got	a car.	You have	not got	a car.
He **hasn't**	got	a brother.	He **has**	not got	a brother.
She **hasn't**	got	a friend.	She **has**	not got	a friend.
It **hasn't**	got	a garden.	It **has**	not got	a garden.
We haven't	got	a radio.	We have	not got	a radio.
You haven't	got	a house.	You have	not got	a house.
They haven't	got	a TV.	They have	not got	a TV.

- In der Verneinung tritt *not* zwischen die Formen *have/has* und *got*; *have not* und *has not* werden in der gesprochenen Sprache zu *haven't* und *hasn't* zusammengezogen (vgl. § 3). Bei diesen Kurzformen fällt das *o* in *not* aus. Für das ausgefallene *o* steht ein Apostroph.
- Verwechsle nicht die Kurzformen von *have got* mit den Kurzformen von *to be*:

⚠ He'**s** got a friend. = He **has** got a friend.
He'**s** my friend. = He **is** my friend.

3. **Fragen und Kurzantworten mit ‚*have got/has got*'**
Questions and short answers with *'have got/has got'*

Have	**you**	**got**	a nice room, Dav**id**?	**Yes, I**	**have.**
Have	**you**	**got**	a small room?	**No, I**	**haven't.**
Has	**Tanja**	**got**	a small room?	**Yes, she**	**has.**
Has	**she**	**got**	a cassette recorder?	**No, she**	**hasn't.**
Have	**the Bensons**	**got**	a cat?	**No, they**	**haven't.**
Haven't	**they**	**got**	a car?	**Yes, they**	**have.**
have/ has	**S** (Subjekt)	**got**	**O** (Objekt)		

- Bei der Kurzantwort läßt man *got* weg. Zur Verwendung von Kurzantworten vgl. § 4.

4. **Fragen mit Fragewörtern** Questions with question words

Where	have	you	got	your car?
What	has	Tanja	got	in her room?
What	have	they	got	in Bristol?
How many books	have	you	got?	
Question word	**have/ has**	**S**	**got**	

- *have/has got* besteht aus zwei Teilen. Bei zweiteiligen Verben erfolgt in der Frage eine Umstellung (sog. Inversion). Das Subjekt steht in der Frage nicht mehr vor den Formen von *have*, sondern zwischen *have/has* und *got*. Diese Wortstellung gilt auch, wenn die Frage mit einem Fragewort beginnt.

§13 Der s-Genitiv und der of-Genitiv The s-genitive and the of-genitive

The s-genitive	The of-genitive
David is Jenny'**s** brother. He is in Tanja'**s** room. This is the Benson**s'** car.	This is a photo **of** our sports centre. Filton is a suburb **of** Bristol.
Der s-Genitiv gibt an, welcher **Person** oder welchen **Personen** etwas gehört. Die Formen lauten: singular: noun + **'s** (Tanja'**s** room) plural: noun + **s'** (the girl**s'** class room)	Der *of*-Genitiv gibt an, welcher **Sache** etwas zugeordnet ist.

⚠ Verwechsle den s-Genitiv nicht mit den Kurzformen von *is* und *has*:
Jenny's brother**'s** got a bike. = Jenny's brother **has** got a bike.
Kevin's bike**'s** in the garden. = Kevin's bike **is** in the garden.

§14 This/these – that/those

Look at **these** photos here:
This is my room and **that** is my brother's room.
These are my books and **those** are his books.
And what about **those** photos over there?

- *These* ist die Pluralform von *this* und *those* ist die Pluralform von *that*. Nach *this/that* folgt immer ein Singular, nach *these/those* immer ein Plural.
- *This/these* verweisen auf Dinge oder Personen, die in der Nähe des Sprechers sind; *that/those* auf Dinge oder Personen, die weiter entfernt sind.
- Bei Gegenüberstellungen von verschiedenen Personen oder Dingen sagt man zuerst *this/these*, dann *that/those*:

This is Tanja and **that** is Kevin.
These are her books and **those** are his books.

§15 Die Grundzahlen The cardinal numbers

1	one	11	eleven	21	twenty-one
2	two	12	twelve	22	twenty-two
3	three	13	thirteen	23	twenty-three
4	four	14	fourteen	24	twenty-four
5	five	15	fifteen	25	twenty-five
6	six	16	sixteen	26	twenty-six
7	seven	17	seventeen	27	twenty-seven
8	eight	18	eighteen	28	twenty-eight
9	nine	19	nineteen	29	twenty-nine
10	ten	20	twenty	30	thirty

- Zwischen den Zehner- und Einerzahlen muß ab 21 ein Bindestrich stehen.

Unit 3

§16 Der Imperativ The imperative

positive forms	**negative forms**
Help your neighbour. **Be** nice to him.	**Don't help** your neighbour now. **Don't be** late.
Der Imperativ hat die gleiche Form wie der Infinitiv (jedoch ohne *to*).	Der verneinte Imperativ wird immer mit *don't* + Infinitiv (ohne *to*) gebildet.

⚠ Beim englischen Imperativ wird kein Unterschied zwischen einer oder mehreren Personen gemacht. Die Formen sind immer gleich (vgl. § 6).

§17 Das Präsens einiger Hilfsverben The present tense of some auxiliaries

1. **Positive and negative forms**

Tanja **can** play volleyball, but she **can't (cannot)** play football.
She **must** be a member before she **can** play volleyball.
Players **must** wear sports clothes, but spectators **needn't (need not)** wear sports clothes.
Players and spectators **mustn't (must not)** bring food or drinks into the gym.

- *Can, can't (cannot), must, needn't (need not)* sowie *mustn't (must not)* sind Hilfsverben. Ihre Formen sind in allen Personen gleich. Wie im Deutschen steht nach Hilfsverben immer ein Infinitiv (ohne *to*).
- Im Gegensatz zum Deutschen stehen jedoch Objekte und andere Satzergänzungen nie zwischen dem Hilfsverb und dem Infinitiv, sondern immer danach:

She	**can**	**play**	volleyball.	
They	**can't**	**go**		into the gym.
He	**cannot**	**play**	football.	
She	**must**	**have**	a note	from her mum and dad.
You	**needn't**	**do**	all the sports.	
They	**mustn't**	**wear**	street shoes	in the gym.

2. **Questions and short answers with auxiliaries**

May	**I**	join	the club?	**Yes, you may.**
May	**we**	take	food into the gym?	**No, you may not/mustn't.**
Can	**Kevin**	bring	a radio?	**No, he mustn't.**
Can	**Tanja**	come,	too?	**Yes, she can.**
Must	**I**	wear	sports shoes?	**Yes, you must.**
Must	**she**	play	football, too?	**No, she needn't.**
Hv	**S**	**V** (Infinitiv)		

- Bei der Frage steht das Hilfsverb vor dem Subjekt. Die restliche Wortstellung bleibt unverändert.
- Bei Kurzantworten (ja/nein) wird nur das Hilfsverb in der bejahten oder verneinten Form wiederholt.
- Statt *may not* kann in der Kurzantwort auch *mustn't* gebraucht werden (stärker als *may not*).
- Statt *may*, das eine sehr höfliche Frage um Erlaubnis ausdrückt, wird oft auch *can* gebraucht.

3. **Questions with question words**

Where	can	Tanja	play	volleyball?
Why	must	she	hurry?	
What	must	members	do?	
Why	can't	Kevin	bring	a radio to the gym?
Question word	**Hv**	**S**	**V** (Infinitiv)	

- Die bereits bekannte Wortstellung bei der Frage ändert sich auch dann nicht, wenn die Frage mit einem Fragewort beginnt.

⚠ Beachte die deutschen Bedeutungen der Hilfsverben:

can	können	can't/cannot	nicht können
may	dürfen	may not	nicht dürfen
must	müssen	**needn't**	**nicht brauchen, nicht müssen**
can	können = dürfen	**mustn't**	**nicht dürfen**

§18 Personal pronouns as objects

1. **Subject**		**Object**	
I	Can you help	**me**?	
you	Sorry, but I can't help	**you**.	
she	Talk to Sandra. Ask	**her**	
he	or go to Jim. Talk to	**him**	
	or go to the notice-board		
it	and read	**it**.	
we	But please help	**us**	
	to keep the gym clean.		
	Oh, here are Jim and Sandra.		
you	They can help	**you**,	Jenny and Tanja.
they	Ask	**them**.	
	Have you got your sports shoes?		
	You must wear	**them**	in the gym.

- Bei den Personalpronomen des Objektfalles wird im Englischen kein Unterschied zwischen den Dativformen (mir, dir usw.) und den Akkusativformen (mich, dich usw.) gemacht; d.h. es gibt nur **eine** Form.
- *it* bezieht sich nur auf Sachen und Tiere; *them* bezieht sich auf Personen oder Sachen.
- Auch für das Personalpronomen des Objektfalls gilt die bereits bekannte Wortstellung:
  I can't see her.
- Das Personalpronomen *you* (vgl. §2) hat auch im Objektfall mehrere Bedeutungen:

I can't see **you**, Tanja.	dich
I can't help **you**, Jenny.	dir
I can't see **you**, Tanja and Jenny.	euch
I can't see **you**, Mr Benson.	Sie
I can't help **you**, Mr Benson.	Ihnen

2. **Zur Verwendung der Personalpronomen des Objektfalles**

Die Personalpronomen des Objektfalles werden gebraucht

a) wenn sie im Satz die Funktion eines Objekts haben.	I can see **them**. I can't help **her**.
b) wenn sie alleine stehen.	Who is it? It's **her**.
c) wenn ihnen eine Präposition *(to, in, on, under, etc.)* vorangeht.	Don't talk **to me**, talk **to her**. She's interested **in you**.

§19 Wieviel Uhr ist es? What time is it?

It's …

three o'clock

(a) quarter to four

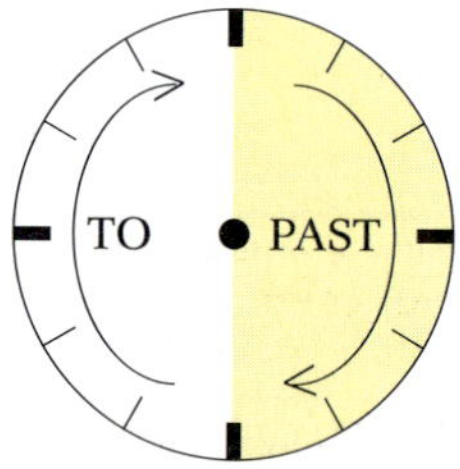

(a) quarter past three

half past three

- Die ersten dreißig Minuten einer Stunde zählt man zur vorhergehenden Stunde dazu; die restlichen neunundzwanzig Minuten zieht man von der folgenden Stunde ab.
- *o'clock* wie auch das *a* vor *quarter* können ausgelassen werden.

§20 Unregelmäßige Pluralformen Irregular plurals

singular		**plural**	
a man	There are three	**men**	in the room.
a woman	There are also two	**women**	there.
a child	They have got two	**children**	with them.
---	The doctor must see seven	**people**.	

- Im Englischen gibt es einige wenige, dafür aber sehr oft gebrauchte Substantive, die einen unregelmäßigen Plural haben.

⚠ *People* in der Bedeutung ‚Leute' besitzt kein Plural-*s*:
There are a lot of **people** in the waiting room.

Unit 4

§21 Die Verlaufsform des Präsens   The present tense: progressive form

1. **Positive forms**

short forms				long forms			
I	**'m**	**watching**	TV.	I	**am**	**watching**	TV.
You	**'re**	**talking**	to Jenny.	You	**are**	**talking**	to Jenny.
He	**'s**	**helping**	her.	He	**is**	**helping**	her.
She	**'s**	**watching**	him.	She	**is**	**watching**	him.
We	**'re**	**waiting**	for them.	We	**are**	**waiting**	for them.
They	**'re**	**coming**	now.	They	**are**	**coming**	now.

2. **Negative forms**

short forms				long forms			
I	**'m not**	**watching**	TV.	I	**am not**	**watching**	TV.
You	**aren't**	**talking**	to Jenny.	You	**are not**	**talking**	to Jenny.
He	**isn't**	**helping**	her.	He	**is not**	**helping**	her.
She	**isn't**	**watching**	him.	She	**is not**	**watching**	him.
We	**aren't**	**waiting**	for them.	We	**are not**	**waiting**	for them.
They	**aren't**	**coming**	now.	They	**are not**	**coming**	now.

- In der Verlaufsform des Präsens wird ein Vorgang beschrieben, der noch nicht zu Ende ist. Diese Form drückt auch aus, daß jemand gerade dabei ist, etwas zu tun (oder nicht zu tun). Sie wird gebildet mit einer Form von *to be*: *am/are/is/are* und dem Infinitiv des Verbs + *ing*-Endung.

⚠ Im Deutschen kennt man die Verlaufsform nicht; die Bedeutung dieser Form wird oft mit **gerade, im Moment, jetzt** usw. ausgedrückt.

§22 Die Bildung des Partizip Präsens   The formation of the present participle

Das *present participle* wird bei den meisten Verben dadurch gebildet, daß man an den Infinitiv eine *ing*-Endung anhängt:

do – do**ing**   play – play**ing**
read – read**ing**   hurry – hurry**ing**

come	She is co**m**ing.
sit	He is si**tt**ing in the garden.
lie	Red is l**y**ing over there.

- Bei Verben, die auf ein stummes *-e* enden, entfällt dieses *-e* vor der *ing*-Endung.
- Verben mit einem kurzen Vokal vor dem Endkonsonanten verdoppeln diesen Endkonsonanten.
- Bei Verben, die auf *-ie* enden, wird das *-ie* zu *-y*.

§23 Questions with the present progressive

1. **Questions with short answers**

Is	**Tanja**	**reading**	her book?	**Yes, she is.**
Is	**Kevin**	**playing**	with Red?	**No, he isn't.**
Are	**you**	**making**	a snack, Mr Benson?	**No, I'm not.**
Are	**Mr and Mrs Brown**	**sitting**	in their garden?	**No, they aren't.**
Are	**they**	**going**	into town?	**Yes, they are.**
Form of 'to be'	**S**	**Present participle**		

2. **Questions with question words**

What	are	you	doing?		I'm learning some German phrases.
Why	aren't	you	listening?		I'm reading a book.
What	is	he	waiting	**for**?	He's waiting for a telephone call.
What	is	she	looking	**at**?	She's looking at a picture of London.
Where	are	they	going?		They're going into town.
Question word	**Form of 'to be'**	**S**	**Pres. part.**	**Preposition**	

- Präpositionen, die mit den entsprechenden Verben eine Einheit bilden (z. B. *to look* **at**, *to wait* **for**), stehen am Ende der Frage.
- Die Verlaufsform des Präsens ist wie *have got* ebenfalls zweiteilig. In der Frage steht daher das Subjekt nach den Formen von *to be*. Dies gilt auch, wenn die Frage mit einem Fragewort beginnt.

§24 Die Grundzahlen The cardinal numbers

30	thirty	50	fifty
31	thirty-one	60	sixty
32	thirty-two	70	seventy
33	thirty-three	80	eighty
34	thirty-f**o**ur	90	ninety
35	thirty-five	100	**a/one** hundred
36	thirty-six	200	two hundred
37	thirty-seven	350	three hundred **and** fifty
38	thirty-eight	399	three hundred **and** ninety-nine
39	thirty-nine	444	f**ou**r hundred **and** forty-f**ou**r
40	forty	1000	**a/one** thousand

- Zahlen über 100 werden durch *and* angeschlossen (999 = nine hundred *and* ninety-nine).
- Vor *hundred* und *thousand* muß immer der unbestimmte Artikel *a* oder ein Zahlwort stehen *(**a** hundred/**one** hundred)*.

§25 Die Wortstellung im bejahten Aussagesatz Word order in positive sentences

Subjekt	**Verb**	**Objekt**	
Kevin	has got	a dog.	
Tanja	has got	a cat.	
The friends	are eating	sandwiches.	
We	are having	lunch	at school.

- Die Wortstellung im englischen Aussagesatz lautet:
  Subjekt – Verb – Objekt
  S – **V** – **O**
  Im Gegensatz zum Deutschen kann man dieses Satzmuster nicht umstellen.

§26 Sätze mit Konjunktionen Clauses with conjunctions

Mit Hilfe von Konjunktionen kann man Sätze verknüpfen.

Hauptsatz (main clause)		Hauptsatz (main clause)
Mr Benson is in the kitchen	**and**	Kevin is talking to him.
Tanja is lying on the sofa	**but**	she is not asleep.
You can watch TV	**or**	you can read the newspaper.
Mr and Mrs Benson are in Wales,	**so**	the girls are alone.

- *And, but, or* und *so* verbinden gleichartige Sätze (z. B. zwei Hauptsätze) miteinander.

Hauptsatz (main clause)		Nebensatz (subordinate clause)
Tanja is shutting the windows	**because**	a nasty wind is blowing.
Don't leave your keys	**where**	burglars can see them.
Tell your neighbours	**when**	you are out for the evening.

- *Because, where* und *when* verbinden einen Hauptsatz mit einem Nebensatz.

⚠ Die Wortstellung **S – V – O** (Subjekt – Verb – Objekt) bleibt auch in untergeordneten Nebensätzen erhalten.

Unit 5

§ 27 Mengenangaben mit ‚of' Expressions of quantity with 'of'

Have we got everything?			
Let me see:	a bar	**of**	chocolate,
	a loaf	**of**	bread,
	a pound	**of**	butter,
	a bottle	**of**	milk,
	a packet	**of**	tea.
Yes, that's everything.			

Im Gegensatz zum Deutschen werden Mengenangaben mit Hilfe des Wörtchens *of* gebildet.

§ 28 Unbestimmte Begleiter Indefinite determiners

Wie im Deutschen, so gibt es auch im Englischen Substantive, die keinen Plural bilden können (z. B. *milk, butter, music, money*). Diese Substantive nennt man *uncountables* (unzählbare Substantive). Substantive, die einen Plural bilden können, werden dagegen *countables* (zählbare Substantive) genannt.

1. **Much / many / a lot of**

Mr Smith has**n't** got **many** things on his shopping list.	He'd like to buy some tea, because he has**n't** got **much** tea at home.
How **many** tea-bags are there in this packet?	How **much** is the tea over there? How **much** are the tea-bags? The tea over there is £2.90. The tea-bags are £1.45.
There are **a lot of** tea-bags in the packet.	That's **a lot of** money.

- Vor Substantiven, die keinen Plural haben, kann nur *much* (viel), vor Substantiven im Plural kann nur *many* (viele) stehen. *A lot of* (viel/viele) wird meistens in bejahten Sätzen gebraucht.
- *How much is/are ...?* bedeutet immer: Wieviel kostet/kosten ...?

2. Some / any

questions	negative statements	positive statements
Have you got **any** apples? Is there **any** milk? Have you got **any** money?	No, we haven't got **any** (apples). No, there isn't **any** (milk). Sorry, I haven't got **any** (money).	Let's buy **some** (apples). I'd like to buy **some** (milk). Let's go to the bank and get **some**.

- Im Englischen wird eine unbestimmte Menge oder Anzahl (im Sinne von ‚etwas' oder ‚einige') durch *some* oder *any* ausgedrückt. In Fragen und verneinten Sätzen wird meistens *any* gebraucht, in bejahten Sätzen *some.*
- Ein bereits erwähntes Substantiv kann nach *some/any* weggelassen werden.
- *Some/any* bleiben oft unübersetzt: *Have you got any money?* – Hast du Geld?
- *Not … any* entspricht dem Deutschen ‚kein/keine'. *Not … any* kann durch *no* ersetzt werden:
  I have**n't** got **any** time. = I've got **no** time.

3. Some / any and their compounds

questions	negative statements	positive statements
Have we got **anything for tea?** (etwas)	No, we have**n't got anything**. (nichts)	Wait, there is **something** in the cupboard. (etwas)
Is there **anyone** / **anybody** in the garden? (jemand)	There isn't **anyone** / **anybody** there. (niemand)	Wait, I can hear **someone**. / **somebody**. (jemand)

- Wie *some/any* selbst werden auch ihre Zusammensetzungen gebraucht:
  somebody (= someone)/*something* werden in bejahten Sätzen, *anybody* (= anyone) / *anything* werden in Fragen und verneinten Sätzen verwendet.

4. Few / a few, little / a little

We've got **a few** second-hand computers downstairs, but very **few** people are interested in them.

The assistant has got very **little** time for David. The young man can offer him **a little** more for his computer.

- *Few* (wenige), *a few* (einige, ein paar) können nur mit Substantiven gebraucht werden, die im Plural stehen; *little* (wenig), *a little* (ein wenig, ein bißchen) können in den angegebenen Bedeutungen nur mit *uncountables* gebraucht werden.
- In der Umgangssprache werden *little* and *few* meistens nach *very, too* und *so* verwendet.

§ 29 Verben mit zwei Objekten   Verbs with two objects

Eine Reihe von englischen Verben können nicht nur ein, sondern zwei Objekte haben. In diesem Fall sind zwei Stellungen möglich:

	ind. obj.	dir. obj.	ind. obj.
Kevin is giving	**Tanja**	a cassette.	
Kevin is giving		a cassette	**to Tanja**.
The shop assistant is showing	**David**	a PC.	
The shop assistant is showing		a PC	**to David**.
Kevin is writing		a letter	**to his friend in Wales**.

- Gewöhnlich steht das indirekte Objekt vor dem direkten Objekt. Soll das indirekte Objekt jedoch betont werden oder ist es besonders lang, so steht es nach dem direkten Objekt und wird mit *to* angeschlossen.
- Ist das direkte Objekt ein Pronomen, so steht das indirekte Objekt meist danach:

	dir. obj.	ind. object
Give	**it** **them**	to your sister.

⚠ Bei einigen englischen Verben wie *to say* wird das indirekte Objekt immer mit *to* angeschlossen:
Don't say that ***to me*** *again!*

Unit 6

§ 30 Das Präsens   The present tense: simple form

a) **Positive forms**

I	**like**	ice-cream.
You	**like**	fruit.
Kevin	**like**s	Tanja.
Tanja	**like**s	Kevin.
A dog	**like**s	other dogs.
We	**like**	English.
You	**like**	tennis.
They	**like**	TV.

- Bis auf die 3. Person Singular hat das Präsens die gleiche Form wie der Infinitiv (ohne *to*).
- In der 3. Person Singular *(he, she, it)* wird jedoch ein **-s** angehängt.
- Bei Verben, die auf einen Zischlaut enden, wird in der 3. Person Singular ein **-es** [ɪz] angehängt: He catch**es** his bus at eight o'clock.

b) **The -s/-es of the third person singular**

School	**starts**	at nine.	
Jenny	**writes**	letters in French.	[s]
Nobody	**helps**	her.	
She	**plays**	in the school band.	[z]
She	**leaves**	school at four o'clock	
Jenny	**fetches**	her things for the sports centre.	[ɪz]
She	**catches**	the bus.	
She	**hurries**	home.	
She	**buys**	some things for her mum.	

- Nach stimmlosen Konsonanten wird das **-s** [s] ausgesprochen.
- Nach Vokalen und stimmhaften Konsonanten wird das **-s** [z] ausgesprochen.
- Nach Zischlauten wird das **-es** [ɪz] ausgesprochen.
- Das auslautende **-y** wird nach einem Konsonanten zu **-ies**. Nach einem Vokal bleibt das **-y** erhalten.

⚠ Für die Aussprache und Schreibung des *-s/-es* in der 3. Person Singular gelten die gleichen Regeln wie bei der Pluralbildung (cf. §10).

c) **Irregular forms** (Unregelmäßige Formen)

Jenny	often	**has**	lunch	at school.
She	always	**does**	her homework	in the evening.
She	usually	**goes**		to bed at nine.

- Bei den Verben *go* und *do* wird in der 3. Person Singular ein *-es* angehängt.
- Die dritte Person Singular von *to have*, das auch als Vollverb gebraucht werden kann, lautet *has*.
- Beachte auch die unregelmäßige Aussprache der Formen *does/says* in der 3. Person Singular:

I	say	[seɪ] :	she says	[sez]
I	do	[du:]:	he does	[dʌz]

§ 31 Die Verneinung mit ‚don't/doesn't'

I	**don't**	**like**	Maths.
You	**don't**	**like**	Art.
Melanie	**doesn't**	**like**	Geography.
Peter	**doesn't**	**like**	History.
We	**don't**	**like**	Civics.
You	**don't**	**like**	Chemistry.
They	**don't**	**like**	French.

Verben wie *to like* sind sogenannte Vollverben. Vollverben werden im *simple present* immer mit *don't/doesn't* verneint. Nach den verneinten Formen von *to do* steht immer der Infinitiv: In der 3. Person Singular wie in den übrigen Formen steht daher **nie** ein *-s/-es*.

- Statt der Kurzformen können natürlich auch die entsprechenden Langformen im geschriebenen Englisch gebraucht werden:

  Tanja doesn't play the saxophone. = Tanja does not play the saxophone.
  They don't wear school uniform. = They do not wear school uniform.

⚠ *to do* und *to have* können auch als Vollverb gebraucht werden.
Die verneinten Formen lauten dann:
He doesn't **do** his homework in the afternoon.
She doesn't **have** lunch at school.

§ 32 Fragen mit ‚do/does'

a) **Yes/no questions and short answers**

Do	you	**like**	English?	Yes, I **do**.
Does	Tanja	**like**	English?	Yes, she **does**.
Does	Tom	**like**	school?	No, he **doesn't**.
Do	they	**like**	Maths?	No, they **don't**.
Hv	**S**	**V**	**O**	

- Wie in der Verneinung werden auch die Frageformen eines Vollverbs mit *to do* gebildet. Dabei steht *do/does (don't/doesn't)* vor dem Subjekt; das Verb folgt als Infinitiv (ohne *to*).
- Bei Entscheidungsfragen, d. h. Fragen, die ein ‚ja' oder ‚nein' zur Antwort haben, muß die entsprechende Form von *do* in der Kurzantwort wiederholt werden. Das Vollverb wird nicht wiederholt.

b) **Questions with question words**

Die oben genannte Wortstellung **(Hv + S + V …?)** bleibt auch dann erhalten, wenn die Frage mit einem Fragewort beginnt:

Where	**does**	Jenny	**go**		to school?
When	**does**	school	**begin**?		
What	**does**	Jenny	**do**		in the lunch break?
Why	**doesn't**	she	**go**		home for lunch?
Why	**do**	they	**wear**	school uniform?	
Why	**don't**	they	**wear**	jeans?	
When	**do**	you	**do**	your homework?	
Question word	**Hv**	**S**	**V**	**O**	

⚠ Wie bei der Verneinung steht das Vollverb immer im Infinitiv (kein *-s/-es*).

§ 33 Der Gebrauch des Präsens The usage of the simple present

Im Gegensatz zum *present progressive*, das Handlungen beschreibt, die noch nicht abgeschlossen sind oder gerade ablaufen (cf. § 21), wird das *simple present* für folgende Handlungen gebraucht:

1. **Wiederholte und gewohnheitsmäßige Handlungen** Mit dem *simple present* drückt man aus, daß etwas regelmäßig, oft, manchmal oder nie geschieht. Signalwörter: *every day, on (Saturdays), often, sometimes, never* usw.	Jenny usually **gets** home at four o'clock. But on Tuesday afternoons she **plays** in the school band. Then she **doesn't get** home until six o'clock. In the evenings Jenny often **watches** TV or **listens** to music. Sometimes she **reads** an interesting book.
2. **Aufeinanderfolgende Handlungen** Man verwendet das *simple present* für abgeschlossene Handlungen, die aufeinander folgen. Signalwörter: *First …, then …, after that …*	Before the concert Tanja **goes** upstairs to the bathroom and **takes** a shower. Then she **puts on** her best blouse and jeans. After that she **looks** for the ticket for the concert.

§ 34 Die Stellung der Adverbien der Häufigkeit The position of adverbs of frequency

Jenny		**usually**	gets up		at half past seven.
She		**sometimes**	takes	a shower.	
She		**never**	sings		in the bathroom.
She	doesn't	**always**	have	time	for breakfast.
She	can	**normally**	walk		to school.
S	**Hv**	**Adverb**	**V**	**O**	

Adverbien der Häufigkeit stehen im Englischen **nie** zwischen Verb und Objekt, sondern unmittelbar **vor** dem Vollverb.

⚠ Bei den Präsensformen von *to be* steht das Adverb der Häufigkeit **nach** dem Verb:
Jenny is **sometimes** late.
She is **often** tired in the morning.

§ 35 Die Stellung von Zeitangaben The position of expressions of time

Zeit (time)	S	V	O	Ort (place)	Zeit (time)
Every morning	we	have	breakfast	in the kitchen.	
On Saturdays	Kevin	takes	Red	to the park.	
	Jenny	practises	the saxophone		every day.
	The girls	play	football	in the park	on Sundays.

- Zeitangaben können am Anfang oder am Ende des Satzes stehen, d. h. vor oder nach der **S-V-O**-Gruppe.
- Wenn man Zeitangaben stärker betonen will, stehen sie am Anfang.
- Stehen eine Orts- und eine Zeitangabe am Satzende, dann gilt: Ort vor Zeit.

[§ 36] Das Gerund The gerund

1. Das *Gerund* wird dadurch gebildet, daß man eine *ing*-Endung an den Infinitiv anhängt. Dabei gelten dieselben Regeln wie für die Bildung des *present participle* (cf. § 22):

do > do**ing**	come > com**ing**	sto**p** > sto**pp**ing	play > play**ing**	**aber:**
read > read**ing**	tak**e** > tak**ing**	si**t** > si**tt**ing	carry > carry**ing**	**lie** > **ly**ing

2. **The gerund as the subject and object of a sentence**

Reading is fun. **Playing** table-tennis is great. **Working** all day is boring.	Das *Gerund* ist hier Subjekt des Satzes.
I **like** **lying** in the sun. Jenny **loves** **going** to school, but she **hates** **doing** homework.	Nach bestimmten Verben wie *to like, to love, to hate,* steht normalerweise ein *Gerund*. Dieses *Gerund* ist Objekt des Satzes.

3. Wie aus den obigen Sätzen hervorgeht, kann das *Gerund* entweder ein Substantiv *(reading)* oder eine Verbform sein. Als Verbform kann das *Gerund* ein Objekt *(playing **table-tennis**)* oder eine Zeit- bzw. Ortsbestimmung *(working **all day**/lying **in the sun**)* nach sich haben.

⚠ Nach *I'd like* und *I'd love* steht immer ein *to* + Infinitiv: *I'd like to go home.*

Unit 7

§ 37 Fragen mit ‚who' und ‚whose' Questions with 'who' and 'whose'

Subject	**Who** **Whose** family	wants to go to Wales? lives in Wales?
Object	**Who** **Whose** bike	can Tanja ask? can Tanja borrow?

- *Who* (wer/wen) kann sowohl nach dem Subjekt als auch nach dem Objekt eines Satzes fragen. Dasselbe gilt auch für *whose* (wessen), das nach dem Besitzer (oder den Besitzern) fragt.

⚠ *Who's* (wer ist) und *whose* (wessen) dürfen nicht verwechselt werden.

§ 38 Gegenüberstellung: present progressive – simple present

a) **The present progressive**

What **are** you **doing** at the moment?

We'**re playing** cards.

I'**m watching** Kevin.
He'**s helping** his dad outside.

- Die Verlaufsform drückt aus, daß etwas **gerade jetzt** geschieht **und noch nicht vorbei** ist.
- Das *present progressive* wird normalerweise nur bei Verben gebraucht, die eine Tätigkeit oder einen Vorgang ausdrücken. Deshalb haben Verben, die einen Zustand (wie z. B. *to be*), einen Besitz *(to have)*, Wünsche *(to want)*, Gefühle *(to like, to love)*, Wissen *(to know)* oder Meinungen *(to think, to believe)* ausdrücken, gewöhnlich keine Verlaufsform.
- *To have* hat in der Verlaufsform verschiedene Bedeutungen, z. B. ‚essen' oder ‚trinken':
  The Bensons **are having** tea now.
  Jenny **is having** a piece of cake.

b) **The simple present**

	Das **simple present** wird gebraucht für:
Jenny **goes** to a comprehensive school in Filton.	Handlungen (oder Zustände), die zeitlich nicht begrenzt sind und länger andauern.
Jenny usually **gets** home at four. In the evening she often **watches** TV or **listens** to music. She sometimes **reads** a good book, too.	gewohnheitsmäßige/wiederholte Handlungen. Signalwörter: *often, always, sometimes, usually,* aber auch Zeitangaben wie *in the morning, every morning, on Sundays* usw.
There is a concert at Jenny's school today. Before the concert Jenny **has** a shower. Then she **puts** on her new blouse. After that she **leaves** the house.	aufeinanderfolgende Handlungen in Erzählungen *(narrative usage)*. Signalwörter: *first, then, after that, the next morning* usw.

§ 39 Wieviel Uhr ist es? What time is it?

1. … o'clock

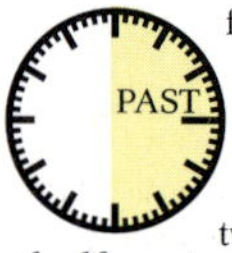

five (minutes) past …
ten (minutes) past …
(a) quarter past …
twenty (minutes) past …
twenty-five (minutes) past …
half past

… o'clock

five (minutes) to …
ten (minutes) to …
(a) quarter to …
twenty (minutes) to …
twenty-five (minutes) to …

Bei Zeitangaben mit Fünferzahlen wird das Wort *minutes* gewöhnlich weggelassen.
Bei allen anderen Minutenangaben muß es stehen:

What time is it?

It's three **minutes** to eleven.

It's eighteen **minutes** past nine.

2. Neben den Zeitangaben mit *to* und *past* (cf. § 19) gibt es auch eine ‚offizielle' Zeitangabe, bei der – wie im Deutschen – zuerst die Stunde und dann die Minuten genannt werden. Solche Uhrzeitangaben finden sich häufig bei Programmansagen (Radio, Fernsehen) und bei Fahrplänen.

6.07	7.15	8.30	10.45	12.15	16.39
six oh seven	seven fifteen	eight thirty	ten forty-five	twelve fifteen	sixteen thirty-nine

[§ 40] Bestätigungsfragen Question tags

Positive statement	**Negative tag**	
Tanja **is** happy,	**isn't**	**she**?
She **is talking** to Kevin,	**isn't**	**she**?
They **have** already **got** their tickets,	**haven't**	**they**?
Tanja **can borrow** Sandra's bike,	**can't**	**she**?
Their train **leaves** at 7.40,	**doesn't**	**it**?
They **change** trains at Newport,	**don't**	**they**?
Negative statement	**Positive tag**	
You **aren't** angry,	**are**	**you**?
Kevin **isn't** late,	**is**	**he**?
Jenny **can't go** with them,	**can**	**she**?
Jenny **hasn't got** a boyfriend,	**has**	**she**?
Jenny **doesn't** play football,	**does**	**she**?
Tanja and Kevin **don't go** to Wales by car,	**do**	**they**?

Wenn man im Deutschen Zustimmung zu einer Aussage oder deren Bestätigung erwartet, so benutzt man oft Ausdrücke wie **nicht wahr?**, **oder?**, **oder nicht?**. Im Englischen werden solche Bestätigungsfragen folgendermaßen gebildet:

- Ist der Aussagesatz bejaht, so wird die Bestätigungsfrage verneint.
- Ist der Aussagesatz dagegen verneint, so wird die Bestätigungsfrage bejaht.
- In Aussagesätzen mit *Hilfsverben* werden diese zusammen mit dem Subjekt des Satzes in der Bestätigungsfrage wieder aufgegriffen.
- Das Subjekt des Aussagesatzes erscheint in der Bestätigungsfrage immer als Personalpronomen. Bei einem Aussagesatz mit *there is* wird *there* in der Bestätigungsfrage wiederholt:

  There isn't much time, is **there**?
- Steht im Aussagesatz ein *Vollverb*, so wird es in der Bestätigungsfrage durch *do/does* ersetzt.

Unit 8

§ 41 Die Ordnungszahlen The ordinal numbers

1st	first	11th	eleventh	21st	twenty-first	100th	(one) hundredth
2nd	second	12th	**twelfth**	22nd	twenty-second	142nd	(one) hundred **and** forty-second
3rd	third	13th	thirteenth	23rd	twenty-third	1,000th	(one) thousandth
4th	fourth	14th	fourteenth	30th	thirtieth		
5th	**fifth**	15th	fifteenth	40th	f**o**rtieth		
6th	sixth	16th	sixteenth	50th	fiftieth		
7th	seventh	17th	seventeenth	60th	sixtieth		
8th	**eighth**	18th	eighteenth	70th	seventieth		
9th	**ninth**	19th	nineteenth	80th	eightieth		
10th	tenth	20th	twentieth	90th	ninetieth		

- *The first, the second, the third* sind unregelmäßige Formen. Sie werden auch bei den zusammengesetzten Ordnungszahlen verwendet. Alle anderen Ordnungszahlen enden auf *-th*.
- Bei Ordnungszahlen steht im Englischen nie ein Punkt, sondern die beiden letzten Buchstaben der Ordnungszahlen: (the) fir**st** = 1st; (the) seco**nd** = 2nd; (the) thi**rd** = 3rd; (the) four**th** = 4th usw.

§ 42 Das Datum The date

Schreibweise	**Aussprache**
May 28th/May 28	May **the** twenty-eigh**th**
28th May/28 May	**The** twenty-eigh**th of** May

- Daten können mit Ordnungszahlen oder Kardinalzahlen geschrieben werden. Beim Sprechen müssen jedoch immer Ordnungszahlen verwendet werden.
- *The* muß beim Sprechen immer vor die Ordnungszahl gesetzt werden.
- **Jahreszahlen** werden wie folgt ausgesprochen: 1900 nineteen hundred; 1901 nineteen hundred and one (nineteen oh one); 1945 nineteen (hundred and) forty-five

§ 43 Die Steigerung von Adjektiven The comparison of adjectives

Die beiden Steigerungsformen des Adjektivs werden verwendet, um Vergleiche zu ziehen:

	positive	comparative	superlative
adjectives with one syllable (Silbe)	clean nice big	clean**er** nice**r** bi**gger**	(the) clean**est** (the) nice**st** (the) bi**ggest**
adjectives with two syllables and *-y, -er, -le* at the end	bus**y** eas**y** clev**er** simp**le**	bus**ier** eas**ier** clever**er** simpl**er**	(the) bus**iest** (the) eas**iest** (the) clever**est** (the) simpl**est**
adjectives with more than two syllables	interesting important	more interesting more important	(the) most interesting (the) most important
irregular forms (unregelmäßige Formen)	good bad much/many	better worse more	(the) best (the) worst — most

- Einsilbig ausgesprochene Adjektive (z. B. *clean, nice*) und zweisilbige Adjektive, die auf *-y* und *-er* enden, werden mit *-er* bzw. *-est* gesteigert.
- Drei- und mehrsilbige Adjektive bilden die Steigerungsformen mit *more* und *most*. Dies gilt auch für die meisten zweisilbigen Adjektive, die **nicht** auf *-y* und *-er* enden (z. B. *boring, famous*).

⚠ Die Steigerungsformen von *good, bad* und von *much/many* sind unregelmäßig. Vor der Superlativform *most* steht kein bestimmter Artikel: **Most** people are nice.

Beachte bei der **Schreibung** und **Aussprache**:
- Bei Adjektiven, die auf *-e* enden (z. B. *nice, fine*), entfällt das auslautende *-e* vor *-er* und *-est*.
- Bei einsilbigen Adjektiven mit kurzem Vokal wird der Endkonsonant verdoppelt:
  big – bigger
  aber: clean – cleaner
- Bei Adjektiven, die auf [ŋ] enden, wird bei den Steigerungsformen ein [g] gesprochen:
  young [jʌŋ] younger [ˈjʌŋgə] (the) youngest [ˈjʌŋgɪst]

§ 44 Vergleiche mit Adjektiven Comparisons with adjectives

Bei einem Vergleich mit Adjektiven wird die Gleichheit oder Ungleichheit folgendermaßen ausgedrückt:

Gleichheit	Ungleichheit	
Jenny is **as** old **as** Tanja. … so alt wie … Football is **as** interesting **as** hockey.	David is old**er than** Tanja. Tanja is **not as** old **as** David. To Tanja, hockey is **more** interesting **than** football. To Tanja, football is **not as** interesting **as** hockey.	… älter als … … nicht so alt wie … … interessanter als …

- Bei (not) **as … as** steht immer die Grundform des Adjektivs.
- Nach einem Komparativ steht immer **than**.

⚠ **Than** (als) darf nicht mit **then** (dann) verwechselt werden.

§ 45 Das going to-Futur The going to-future

I	**am**	**going to**	have a look at the Computer Show.	
Wendy	**is**	**going to**	come, too.	
We	**are**	**going to**	meet her at the snack bar,	
but we	**aren't**	**going to**	stay long.	
What	**are you**	**going to**	do on Saturday?	
	Are you	**going to**	have a look at the show, too?	Yes, I am./No, I'm not.

- Mit den *going to*-Futur kann man eine Absicht ausdrücken oder sich erkundigen, was jemand in naher Zukunft oder später vorhat.
- Das *going to*-Futur bildet man mit *am/are/is* + *going to* + Infinitiv.
- Für die Verneinung, die Fragestellung und für Kurzantworten gelten die gleichen Regeln wie für *to be* (§§ 3–4).

⚠ Verwechsle nicht das *going to*-Futur mit der entsprechenden Verlaufsform von *to go*:

I'm going home.	**I'm going to go** home.
Ich gehe (gerade) nach Hause.	Ich habe vor, nach Hause zu gehen.

§46] **Das will-Futur** The will-future

Jenny	**will**	**be**	14 next Saturday.
All her friends	**will**	**come**	to her party.
I	**will**	**be**	there, too.
She	**will not**	**be**	alone that day.
She	**'ll**	**get**	a lot of presents.
She	**won't**	**be**	unhappy on her birthday.

- Das *will*-Futur wird mit *will* + **Infinitiv** (ohne *to*) gebildet. Die Formen des *will*-Futur sind für alle Personen gleich.
- Häufig werden statt *will* und *will not* die Kurzformen *'ll* und *won't* [wəʊnt] verwendet.
- Bei der Frage steht *will* vor dem Subjekt:

	Will	**she get**	a present from Kevin?
What	**will**	**she get?**	

§47] **Das going to-Futur und das will-Futur** The going to-future and the will-future

The will-future	The going to-future
Next Saturday Jenny **will be** fourteen. I don't think **it'll rain** then.	On her birthday Jenny **is going to have** a party. She **is going to invite** all her friends.
Mit dem *will*-Futur drückt man aus, daß zukünftige Ereignisse nicht von persönlichen Entscheidungen, sondern von äußeren Umständen (z. B. Geburtstag, Wetter usw.) abhängen.	Das *going to*-Futur drückt eine Absicht aus, d. h. was jemand in naher Zukunft oder später vorhat.

Unit 9

§48 **Das Present Perfect: regelmäßige Formen** The present perfect: regular forms

1. **Positive and negative forms**

I	**have**		**asked**	David about the lights.
You	**have**		**invited**	all the guests.
Dad	**has**		**moved**	the bikes.
Work	**has**	**not**	**ended**	yet.
We	**have**	**not**	**finished**	the job yet.
We	**have**	**not**	**tidied**	up the barn yet.
They	**have**	**not**	**started**	to make the sandwiches.
S	Present of 'have'	+	Past Participle	

- Im Gegensatz zum Deutschen (cf. sie *hat* gearbeitet, er *ist* gefallen) wird das *present perfect* im Englischen immer mit dem Präsens von *to have* und dem *past participle* gebildet. Verneinte Formen werden mit *have not/has not* gebildet.

- Beim *present perfect* gibt es auch Kurzformen:

I'**ve** asked Sandra.	I **haven't** asked Peter.
He'**s** moved the bikes.	He **hasn't** moved the boxes.
They'**ve** started work.	They **haven't** finished the job yet.

⚠ Verwechsle die Kurzformen von *to have* nicht mit den Kurzformen von *to be*:
She'**s** opened the shop. It'**s** open now.
She **has** opened the shop. It **is** open now.

2. The past participle

Das *past participle* wird bei regelmäßigen Verben dadurch gebildet, daß man an den Infinitiv die Endung *-ed* anhängt. Bei der Schreibung und Aussprache muß man auf folgende Besonderheiten achten:

Schreibung:

to move – mov**ed** to change – chang**ed**	Das stumme End-**e** entfällt.
to car**ry** – carr**ied** to ti**dy** – tid**ied**	Bei Verben, die auf Konsonant + *y* enden, ist die Endung *-ied*.
to sto**p** – sto**pped** aber: to loo**k** – look**ed**	Nach kurzem, einfachem Vokal wird ein auslautender Konsonant verdoppelt.

Aussprache:

[d]	pla**y**ed answe**r**ed ca**ll**ed	Nach Vokalen und stimmhaften Konsonanten wird die Endung *-ed* [d] ausgesprochen.
[t]	as**k**ed fet**ch**ed sto**pp**ed	Nach stimmlosen Konsonanten wird die Endung *-ed* [t] ausgesprochen.
[ɪd]	en**d**ed star**t**ed invi**t**ed	Nach auslautendem *-d* und *-t* wird die Endung *-ed* [ɪd] ausgesprochen.

3. Questions and short answers

Have	**you**	**fetched**	the chairs yet?	Yes, **I have**.
Have	**you**	**talked**	to Tanja?	No, **I haven't**.
Hasn't	**work**	**ended**	for today?	No, **it hasn't**.
Has	**dad**	**moved**	the bikes?	Yes, **he has**.
Haven't	**you**	**tried**	to call Rajiv?	Yes, **we have**.
Haven't	**they**	**invited**	Peter yet?	No, **they haven't**.
Hv	**S**	**V**		

- Im *present perfect* wird die Frage durch Umstellung von Subjekt und Hilfsverb (Inversion) gebildet. Diese Regel gilt auch, wenn die Frage mit einem Fragewort beginnt:

Why	haven't	they	invited	Peter	yet?
Question word	**Hv**	**S**	**V**	**O**	

- Kurzantworten werden auch im *present perfect* nach dem bereits bekannten Muster gebildet; das *past participle* wird weggelassen.

Yes / No, Subject (pronoun) + long form (positive form). / short form (negative form).

§49 Das Present Perfect: unregelmäßige Formen The present perfect: irregular forms

Eine Reihe häufig gebrauchter englischer Verben haben unregelmäßige Formen für das *past participle*. Für die Bildung dieser Formen gibt es keine Regel. Sie müssen daher einzeln gelernt werden.

Infinitive	**Past Participle**	**Present Perfect**
to do	**done**	What **have** you **done**?
to put	**put**	I **have put** the food in the barn.
to leave	**left**	Where **have** you **left** the key?
to see	**seen**	**Haven't** you **seen** it?
to tell	**told**	**Have** you **told** David about the party?

§50 Die Wortstellung beim Present Perfect Word order with the present perfect

question	short answer	statement
Has she started **work**?	Yes, she has.	She has started **it**.
Have you seen **my keys**?	No, I haven't.	I haven't seen **them**.
Have they asked **David** yet?	No, they haven't.	They haven't asked **him** yet.
Hv S V O		**S Hv V O**

- Im Gegensatz zum Deutschen steht im Englischen das Objekt **nie** zwischen Hilfsverb und Verb, sondern immer **nach** dem *past participle*.

⚠ *Yet* steht immer am Satzende. Adverbien wie *just, never, already* stehen dagegen nach dem Hilfsverb, d. h. vor dem *past participle*:

I have	**never**	been	to England.
He has	**just**	arrived.	

§ 51 Der Gebrauch des Present Perfect The usage of the present perfect

Action/Handlung	Result/Ergebnis
Look at these glasses. I **have washed** them.	They are clean now.
Dad **has moved** the bikes.	They are no longer there.
Mum **has remembered** the sausages.	They are on the table.
Tanja **has asked** Kevin to come to Hanover.	Kevin is very happy.

- Das *present perfect* wird für Handlungen verwendet, die zwar vorbei sind, deren Ergebnis jedoch in der Gegenwart sichtbar oder spürbar ist.
- Dies gilt auch für Handlungen, die nicht stattgefunden haben. Auch etwas, das nicht geschehen ist, kann Auswirkungen auf die Gegenwart haben:

I **haven't cleaned** my room yet. = It's still the same mess.

⚠ Im Gegensatz zur deutschen Umgangssprache kann das *present perfect* nicht als Erzählzeit der Vergangenheit verwendet werden. Dafür wird die in den folgenden Paragraphen beschriebene Zeit *(simple past)* gebraucht.

[Unit 10]

[§ 52] The past tense: simple form (simple past)

1. **Regular forms**

Infinitive	The Simple Past
to **sail**	Around 1850 a Benson **sailed** to the USA.
to **work**	He **worked** on a ship.
to **mail**	He **mailed** a letter home from New York.

- Das *simple past* regelmäßiger Verben wird auf die gleiche Weise wie das *past participle* gebildet. Wie beim *past participle* hängt man auch hier die Endung *-ed* an den Infinitiv (ohne *to*) an.
- Daher gelten für die Bildung des *simple past* auch die gleichen Schreib- und Ausspracheregeln (cf. § 47,2):

[d]	Aussprache der Endung nach Vokalen und stimmhaften Konsonanten: he sail**ed** [seɪld]
[t]	Aussprache der Endung nach stimmlosen Konsonanten: he work**ed** [wɜːkt]
[ɪd]	Aussprache der Endung nach auslautendem [-d] und [-t]: he visit**ed** [ˈvɪzɪtɪd]

– Ausfall des nicht gesprochenen End-*e*:	invite	– invit**ed**
– *-y* wird nach Konsonanten zu *-ied*:	carry	– carr**ied**
– Verdoppelung des Endkonsonanten:	stop	– sto**pped**

- Die Form des *simple past* ist für alle Personen gleich.

2. **Irregular forms**

Infinitive	The Simple Past		
to **wake**	David	**woke**	up in his hotel room.
to **go**	He	**went**	to the window.
to **stand**	He	**stood**	by the window for a minute.
to **run**	Then	**ran**	into the bathroom
to **have**	and	**had**	a shower.

- Wie beim *past participle* gibt es auch beim *simple past* unregelmäßige Formen. Für ihre Bildung gibt es ebenfalls keine Regeln: Sie müssen einzeln gelernt werden.
- Auch bei den unregelmäßigen Verben sind die Formen des *simple past* für alle Personen gleich.

3. **Negative forms**

David	**didn't see**	much of San Francisco.
He	**didn't have**	much time.
Sometimes he	**didn't know**	where he was.
S	**Hv V**	

- Wie im Präsens (cf. § 31) wird auch im *simple past* die Verneinung mit einer Form von *to do* gebildet, und zwar mit *didn't/did not* + Infinitiv. Die Form *didn't* ist für alle Personen gleich.

4. **Questions and short answers**

Did	you	**like**	New York,	David?	**Yes, I did.**
Did	the guide	**show**	you	around?	**Yes, she did.**
Did	you	**have**	enough time?		**No, I didn't.**
Did	people	**help**	you?		**Yes, they did.**
Hv	**S**	**V**	**O**		

- Entscheidungsfragen werden im *simple past* mit *did* gebildet, Kurzantworten nach dem bereits bekannten Muster.

$$\frac{\text{Yes}}{\text{No}}\text{, Subject (pronoun) + }\frac{\text{long form (= did).}}{\text{short form (= didn't).}}$$

5. **Questions with question words**

What	did	Jan	tell	David?
Where	did	'their' Benson	come	from?
What	did	grandfather	say	about David?
Question word	**Hv**	**S**	**V**	

⚠ Nach einer Form von *to do* steht immer der Infinitiv!

[§ 53] Das Simple Past von ‚to be' The simple past of 'to be'

1. **Positive forms**

I	**was**	in England last year.
You	**were**	in Switzerland.
David	**was**	in California.
Tanja	**was**	in Bristol.
It	**was**	a nice holiday.
We	**were**	in England, too.
You	**were**	in Germany.
The Bensons	**were**	in Wales.

- Die Vergangenheitsformen von *to be* sind unregelmäßig. Sie lauten *was* und *were*.

2. **Negative forms**

Long forms			**Short forms**		
I	**was not**	in Bristol yesterday.	I	**wasn't**	in Bristol yesterday.
You	**were not**	at home.	You	**weren't**	at home.
Sandra	**was not**	surprised.	She	**wasn't**	surprised.
We	**were not**	late.	We	**weren't**	late.
They	**were not**	in town.	They	**weren't**	in town.

- Wie im Präsens werden die verneinten Formen von *to be* auch in der Vergangenheit nur mit *not* gebildet. Die Kurzformen lauten: *wasn't/weren't*.

3. **Questions and short answers**

Were	**you**	late for your tour, David?	Yes, I	**was**.
Wasn't	**Jan**	your guide in New York?	No, she	**wasn't**.
Was	**there**	enough time to see New York?	No, there	**wasn't**.
Were	**people**	nice to you, David?	Yes, they	**were**.
V	**S**			

- Wie im Präsens werden auch in der Vergangenheit Fragen mit *to be* durch die Umstellung von Subjekt und Verb (Inversion) gebildet. Für Kurzantworten gelten die bereits bekannten Regeln.

4. **Questions with question words**

When	**were**	**you**	in California, David?
Why	**wasn't**	**Sandra**	with you?
How long	**were**	**you**	in California?
Question word	**V**	**S**	

⚠ Bei allen Formen von *to be* darf nie eine Form von *to do* gebraucht werden. Eine Ausnahme bildet allein der verneinte Imperativ (vgl. § 16).

§54] Der Gebrauch des Simple Past The usage of the past tense: simple form

When **did** you **see** David? I **saw** him yesterday. He **was** in California.	Das *simple past* wird für Handlungen und Zustände verwendet, die in der Vergangenheit liegen und als abgeschlossen betrachtet werden. Signalwörter: *yesterday, last (week, month, year), ago, in 1970* usw.
In San Francisco a bus **picked** David up at the airport. After lunch he **walked** around downtown until he **was** tired. Then he **went** back to his hotel.	Das *simple past* wird auch benutzt, um aufeinanderfolgende Handlungen wiederzugeben, die in der Vergangenheit stattgefunden haben. Das *simple past* ist deshalb die Zeitform für Erzählungen und Berichte über vergangene Ereignisse. Signalwörter: *first, then, after that, the next morning* usw.

§55] Bedingungssätze Conditional sentences

if-clause (if-Satz)	main clause (Hauptsatz)
If David **wins** the first prize, **If** he **doesn't win** it,	he **will fly** to the USA. he **won't be** unhappy.
if + simple present	will-future

- Ein Bedingungssatz besteht aus einem *if*-Satz und einem Hauptsatz. Der Hauptsatz drückt aus, was geschieht, wenn die in dem *if*-Satz ausgesprochene Bedingung erfüllt wird.

⚠ Auch wenn sich die Bedingung auf die Zukunft bezieht, darf im *if*-Satz nie das *will*-Futur stehen.

§56] Adverbien der Art und Weise Adverbs of manner

1. Im Deutschen sind Adjektive und Adverbien oft formgleich, z. B.:
   Sie ist **schön** (Adjektiv) – Sie singt **schön** (Adverb).
   Im Englischen dagegen haben sie meist unterschiedliche Formen:

Adjective	**Adverb**
Nivruti has a **beautiful** voice. Tanja is **happy**.	She sings **beautifully**. She is talking **happily** to Kevin.

- Adjektive geben an, wie jemand oder etwas ist.
- Ein Adjektiv steht vor einem Substantiv oder nach dem Verb *to be*.

- Adverbien geben an, wie etwas getan wird. Sie geben Antwort auf Fragen mit *how*: *How does she sing? She sings **beautifully**.*
- Adverbien der Art und Weise werden meistens mit der Endung *-ly* von Adjektiven abgeleitet:
  nice + ly → nicely

⚠ Beachte beim Schreiben: happy – happily

⚠ Beachte die Sonderformen: good – well
hard – hard

⚠ Adverbien stehen nie vor einem Substantiv und nie nach einer Form von *to be*!

[§ 57] Can, mustn't und ihre ‚Ersatzverben' 'Can', 'mustn't' and their substitutes

Can drückt eine Fähigkeit aus. Für *can* kann das ‚Ersatzverb' *to be able to* verwendet werden:

Tanja **can** walk again but she **can't** do judo yet.	Tanja **is able to** walk again but she **isn't able to** do judo yet.

Ein Verbot wird im Englischen durch *mustn't* (= nicht dürfen) ausgedrückt. Für *mustn't* kann das ‚Ersatzverb' *not to be allowed to* verwendet werden:

You **mustn't** turn left here. You **mustn't** stop here.	You **are not allowed to** turn left here. You **aren't allowed to** stop here.

Useful grammatical terms

adjective ['ædʒɪktɪv] Adjektiv
adverbial [æd'vɜ:bɪəl] adverbiale Bestimmung
adverb of frequency ['ædvɜ:b‿əv 'fri:kwənsɪ] Adverb der Häufigkeit
adverb of manner ['ædvɜ:b‿əv 'mænə] Adverb der Art und Weise
auxiliary verb [ɔ:g'zɪljərɪ ˌvɜ:b] Hilfsverb
cardinal number ['kɑ:dɪnl 'nʌmbə] Grundzahl
comparative [kəm'pærətɪv] Komparativ
comparison [kəm'pærɪsn] Steigerung
conditional sentence [kən'dɪʃənl 'sentəns] Bedingungssatz
conjunction [kən'dʒʌŋkʃən] Konjunktion
definite article ['defənɪt 'ɑ:tɪkl] bestimmter Artikel
determiner [dɪ'tɜ:mɪnə] Begleiter
direct object ['daɪrekt 'ɒbdʒɪkt] direktes Objekt
expression of quantity [ɪk'spreʃn‿əv 'kwɒntɪtɪ] Mengenangabe
expression of time [ɪk'spreʃn‿əv 'taɪm] Zeitangabe
future ['fju:tʃə] Futur
genitive ['dʒenɪtɪv] Genitiv
gerund ['dʒerənd] ‚Gerund'
going to-future ['gəʊɪŋˌtu: 'fju:tʃə] going to-Futur
imperative [ɪm'perətɪv] Imperativ
indefinite article [ɪn'defənɪt 'ɑ:tɪkl] unbestimmter Artikel
indefinite determiner [ɪn'defənɪt dɪ'tɜ:mɪnə] unbestimmter Begleiter
indirect object ['ɪndaɪˌrekt 'ɒbdʒɪkt] indirektes Objekt
main clause ['meɪn 'klɔ:z] Hauptsatz
noun [naʊn] Substantiv
ordinal number ['ɔ:dɪnl 'nʌmbə] Ordnungszahl
personal pronoun ['pɜ:snl 'prəʊnaʊn] Personalpronomen
plural ['plʊərəl] Plural
possessive determiner [pə'zesɪv dɪ'tɜ:mɪnə] Possessivbegleiter
preposition [ˌprepə'zɪʃn] Präposition
present participle [ˌpreznt 'pɑ:tɪsɪpl] Partizip Präsens
present progressive [ˌpreznt prə'gresɪv] Verlaufsform des Präsens
present perfect [ˌpreznt 'pɜ:fɪkt] Perfekt
present tense ['preznt ˌtens] Präsens
progressive form [prə'gresɪv ˌfɔ:m] Verlaufsform
pronoun ['prəʊnəʊn] Pronomen
question tag ['kwestʃən ˌtæg] Bestätigungsfrage
question word ['kwestʃən ˌwɜ:d] Fragewort
sentence ['sentəns] Satz
short answer ['ʃɔ:t ˌɑ:nsə] Kurzantwort
simple past [ˌsɪmpl 'pɑ:st] Imperfekt
singular ['sɪŋgjʊlə] Singular
subject ['sʌbdʒɪkt] Subjekt
subordinate clause [sə'bɔ:dɪnɪt 'klɔ:z] Nebensatz
substitute ['sʌbstɪtju:t] Ersatzverb
tense [tens] Zeit
verb [vɜ:b] Vollverb
will-future ['wɪl ˌfju:tʃə] will-Futur
word order ['wɜ:d ˌɔ:də] Wortstellung

Vocabulary

Lautzeichen (Phonetic Symbols)

Vokale (Vowels)

[ɑː] **father**, **cards**; langes *a*, weiter hinten gesprochen als in *Vater*

[ʌ] **mother**, **does**, **but**; kurzes *a*, etwa wie in *Mann*

[e] **pen**, **head**; etwa wie das *e* in *nett*

[ə] **a** bar **of** chocolate, sist**er**; kurzer, unbetonter Laut, wie der Endlaut in *bitte*

[ɜː] **girl**, **her**, **word**; etwa ein verlängertes [ə]. Dieser Laut wird weiter hinten gesprochen als das deutsche *ö* (Lippen nicht vorstülpen!)

[æ] **flat**, **can**; kurzes, ganz offenes *ä*, offener als in *Männer*

[ɪ] **it**, favour**i**te, mark**e**t; kurzes *i* wie in *Lippe*, doch weniger spitz, etwas zum [ə] hin

[iː] t**ea**cher, sh**e**, p**ie**ce; langes *i* wie in *tief*

[ɒ] sh**o**p, wh**a**t; kurzes, offenes *o*

[ɔː] **or**, d**oor**, f**our**; langes, offenes *o* (Lippen leicht vorstülpen!)

[ʊ] p**u**llover, l**oo**k; kurzes *u* wie in *Schutt*

[uː] y**ou**, t**oo**, bl**ue**; langes *u*, etwa wie in *du* (Lippen kaum vorstülpen!)

Doppellaute (Diphthongs)

[aɪ] n**i**ne, b**y**, r**igh**t; wie *ai* in *Mai, Kaiser*

[aʊ] n**ow**, h**ou**se; helles *a* mit nachklingendem *u*, etwa wie in *Zauber*

[eə] th**ere**, ch**air**; kurzes, offenes *ä* mit nachklingendem [ə], etwa wie in *Bär*

[eɪ] n**a**me, th**ey**, **eigh**t; englisches [e] mit nachklingendem [ɪ]

[ɪə] h**ere**, id**ea**; etwa wie in *mir*

[ɔɪ] b**oy**; kurzes offenes *o* mit nachklingendem [ɪ], ähnlich wie in *Freude*

[əʊ] hell**o**, r**oa**d; [ə] mit nachklingendem [ʊ]

[ʊə] t**ou**rist; [ʊ] mit nachklingendem [ə]

Konsonanten (Consonants)

[j] **y**es, n**e**w, wie das deutsche *j*

[l] **l**isten, b**l**ue; am Wortanfang und vor Vokalen etwa wie das deutsche *l*
*schoo***l**, she**l**f; am Wortende und vor Konsonanten wie das *l* der Rheinländer, z. B. in *Köln*

[ŋ] morni**ng**, lo**ng**; wie der *-ng*-Laut in *singen* (kein [g] sprechen!)

[ŋg] E**ng**lish; wie [ŋ] jedoch mit nachfolgendem gesprochenem [g]

[r] **r**ed, b**r**oken; Gaumen-*r*, Zungenspitze gegen Gaumen anheben und leicht zurückbiegen; der austretende Luftstrom erzeugt [r]

[s] **s**ister, thi**s**; stimmloses, d. h. hartes *s* wie in *Laus*

[z] i**s**, dog**s**; stimmhaftes, d. h. weiches *s* wie in *summen*

[ʒ] gara**g**e; stimmhaftes *sch* wie in *Gelee*

[dʒ] **j**eans, **G**erman; [ʒ] mit vorausklingendem [d]

[ʃ] **sh**e, sta**ti**on; stimmloses *sch* wie in *Tisch*

[tʃ] tea**ch**er, **ch**ild; [ʃ] mit vorausklingendem [t]

[st/sp] **st**ory, **sp**ort; wird [st] und [sp] gesprochen, nicht [ʃt] und [ʃp]

[ð] **th**e, mo**th**er; stimmhafter Lispellaut (Zunge zwischen den Zähnen!)

[θ] **th**anks, no**th**ing; stimmloser Lispellaut (Zunge zwischen den Zähnen!)

[v] **v**isit, o**f**; wie *w* in *Winter*

[w] **w**eek, **wh**en, **o**ne; vom [ʊ] ausgehenden und zum folgenden Laut hinübergleiten

ˈ = Hauptbetonung

ˌ = Nebenbetonung

(Die Betonungsstriche stehen immer **vor** der betonten Silbe.)

‿ = besonders enge Bindung zweier Wörter aneinander

⟨⟩ Stücke, deren Überschriften, und Übungen, deren Ziffern in Winkelklammern stehen, sind fakultativ.
[ ] Stücke, deren Überschriften, und Übungen, deren Ziffern in eckigen Klammern stehen, sind in Bayern obligatorisch.
– Diese Übungen enthalten keinen neuen Wortschatz.

Unit 1

7	**unit**	['ju:nɪt]	Einheit, *hier:* Lektion
	Welcome to Bristol!	['welkəm tə 'brɪstl]	Willkommen in Bristol!
	to **welcome**		willkommen heißen
	This is Bristol.	['ðɪs‿ɪz 'brɪstl]	Dies ist Bristol.
	this		dies, das
	is		ist
	It is in England.	[ɪt‿ɪz‿ɪn‿'ɪŋglənd]	Es ist in England.
	it		es
	in		in

A Welcome to Bristol

8a)	**Mr Benson**	['mɪstə 'bensn]	Herr Benson
	He is (He's) from Bristol.	['hi:‿ɪz (hi:z) frəm 'brɪstl]	Er ist aus Bristol.
	he		er
	from		von, *hier:* aus
	Mrs Benson	['mɪsɪz]	Frau Benson
	She is (She's) from Bristol, too.	['ʃi:‿ɪz (ʃi:z) frəm 'brɪstl 'tu:]	Sie ist auch aus Bristol.
	she		sie *(Singular)*
	too		*am Ende eines Satzes:* auch
	Jenny is English.	['dʒenɪ‿ɪz‿'ɪnglɪʃ]	Jenny ist Engländerin.
	English		englisch; Engländer(in)
9b)	**teacher**	['ti:tʃə]	Lehrer, Lehrerin
	here	[hɪə]	hier
	Hello.	[hə'ləʊ]	Hallo! Guten Tag!
	Is this your suitcase?	[ɪz 'ðɪs jɔ: 'su:tkeɪs]	Ist das dein Koffer?
	your		dein(e), euer (eure); Ihr(e)
	suitcase		Koffer
	Yes, it is.	['jes‿ɪt‿'ɪz]	*hier:* Ja.
	yes		ja
	and	[ænd/ənd]	und
	bag	[bæg]	Tasche, Reisetasche
	No, it isn't.	['nəʊ‿ɪt‿'ɪznt]	*hier:* Nein.
	no		nein
	This is my bag.	['ðɪs‿ɪz maɪ 'bæg]	Dies ist meine Tasche.
	Put the bag in the car.	['pʊt ðə 'bæg ɪn ðə 'kɑ:]	Leg/Stell die Tasche ins Auto.
	to **put**		legen, setzen, stellen
	the		der, die, das; die *(Plural)*
	car		Auto
	please	[pli:z]	bitte
	OK.	[ˌəʊ'keɪ]	In Ordnung./Okay.
9c),1	**My name's David.**	['maɪ 'neɪmz‿'deɪvɪd]	Ich heiße David.
	name		Name
	I'm English.	[aɪm‿'ɪŋglɪʃ]	Ich bin Engländer(in).
	I am	[aɪ‿'æm]	ich bin
	you	[ju:]	du, ihr; Sie
	What's your name?	['wɒts‿jɔ: 'neɪm]	Wie heißt du? Wie heißen Sie?
	what		was
	Where are you from?	['weər‿ə ju: 'frɒm]	Woher kommst du? Woher kommen Sie?
	where		wo
	you are	[ju:‿'ɑ:]	du bist, ihr seid; Sie sind

9c),2	I'm **German.**	[aɪm‿ˈdʒɜ:mən]	Ich bin Deutsche(r).
	German		deutsch
9c),3	**Over to you.**	[ˈəʊvə‿tə‿ˈju:]	Du bist/Ihr seid/Sie sind dran.
	I'm **Swiss.**	[aɪm‿ˈswɪs]	Ich bin Schweizer(in).
	Go on.	[ˌgəʊ‿ˈɒn]	Mach(t) weiter!
	to **go on**		weitermachen, fortfahren
10,1a)	to **ask**	[ɑ:sk]	fragen
	to **answer**	[ˈɑ:nsə]	antworten
b)	**No, I'm not.**	[ˈnəʊ‿aɪm ˈnɒt]	Nein.
	not		nicht
10,2	–		

B Upstairs, downstairs

11	**upstairs**	[ˌʌpˈsteəz]	(nach) oben
	downstairs	[ˌdaʊnˈsteəz]	(nach) unten
a)	**Here we are.**	[ˈhɪə wi: ˈɑ:]	Hier sind wir.
	we		wir
	This is our house.	[ˈðɪs‿ɪz‿aʊə ˈhaʊs]	Dies ist unser Haus.
	nice	[naɪs]	nett, schön
	to come in	[kʌm‿ˈɪn]	hereinkommen
	room	[ru:m/rʊm]	Zimmer
	David's bedroom	[ˈdeɪvɪdz ˈbedrʊm]	Davids Schlafzimmer *(s-Genitiv)*
	his	[hɪz]	sein(e)
	bathroom	[ˈbɑ:θrʊm]	Badezimmer, Bad
	Oh!	[əʊ]	Oh!
	The toilet is **next to** the bathroom.	[ðə ˈtɔɪlɪt‿ɪz neks‿tə ðə ˈbɑ:θrʊm]	Die Toilette ist neben dem Bad.
	next to		(direkt) neben
	little	[ˈlɪtl]	klein
	Thanks.	[θæŋks]	Danke.
b)	We're upstairs, **Mum**	[mʌm]	Wir sind oben, Mutti.
	her	[hɜ:]	ihr(e) *(Singular)*
	to come	[kʌm]	kommen
	It's **tea-time.**	[ˈti:taɪm]	Es ist Zeit für 'tea'.
	tea	[ti:]	Tee; *leichte Mahlzeit am späten Nachmittag, gewöhnlich mit Tee*
	small	[smɔ:l]	klein
11,1	–		
11,2	–		
12,3	–		
12,4	**Look, listen and say.**	[ˈlʊk ˈlɪsn‿ən ˈseɪ]	Schau(t) hin, hör(t) zu und sprich (sprecht) nach.
	to look		sehen, schauen
	to listen		zuhören
	to say		sagen

C Tanja's room

12	**a big room**	[ə ˈbɪg ˈrʊm]	ein großes Zimmer
	a		ein(e)
	big		groß
	There is an old desk in her room.	[ˌðeər‿ɪz‿ən‿ˈəʊld‿ˈdesk]	In ihrem Zimmer steht ein alter Schreibtisch.
	there is (there's)	[ðeər‿ˈɪz/ðeəz]	es gibt, da ist
	an		ein(e)
	apple	[ˈæpl]	Apfel
	orange	[ˈɒrɪndʒ]	Apfelsine, Orange
	on the desk	[ɒn ðə ˈdesk]	auf dem Schreibtisch
	plate	[pleɪt]	Teller

	new	[nju:]	neu
	book	[bʊk]	Buch
	a book **about** Bristol	[ə ˈbʊk‿əˈbaʊt ˈbrɪstl]	ein Buch über Bristol
	notebook	[ˈnəʊtbʊk]	Notizheft, -buch
	note	[nəʊt]	Notiz, kurze Mitteilung
	exercise book	[ˈeksəsaɪz ˈbʊk]	(Schul-)Heft
	exercise	[ˈeksəsaɪz]	Übung
	pen	[pen]	Füller
	pencil	[ˈpensl]	Bleistift
	card	[kɑ:d]	Karte; Postkarte
	The book is **for** you.	[ðə ˈbʊk‿ɪz fə ˈju:]	Das Buch ist für dich.
13,1	–		
13,2	–		
13,3	**classroom**	[ˈklɑ:srʊm]	Klassenzimmer
13,4	–		

D Tea-time

14	He's **late.**	[ˌhi:z‿ˈleɪt]	Er kommt zu spät.
	late		spät
	Sit here, Tanja.	[ˌsɪt ˈhɪə ˈtæ:njə]	Setz dich hierhin, Tanja.
	to sit		sitzen; sich hinsetzen
	a cup of tea	[ə ˈkʌp‿əv ˈti:]	eine Tasse Tee
	cup		Tasse
	Here you are.	[ˌhɪə ju:‿ˈɑ:]	Bitte schön.
	sugar	[ˈʃʊgə]	Zucker
	or	[ɔ:]	oder
	milk	[mɪlk]	Milch
	sandwich	[ˈsænwɪdʒ]	Butterbrot, Sandwich
	a piece of cake	[ə ˈpi:s‿əv‿ˈkeɪk]	ein Stück Kuchen
	to **meet**	[mi:t]	(sich) treffen, begegnen *hier:* kennenlernen
	I'm **Jenny's brother.**	[aɪm ˈdʒenɪz ˈbrʌðə]	Ich bin Jennys Bruder.
	glass	[glɑ:s]	Glas
	table	[teɪbl]	Tisch
14,1	–		
14,2	–		

You = du, ihr; Sie	
You're late, David.	**Du** kommst zu spät, David.
You're late, Tanja and Jenny.	**Ihr** kommt zu spät, Tanja und Jenny.
You're late, Mrs Benson.	**Sie** kommen zu spät, Mrs Benson.
Your = dein(e), euer(e); Ihr(e)	
Is that **your** bag, Tanja?	Ist das **deine** Tasche, Tanja?
Is that **your** house, Jenny and David?	Ist das **euer** Haus, Jenny und David?
Is that **your** car, Mr Benson?	Ist das **Ihr** Auto, Mr Benson?

E Tanja's house

15	**Who's this?**	[ˈhu:z‿ˈðɪs]	Wer ist das?
	who?	[hu:]	wer?
	in front of the house	[ɪn ˈfrʌnt‿əv ðə ˈhaʊs]	vor dem Haus
	It's me.	[ɪts ˈmɪ:]	Ich bin's./Das bin ich.
	of course	[əvˈkɔ:s]	natürlich, selbstverständlich
	This is my mum and **dad**.	[dæd]	Papi, Papa
	They're in Switzerland.	[ˌðeər‿ɪn ˈswɪtsələnd]	Sie sind in der Schweiz.
	they are	[ðəɪ‿ˈɑ:]	sie sind

	photo	[ˈfəʊtəʊ]	Foto
	Who's this **in the photo?**	[ˈhuːz‿ˈðɪs ɪn ðə ˈfəʊtəʊ]	Wer ist das auf dem Foto?
	behind the tree	[bɪˈhaɪnd ðə ˈtriː]	hinter dem Baum
	He's **on his bike.**	[ɒn hɪz ˈbaɪk]	Er sitzt auf seinem Fahrrad.
	with his friend	[wɪð hɪz ˈfrend]	mit seinem Freund
	with		mit; bei
	friend		Freund(in)
	How old is he?	[haʊ‿ˈəʊld ˈɪz hɪ]	Wie alt ist er?
	how?		wie?
	He's **ten.**	[ˈten]	Er ist zehn (Jahre alt).
	to **look at**	[ˈlʊk‿æt]	(jdn./etw.) ansehen, anschauen
	in the garden	[ɪn ðə ˈɡɑːdn]	im Garten
	They're **under** the tree.	[ðeər‿ˈʌndə ðə ˈtriː]	Sie sind unter dem Baum.
	their	[ðeə]	ihr(e) *(Plural)*
	dog	[dɒɡ]	Hund
	cat	[kæt]	Katze
	lovely	[ˈlʌvlɪ]	schön
	three	[θriː]	drei

Hello, **Mum**. Hello **Dad**. Is Tanja upstairs?	Hallo **Mutti**. Hallo **Vati**. Ist Tanja oben?
Mrs Benson is Jenny's **mum**.	Mrs Benson ist Jennys **Mutter**.
Mr Benson is David's **dad**.	Mr Benson ist Davids **Vater**.

15,1	**picture**	[ˈpɪktʃə]	Bild
	page	[peɪdʒ]	(Buch-)Seite
	partner	[ˈpɑːtnə]	Partner
16,2	–		
16,3	to **complete**	[kəmˈpliːt]	vervollständigen

Their bedroom is upstairs.	**Ihr** Schlafzimmer ist oben.
They're in the garden.	**Sie sind** im Garten.
There is a desk in Tanja's room.	In Tanjas Zimmer **steht** ein Schreibtisch.
There is tea and **there** is milk.	**Es gibt** Tee und Milch (zu trinken).
That's David **there**.	Das **dort** ist David.

F Kevin

17	**Aren't you** Jenny's friend?	[ˈɑːnt‿juː ˈdʒenɪz ˈfrend]	Bist du nicht Jennys Freundin?
	brown	[braʊn]	braun
	I'm Jenny's **neighbour.**	[aɪm ˈdʒenɪz ˈneɪbə]	Ich bin Jennys Nachbar.
	neighbour		Nachbar(in)
	red	[red]	rot
	She's **at home.**	[ʃiːz‿ət‿ˈhəʊm]	Sie ist zu Hause.
	They're **in town.**	[ðeər‿ɪn‿ˈtaʊn]	Sie sind in der Stadt.
	town		(kleinere) Stadt
	Come on.	[ˈkʌm‿ˈɒn]	Komm, beeil dich!
	Bye./Bye-bye.	[baɪ/ˈbaɪˈbaɪ]	Tschüß.
	She's a nice **girl.**	[ˈʃiːz‿ə ˈnaɪs ˈɡɜːl]	Sie ist ein nettes Mädchen.
	Woof!	[wʊf]	Wau!
17,1	–		
17,2	–		
18,3	**dialogue**	[ˈdaɪəlɒɡ]	Dialog
18,4	**quiz**	[kwɪz]	Ratespiel, Quiz
18,5	**best**	[best]	der, die, das beste
18,⟨6⟩	**listening comprehension**	[ˈlɪsnɪŋ ˌkɒmprɪˈhenʃn]	Hörverständnis
	man	[mæn]	Mann, *hier:* Mensch

Unit 2

A 10 York Road

	road	[rəʊd]	Straße, Landstraße
19a)	**city (cities)**	[ˈsɪtɪ (ˈsɪtɪz)]	(Groß-)Stadt (Großstädte)
	West	[west]	Westen
	Filton is a **suburb** of Bristol.	[ˈfɪltən‿ɪz‿ə ˈsʌbɜ:b‿əv ˈbrɪstl]	Filton ist ein Vorort von Bristol.
	There are a lot of streets like York Road.	[ˌðeər‿ə‿əˈlɒt‿əv ˈstri:ts laɪk ˈjɔ:k ˈrəʊd]	Es gibt viele Straßen wie York Road.
	there are		es gibt; da sind
	a lot of		viel(e)
	street		Straße *(meistens in einer Stadt)*
	like		wie
	on the left	[ɒn ðə ˈleft]	links
	number	[ˈnʌmbə]	Nummer, Zahl
	on the right	[ɒn ðə ˈraɪt]	rechts
	There are **some** cars in York Road.	[ˌðeər‿ə səm ˈkɑ:z‿ɪn ˈjɔ:k ˈrəʊd]	Da sind einige Autos in York Road.
	some	[sʌm/səm]	einige
	But there are **no buses.**	[bət ˌðeər‿ə ˈnəʊ ˈbʌsɪz]	Aber da sind keine Busse.
	but	[bʌt/bət]	aber
	no	[nəʊ]	*hier:* kein(e)
	bus (buses)	[bʌs (ˈbʌsɪz)]	Bus(se)
	lorry (lorries)	[ˈlɒrɪ (ˈlɒrɪz)]	Lastwagen
	It is a **quiet** street.	[ɪt‿ɪz‿ə ˈkwaɪət ˈstri:t]	Es ist eine ruhige Straße.
	quiet		ruhig, still
	singular	[ˈsɪŋgjʊlə]	Einzahl, Singular
	plural	[ˈplʊərəl]	Mehrzahl, Plural
20b)	**back door**	[ˈbæk ˈdɔ:]	Hintereingang
	door		Tür
	kitchen	[ˈkɪtʃɪn]	Küche
	cupboard	[ˈkʌbəd]	Schrank
	four	[fɔ:]	vier
	six	[sɪks]	sechs
	chair	[tʃeə]	Stuhl
	dining room	[ˈdaɪnɪŋrʊm]	Eßzimmer
	hall	[hɔ:l]	Flur
	window	[ˈwɪndəʊ]	Fenster
	living room	[ˈlɪvɪŋrʊm]	Wohnzimmer
	sofa	[ˈsəʊfə]	Sofa
	armchair	[ˈɑ:mtʃeə]	Sessel
	TV	[ˈti:ˈvi:]	Fernsehen
	front door	[ˈfrʌnt ˈdɔ:]	Haus-, Eingangstür
	now	[naʊ]	jetzt
	to **make up**	[ˈmeɪk ˈʌp]	erstellen
	text	[tekst]	Text
21c)	**bed**	[bed]	Bett
	Beside her sofa there are two chairs.	[bɪˈsaɪd hɜ: ˈsəʊfə ðeər‿ə ˈtu: ˈtʃeəz]	Neben ihrem Sofa stehen zwei Stühle.
	radio	[ˈreɪdɪəʊ]	Radio
	cassette recorder	[kəˈset rɪˈkɔ:də]	Cassettenrecorder
	saxophone	[ˈsæksəfəʊn]	Saxophon
	There is a **place** in the **corner** for her **clothes.**	[ˌðeər‿ɪz‿ə ˈpleɪs‿ɪn ðə ˈkɔ:nə fɔ: hɜ: ˈkləʊðz]	In der Ecke ist Platz für ihre Kleidung.
	clothes		Kleider, Kleidung
	shoe	[ʃu:]	Schuh
	wardrobe	[ˈwɔ:drəʊb]	Kleiderschrank

	shelf (shelves)	[ʃelf (ʃelvz)]	Regal(e)
	on the wall	[ɒn ðə ˈwɔ:l]	an der Wand
	wall		Wand; Mauer
	school book	[ˈsku:l bʊk]	Schulbuch
	school		Schule
	other	[ˈʌðə]	andere
	thing	[θɪŋ]	Sache, Ding
	poster	[ˈpəʊstə]	Plakat, Poster
	only	[ˈəʊnlɪ]	nur
	very	[ˈverɪ]	sehr

B In Bristol and Hanover

21a)	**Tanja has got a desk.**	[ˈtænjə həz ˈgɒt‿ə ˈdesk]	Tanja hat einen Schreibtisch.
	She has not got a wardrobe.	[ˈʃɪ həz ˈnɒt gɒt‿ə ˈwɔ:drəʊb]	Sie hat keinen Kleiderschrank.
b)	**How many rooms have you got?**	[ˈhaʊ menɪ ˈrʊmz]	Wie viele Zimmer habt ihr?
22,1	–		
22,2	–		
22,3	–		
22,4	to **describe**	[dɪˈskraɪb]	beschreiben

C TV or an evening at the youth club?

23	**evening**	[ˈi:vnɪŋ]	Abend
	youth club	[ˈju:θ ˌklʌb]	Jugendklub
a)	**Let's go to** the club.	[ˈlets ˈgəʊ tə ðə ˈklʌb]	Gehen wir zum Klub.
	let's		laß(t) uns, lassen Sie uns
	to	[tʊ/tə]	zu, nach
	to **go (to)**		gehen; hingehen
	this evening	[ðɪs‿ˈi:vnɪŋ]	heute abend
	Good idea.	[ˈgʊd‿aɪˈdɪə]	Gute Idee.
	I'd like to watch TV.	[ˈaɪd ˈlaɪk tə ˈwɒtʃ ˈti:ˈvi:]	Ich möchte (gern) fernsehen.
	I'd like (to)		Ich möchte (gern)
	to **watch**		(an-)sehen, zusehen; beobachten
	to **watch TV**		fernsehen
	to **see**	[si:]	sehen
	on (TV)	[ɒn (ˈti:ˈvi:)]	*hier:* im Fernsehen
	Give me the newspaper.	[ˈgɪv mi: ðə‿ˈnju:sˌpeɪpə]	Gib mir/Geben Sie mir die Zeitung.
	me		mir
	to **give**		geben
	programme	[ˈprəʊgræm]	Sendung; Programm
	sport(s)	[spɔ:t(s)]	Sportart, Sport, Sport-
	in five minutes	[ɪn ˈfaɪv ˈmɪnɪts]	in fünf Minuten
	minute		Minute
	basketball	[ˈbɑ:skɪtbɔ:l]	Basketball
	tennis	[ˈtenɪs]	Tennis
	that	[ðæt]	das; jene(r/s)
	also	[ˈɔ:lsəʊ]	auch
	on the radio	[ˈreɪdɪəʊ]	im Radio
	Listen to that!	[ˈlɪsn tə ˈðæt]	Hör dir/Hört euch/Hören Sie sich das mal an!
	to **listen to**		sich (etwas) anhören, zuhören
b)	**everybody**	[ˈevrɪˌbɒdɪ]	jeder, *hier:* alle
	to **find**	[faɪnd]	finden
	football	[ˈfʊtbɔ:l]	Fußball
	Let's play table-tennis.	[lets ˈpleɪ ˈteɪbltenɪs]	Laßt uns Tischtennis spielen.
	to **play**		spielen
	table-tennis		Tischtennis
	to **have a coke**	[hæv‿ə ˈkəʊk]	Cola trinken
	to **have**		*hier:* trinken

23,1	to **do**	[du:]	tun, machen
	something	[ˈsʌmθɪŋ]	etwas
	to **put in**	[ˈpʊt‿ˈɪn]	einsetzen
	verb	[vɜ:b]	Verb
	to **make**	[meɪk]	machen, bilden
	sentence	[ˈsentəns]	Satz
24,2	**example**	[ɪgˈzɑ:mpl]	Beispiel

D Horfield Sports Centre

	sports centre	[ˈspɔ:ts‿ˌsentə]	Sportzentrum
	Kevin is **there**, too.	[ˈkevɪn‿ɪz ˈðeə ˈtu:]	Kevin ist auch da.
	to **join**	[dʒɔɪn]	Mitglied werden; sich anschließen
	centre	[ˈsentə]	*hier:* Mitte; Stadtmitte
	a football team	[ə ˈfʊtbɔ:l ˌti:m]	eine Fußballmannschaft
	group	[gru:p]	Gruppe
	volleyball	[ˈvɒlɪbɔ:l]	Volleyball
	coach	[kəʊtʃ]	*hier:* Trainer
	He hasn't got **a job.**	[hɪ ˈhæznt gɒt‿ə ˈdʒɒb]	Er ist arbeitlos.
	job		Arbeit, Job; Arbeitsstelle
	at the moment	[ˈət ðə ˈməʊmənt]	im Augenblick, zur Zeit
	Would you like to play basketball?	[ˌwʊd‿ju: ˈlaɪk‿tə ˈpleɪ ˈbɑ:skɪtbɔ:l]	Möchtest du/Möchtet ihr/Möchten Sie Basketball spielen?
	hockey	[ˈhɒkɪ]	(Feld-)Hockey
	captain	[ˈkæptɪn]	Mannschaftskapitän
	at my school	[ət maɪ ˈsku:l]	in meiner Schule
	at school	[ət ˈsku:l]	in der Schule
	I'm sorry.	[ˌaɪm ˈsɒrɪ]	Es tut mir leid.
	Is it **open** to everybody?	[ɪz‿ɪt‿ˈəʊpən tə ˈevrɪbɒdɪ]	Kann jeder Mitglied werden?
	open		offen
	I'm sure.	[ˌaɪm ˈʃʊə]	Ich bin sicher.
	boy	[bɔɪ]	Junge
25,1	–		
25,2	–		

A cup of tea, Tanja? – **Yes, Please**	Eine Tasse Tee, Tanja? – **Ja, bitte.**
A piece of cake? – **No, thanks.**	Ein Stück Kuchen? – **Nein, danke.**
I'm sorry, Tanja. – There's no milk.	**Es tut mir leid,** Tanja. – Wir haben keine Milch.

E Filton and Westbury

26	**these**	[ði:z]	diese
	sports field	[ˈspɔ:ts ˈfi:ld]	Sportplatz
	field		Feld
	over there	[ˌəʊvə ˈðeə]	da drüben, dort drüben
	those	[ðəʊz]	jene
	all	[ɔ:l]	alle
26,1	**Hey!**	[heɪ]	Hey!
27,2	–		
28,4	–		
28,⟨5⟩	Let's sing a song.	[lets‿sɪŋ‿ə sɒŋ]	Singen wir ein Lied.
	to sing		singen
	song		Lied
	green	[gri:n]	grün
	bottle	[ˈbɒtl]	Flasche
	to hang	[hæŋ]	hängen

	if	[ɪf]	wenn, falls
	should	[ʃu:d]	sollte, -n
	accidentl'y	[ˌæksɪˈdentəlɪ]	versehentlich
	to fall	[fɔ:l]	(herunter-)fallen
	there'd (there would) be nine	[ˈðeəd ˈbɪ ˈnaɪn]	würden es (nur noch) neun sein
28,6	–		

F A city with something for everybody

29a)	**young**	[jʌŋ]	jung
	people	[ˈpi:pl]	Leute
	disco	[ˈdɪskəʊ]	Disco
	cinema	[ˈsɪnəmə]	Kino
	large	[lɑ:dʒ]	groß
	park	[pɑ:k]	Park
	even	[ˈi:vən]	sogar
	balloon festival	[bəˈlu:n ˈfestɪvəl]	Ballonfest
b)	Are you **interested in ships?**	[ˌɑ: ju:‿ˈɪntrɪstɪd‿ɪn ˈʃɪps]	Interessierst du dich/Interessiert ihr euch/ Interessieren Sie sich für Schiffe?
	interested in		interessiert an
	docks	[dɒks]	Hafenanlagen
	Great Britain	[ˌgreɪt ˈbrɪtən]	*hier: Name eines Dampfschiffes*
	steamer	[ˈsti:mə]	Dampfschiff
c)	Have you got **time** for a cup of tea?	[ˈhæv ju: gɒt‿ˈtaɪm fər‿ə ˈkʌp‿əv ˈti:]	Haben Sie Zeit für eine Tasse Tee?
	time		Zeit
	café	[ˈkæfeɪ]	Café
	Have a hamburger.	[ˈhæv‿ə ˈhæmbɜ:gə]	Iß doch einen Hamburger.
	to **have**		*hier:* essen
	hamburger		Hamburger
	snack	[snæk]	(kleiner) Imbiß
	music	[ˈmju:zɪk]	Musik
d)	**shop**	[ʃɒp]	Geschäft, Laden
	shopping centre	[ˈʃɔpɪŋˌsentə]	Einkaufszentrum
	interesting	[ˈɪntrɪstɪŋ]	interessant
30,1	**right**	[raɪt]	richtig
	wrong	[rɒŋ]	falsch
30,2b)	**question**	[ˈkwestʃən]	Frage
30,3	–		

Tanja is **interested in** sport.	Tanja **interessiert sich für** Sport.
Bristol is a very **interesting** city.	Bristol ist eine sehr **interessante** Stadt.

G A snack with friends

31a)	**near**	[nɪə]	in der Nähe von
	enough	[ɪˈnʌf]	genug
	today	[təˈdeɪ]	heute
	Let's go into this café.	[ˈlets ˈgəʊ‿ɪntə ðɪs ˈkæfeɪ]	Gehen wir in dieses Café (hinein).
	into		in, in ... hinein
	What about this café?	[ˈwɒt‿əˈbaʊt ˈðɪs ˈkæfeɪ]	Wie wär's mit diesem Café?
	black	[blæk]	schwarz
	the next	[ðə ˈnekst]	der, die, das nächste
b)	**modern**	[ˈmɒdən]	modern
	tourist	[ˈtʊərɪst]	Tourist(in)
	Is this **seat free?**	[ˌɪz ˈðɪs‿ˈsi:t ˈfri:]	Ist dieser Platz frei?
	seat		(Sitz-)Platz
	free		frei; kostenlos

	girlfriend	[ˈgɜːlfrend]	Freundin
	at the table	[ˌət ðə ˈteɪbl]	am Tisch
	to **sit down**	[ˌsɪt ˈdaʊn]	sich setzen
	Hi!	[haɪ]	Hallo!
	us	[ʌs/əs]	uns
	waitress	[ˈweɪtrɪs]	Kellnerin, Bedienung
31,1	–		
32,2b)	**coffee**	[ˈkɒfɪ]	Kaffee
32,3	–		
32,4	–		
32,⟨5⟩	–		

Some prepositions

At the moment	**Im** Augenblick
At home	**Zu** Hause
At the youth club	**Im** Jugendclub
Behind the tree	**Hinter** dem Baum
There are two chairs **beside** the sofa.	**Neben** dem Sofa stehen zwei Stühle.
Mr Benson is **from** Bristol.	Mr Benson ist **aus** Bristol.
In the corner	**In** der Ecke
In the street	**Auf** der Straße
In front of the house	**Vor** dem Haus
Next to the table	**Neben** dem Tisch
On the radio/**On** TV	**Im** Radio/**Im** Fernsehen
On the table	**Auf** dem Tisch
On the wall	**An** der Wand
There's a sports programme **on in** five minutes.	**In** fünf Minuten gibt es eine Sportsendung. (**Im** Radio/Fernsehen)
Welcome **to** Bristol.	Willkommen **in** Bristol.
Under the window	**Unter** dem Fenster
A small table **with** two chairs	Ein kleiner Tisch **mit** zwei Stühlen

Unit 3

A All about Horfield Sports Centre

33	**fan**	[fæn]	begeisterter Anhänger, Fan
	every	[ˈevrɪ]	jede(r,s)
	afternoon	[ˌɑːftəˈnuːn]	Nachmittag
	outdoor sport	[ˈaʊtdɔː ˈspɔːt]	Sport im Freien
	indoor sport	[ˈɪndɔː ˈspɔːt]	Sport in der Halle
	ball	[bɔːl]	Ball
	game	[geɪm]	Spiel, Sport
	outdoors	[ˈaʊtdɔːz]	draußen, im Freien
	gym	[dʒɪm]	Sporthalle
	to **do judo**	[duː ˈdʒuːdəʊ]	Judo machen
	to **learn**	[lɜːn]	lernen
	New **members** are welcome!	[ˈnjuː ˈmembəz‿ə ˈwelkəm]	Neue Mitglieder sind willkommen!
	member		Mitglied
	Why (not)?	[waɪ (nɒt)]	Warum (nicht)?
	to **start**	[stɑːt]	anfangen, beginnen
	to **bring**	[brɪŋ]	(mit-)bringen
	to **wear** sports clothes	[weə ˈspɔːts ˈkləʊðz]	Sportkleidung tragen
	to **talk to** Jeff Brown	[ˈtɔːk tə ˈdʒef ˈbraʊn]	mit Jeff Brown reden

Let's go to a café.	**Komm(t), wir gehen** in ein Café.
Let's play tennis.	**Spielen wir** Tennis.

33,1 **father**	[fa:ðə]	Vater
33,2 **word**	[wɜ:d]	Wort
phrase	[freɪz]	Redewendung, Redemittel; Phrase

B A new member at Horfield Sports Centre

34a) What games **can you play?**	[ˌwɒt ˈgeɪmz kən ju: ˈpleɪ]	Was spielst du?
She **can't start** judo today.	[ʃɪ ˈkɑ:nt ˈstɑ:t ˈdʒu:dəʊ təˈdeɪ]	Heute kann sie mit dem Judo nicht anfangen.
can't/cannot	[kɑ:nt/ˈkænɒt]	nicht können
You **needn't play** football.	[ju: ˈni:dnt pleɪ ˈfʊtbɔ:l]	Du brauchst nicht Fußball zu spielen.
needn't/need not		
Let's **talk about it.**	[lets ˈtɔ:k‿əˈbaʊt‿ɪt]	Laß uns darüber reden.
to **talk about**		über (etwas) reden
b) **May I** join the judo group?	[ˌmeɪ‿aɪ ˈdʒɔɪn ðə ˈdʒu:dəʊ ˌgru:p]	Darf ich in die Judogruppe eintreten?
I **must have** a note.	[ˌaɪ ˈmʌst‿hæv‿ə ˈnəʊt]	Ich muß einen ‚Zettel' haben./Ich muß das Einverständnis Ihrer Eltern haben.
must	[mʌst/məst]	
You **mustn't** wear street shoes.	[ju: ˈmʌsnt weə ˈstri:t‿ʃu:z]	Du darfst keine Straßenschuhe tragen.
mustn't/must not		nicht dürfen
34,1 –		
35,2 **short**	[ʃɔ:t]	kurz
answer	[ˈɑ:nsə]	Antwort
35,3 **role play**	[ˈrəʊl ˌpleɪ]	Rollenspiel
35,4 **long**	[lɒŋ]	lang

C Rules for the gym

36 **rules**	[ru:lz]	Regeln
a) to **read**	[ri:d]	lesen
notice-board	[ˈnəʊtɪsˌbɔ:d]	Schwarzes Brett
player	[ˈpleɪə]	Spieler(in)
spectator	[spekˈteɪtə]	Zuschauer(in)
always	[ˈɔ:lweɪz]	immer
to **use**	[ju:z]	benutzen
to **keep clean**	[ˈki:p ˈkli:n]	sauber halten
to **keep**		halten, behalten
clean		sauber; rein
food and drinks	[ˈfu:d‿n ˈdrɪŋks]	Essen und Getränke
to **book**	[bʊk]	buchen, reservieren
match	[mætʃ]	Spiel, Match
first	[fɜ:st]	zuerst
b) to **be late for s.th.**	[bi: ˈleɪt fə]	zu spät zu etwas kommen
them	[ðem/ðəm]	sie *(Plural/Objektfall)*
to **help**	[help]	helfen
her	[hɜ:]	sie *(Singular/Objektfall)*
him	[hɪm]	ihn; ihm
white	[waɪt]	weiß
36,1 –		
36,2 –		
37,3 –		
37,4 **pronoun**	[ˈprəʊnaʊn]	Pronomen
37,5 –		

D The volleyball match

38a) It is **seven o'clock.**	[ˌɪt‿ɪz ˈsevn‿əˈklɒk]	Es ist sieben Uhr.
Friday evening	[ˈfraɪdɪ‿ˈi:vnɪŋ]	Freitag abend
Are you **ready?**	[ˌɑ: jʊ ˈredɪ]	Bist du fertig?
to **write**	[raɪt]	schreiben
letter	[ˈletə]	Brief
later	[ˈleɪtə]	später
at a quarter past seven	[ət‿ə ˈkwɔ:tə ˌpɑ:st ˈsevn]	um Viertel nach sieben
What time is it?	[wɒt ˈtaɪm‿ɪz‿ɪt]	Wieviel Uhr ist es?
Just a minute, please.	[ˌdʒʌst‿ə ˈmɪnɪt ˈpli:z]	Einen Moment, bitte.
to **fetch**	[fetʃ]	holen
Hurry up!	[ˈhʌrɪ‿ˈʌp]	Beeil dich!/Beeilt euch!/Beeilen Sie sich!
to **hurry**		sich beeilen
(not) far	[(nɒt) fɑ:]	(nicht) weit entfernt
so	[səʊ]	daher, deshalb
to **take a bus**	[teɪk]	mit dem Bus fahren
to **take**		nehmen
in each team	[ɪn ˈi:tʃ ˈti:m]	in jeder Mannschaft
each		jede(r,s)
b) It is **half past seven.**	[ɪt‿ɪz ˈhɑ:f ˈpɑ:st ˈsevn]	Es ist halb acht.
The score is 8-7.	[ðə ˈskɔ:r‿ɪz‿ˈeɪt ˈsevn]	Es steht 8 zu 7.
score		Spielstand
to **stop**	[stɒp]	stoppen; anhalten
accident	[ˈæksɪdənt]	Unfall
on the floor	[ɒn ðə ˈflɔ:]	auf dem Boden
Ouch!	[aʊtʃ]	Au! *(Ausruf des Schmerzes)*
leg	[leg]	Bein
What's the matter?	[ˌwɒts ðə ˈmætə]	Was ist los?
There's something wrong.	[ðeəz‿ˈsʌmθɪŋ ˈrɒŋ]	(Irgend)etwas stimmt nicht.
I can't **move** it.	[aɪ ˈkɑ:nt ˈmu:v‿ɪt]	Ich kann es nicht bewegen.
to **move**		(sich/etwas) bewegen
well	[wel]	also, nun, tja
to **try**	[traɪ]	versuchen
then	[ðen]	dann
It isn't broken.	[ɪt‿ˈɪznt ˈbrəʊkən]	Es ist nicht gebrochen.
You must see **a doctor.**	[ˈju: məst ˈsi:‿ə ˈdɒktə]	Du mußt zum Arzt gehen.
Call an ambulance.	[ˈkɔ:l‿ən‿ˈæmbjʊləns]	Ruf einen Krankenwagen.
to **call**		rufen, anrufen
ambulance		Krankenwagen
at a quarter to eight	[ət‿ə ˈkwɔ:tə tə‿ˈeɪt]	um Viertel vor acht
38,1 –		

What time is it?	Wie spät ist es?
It's **four o'clock**.	Es ist **vier Uhr**.
No, it's not. It's a **quarter past four**.	Nein, es ist **Viertel nach vier.**
We must go at **a quarter to five.**	Um **Viertel vor fünf** müssen wir gehen.
It is **half past five**.	Es ist **halb sechs**.

39,2 –		
39,3 –		
39,4 –		
39,5 **Take Kevin's role.**	[teɪk ˈkevɪnz ˈrəʊl]	Spiel Kevins Rolle.
to **take a role**		eine Rolle spielen

I'm afraid you must stay in bed.	**Es tut mir leid**, aber du mußt im Bett bleiben.
Of course you may go to the cinema.	**Selbstverständlich** darfst du ins Kino.
What's the matter? Is your ankle painful?	**Was ist los?** Tut dir dein Knöchel weh?

E Southmead Hospital

40	**hospital**	[ˈhɒspɪtl]	Krankenhaus
	waiting room	[ˈweɪtɪŋ rʊm]	Wartezimmer
	nurse	[nɜːs]	Krankenschwester
	patient	[ˈpeɪʃnt]	Patient
	bandage	[ˈbændɪdʒ]	Verband
a)	**man (men)**	[mæn (men)]	Mann (Männer)
	woman (women)	[ˈwʊmən (ˈwɪmɪn)]	Frau (Frauen)
	child (children)	[tʃaɪld (ˈtʃɪldrən)]	Kind (Kinder)
	mother	[ˈmʌðə]	Mutter
	There is **a bandage over her left eye.**	[ðeər‿ɪz‿ə ˈbændɪdʒ‿ˌəʊvə hɜː ˈleft‿ˈaɪ]	Ihr linkes Auge ist verbunden.
	over		über
	eye		Auge
	to **walk**	[wɔːk]	gehen
	a sprained ankle	[ə ˈspreɪnd‿ˈæŋkl]	ein verstauchter Knöchel
	sprained		verstaucht
	ankle		(Fuß-)Knöchel
	because	[bɪˈkɒz]	weil
b)	She has got a bandage **round** her left **arm.**	[ʃɪ həz gɒt‿ə ˈbændɪdʒ raʊnd hɜː ˈleft‿ˈɑːm]	Ihr linker Arm ist verbunden.
	round		um ... herum
	arm		Arm
	hand	[hænd]	Hand
	wrist	[rɪst]	Handgelenk
	It is **very painful.**	[ɪt‿ɪz ˈverɪ ˈpeɪnfʊl]	Es tut sehr weh.
	painful		schmerzhaft
	He must **stay at home.**	[hɪ məs‿ˈsteɪ‿ət ˈhəʊm]	Er muß zu Hause bleiben.
	to **stay**		bleiben
	He needn't go **to school.**	[hɪ ˈniːdnt gəʊ tə ˈskuːl]	Er braucht nicht zur Schule gehen.
41,1	–		
41,2	–		

F At the hospital

42a)	**outside**	[ˌaʊtˈsaɪd]	draußen vor; draußen
	Can you **spell** it?	[ˌkæn juː ˈspel‿ɪt]	Kannst du/Könnt ihr/Können Sie es buchstabieren?
	to **spell**		buchstabieren
	address	[əˈdres]	Adresse
	to wait for s.th.	[weɪt (fɔː)]	auf etwas warten
	before	[bɪˈfɔː]	vor
b)	I must **put** a bandage **on it.**	[aɪ məs(t) ˈpʊt‿ə ˈbændɪdʒ‿ˈɒn‿ɪt]	Ich muß einen Verband anlegen.
	to **put on**		anlegen
	You can **go home.**	[ˌjuː kən ˈgəʊ ˈhəʊm]	Du kannst nach Hause gehen/fahren.
	in bed	[ɪn ˈbed]	im Bett
	day	[deɪ]	Tag
	week	[wiːk]	Woche
	I'm afraid ...	[aɪm‿əˈfreɪd]	Es tut mir leid .../Leider ...
	Oh dear!	[ˈəʊ ˌdɪə]	O je!

43c) She must **lie** in bed.	[ʃɪ məst‿ˈlaɪ ɪn ˈbed]	Sie muß im Bett liegen.
to **lie**		liegen
unhappy	[ʌnˈhæpɪ]	unglücklich
She can **speak** English.	[ʃɪ kən ˈspiːk‿ˈɪŋglɪʃ]	Sie kann Englisch (sprechen).
to **speak**		sprechen
tomorrow	[təˈmɒrəʊ]	morgen
Saturday	[ˈsætədɪ]	Samstag, Sonnabend
all day	[ˈɔːl ˈdeɪ]	den ganzen Tag
Can Tanja call **in the morning?**	[kən ˈtænjə ˈkɔːl‿ɪn ðə ˈmɔːnɪŋ]	Kann Tanja vormittags anrufen?
in the morning		morgens, vormittags
We'd like to **go shopping.**	[wiːd ˈlaɪk tə gəʊ ˈʃɒpɪŋ]	Wir möchten gerne einkaufen gehen/fahren.
a (telephone) call	[kɔːl]	Anruf

You can stay at home **on Friday.**	**Am Freitag** kannst du zu Hause bleiben.
We must go **at half past three.**	Wir müssen **um halb vier** gehen.
Mrs Schulz would like to go shopping **in the morning.**	Frau Schulz möchte gern **vormittags** einkaufen gehen.
Tanja must go to school **in the afternoon.**	Tanja muß **nachmittags** in die Schule.
Jenny can play volleyball **in the evening.**	Jenny kann **abends** Volleyball spielen.
We have got judo **today.**	Wir haben **heute** Judo.
I would like to play hockey **tomorrow.**	**Morgen** möchte ich Hockey spielen.
In England there is school **all day.**	In England haben die Schüler **den ganzen Tag** Schule.

43,1 –		
43,2 **alphabet**	[ˈælfəbet]	Alphabet
capital letter	[ˈkæpɪtl‿ˈletə]	Großbuchstabe
letter		Buchstabe
double	[ˈdʌbl]	Doppel-, doppelt
44,3 **etc.**	[etˈsetərə]	usw.
boxing	[ˈbɒksɪŋ]	Boxen
44,4 –		
44,5 –		
45,6 –		
45,7 **pair**	[peə]	Paar
45,8 to **explain**	[ɪkˈspleɪn]	erklären
45,⟨9⟩ –		

Unit 4

A A Saturday morning in York Road

46a) to **make a cake**	[ˌmeɪk‿ə ˈkeɪk]	einen Kuchen backen
earth	[ɜːθ]	Erde
homework *(sg. only)*	[ˈhəʊmwɜːk]	Hausaufgaben
47b) to **put a leg up**	[ˈpʊt‿ə ˈleg ˈʌp]	ein Bein hochlegen
Thanks a lot!	[ˈθæŋks‿ə ˈlɒt]	Tausend Dank!
47,1 –		
47,2 –		
48,3 –		
48,4 to **know**	[nəʊ]	wissen; kennen
everything	[ˈevrɪθɪŋ]	alles
48,5 **postcard**	[ˈpəʊstˌkɑːd]	Postkarte
to **begin**	[bɪˈgɪn]	beginnen, anfangen

B Later that morning

49	**love**	[lʌv]	Liebe; *hier:* Schatz
	bad	[bæd]	schlimm; schlecht
	Don't worry.	[ˈdəʊnt ˈwʌrɪ]	Mach dir keine Sorgen.
	to **worry**		sich Sorgen machen
	How are Mr and Mrs Benson?	[ˈhaʊ‿ə ˈmɪstər‿n ˌmɪsɪz ˈbensn]	Wie geht's Herrn und Frau Benson?
	They have got **an invitation.**	[ˌðeɪ həv ˈgɒt‿ən‿ˌɪnvɪˈteɪʃn]	Sie sind eingeladen.
	invitation		Einladung
	next door	[ˌnex‿ˈdɔ:]	nebenan
	on the phone/telephone	[ɒn ðə ˈfəʊn/ˈteləfəʊn]	am Telefon
	band	[bænd]	Musikkapelle, Band
	weather	[ˈweðə]	Wetter
	storm	[stɔ:m]	Sturm
	on the way	[ˌɒn‿ðə‿ˈweɪ]	unterwegs
	way		Weg
	about	[əˈbaʊt]	etwa, circa
	all right	[ˈɔ:l ˈraɪt]	in Ordnung
	Aerospace Club	[ˈeərəspeɪs ˈklʌb]	*Klub für (innerbetriebliche) Freizeitgestaltung*
	list	[lɪst]	Liste
	to **ring**	[rɪŋ]	läuten
	Hello. Bristol **317 509.**	[həˈləʊ ˈbrɪstl ˈθri: ˈwʌn ˈsevn ˈfaɪv ˈəʊ ˈnaɪn]	Hallo. Hier Bristol 317 509.
	I'm **so angry.**	[aɪm ˈsəʊ ˈæŋgrɪ]	Ich bin wirklich böse./Ich bin wütend.
	Pamela Benson speaking.	[ˈpæmələ ˈbensn ˈspi:kɪŋ]	Pamela Benson am Apparat.
	Just a moment. (Hang on!)	[ˈdʒʌst‿ə ˈməʊmənt]	(Einen) Moment bitte.
49,1	**after**	[ɑ:ftə]	nach
50,2	**film**	[fɪlm]	Film
	plan	[plæn]	Plan

C Numbers and colours

51	**number**	[ˈnʌmbə]	*hier:* Zahl
	colour	[ˈkʌlə]	Farbe
51,1	**What colour is it?**	[ˌwɒt ˈkʌlər‿ɪz‿ɪt]	Welche Farbe ist (hat) es?
	green	[gri:n]	grün
	yellow	[ˈjeləʊ]	gelb
	pink	[pɪŋk]	rosa, pink
	orange	[ˈɒrɪndʒ]	orange
	purple	[ˈpɜ:pl]	violett, lila
	blue	[blu:]	blau
	grey	[greɪ]	grau
51,⟨2⟩	rainbow	[ˈreɪnbəʊ]	Regenbogen
	to sing along	[ˈsɪŋ‿əˈlɒŋ]	mitsingen

D A message from the police

52	**message**	[ˈmesɪdʒ]	Nachricht; *hier:* Mitteilung
	police	[pəˈli:s]	Polizei
a)	They are **alone.**	[ˌðeɪ‿ər‿əˈləʊn]	Sie sind allein.
	away	[əˈweɪ]	fort, weg
	weekend	[ˌwi:kˈend]	Wochenende
	Kevin is **out.**	[ˈkevɪn‿ɪz‿ˈaʊt]	Kevin ist nicht zu Hause.
	dark	[dɑ:k]	dunkel
	nasty	[ˈnɑ:stɪ]	scheußlich, widerlich; unangenehm

wind	[wɪnd]	Wind
to **blow**	[bləʊ]	blasen, wehen
to **shut**	[ʃʌt]	schließen
to **hear**	[hɪə]	hören
burglar	[ˈbɜːglə]	Einbrecher
burglary	[ˈbɜːglərɪ]	Einbruch
What are you doing, anyway?	[ˈwɒt‿ə juː ˈduːɪŋ ˈenɪweɪ]	Was machst du überhaupt?
anyway		überhaupt, immerhin
something **special**	[ˈsʌmθɪŋ ˈspeʃl]	etwas Besonderes
magazine	[mægəˈziːn]	Zeitschrift, Illustrierte

Am I right?	**Habe ich recht?**
Am I wrong?	**Habe ich unrecht?**
The house is **on the right.**	Das Haus steht **auf der rechten Seite.**
Is the sentence **right** or **wrong**?	Ist der Satz **richtig** oder **falsch**?
There is something **wrong** with his **right** eye.	Mit seinem **rechten** Auge ist etwas **nicht in Ordnung.**
Is everything **all right**?	Ist alles **in Ordnung**?

52b) Bristol and **its** suburbs.	[ɪts]	Bristol und seine Vororte.
its		sein(e,n), ihr(e,n)
Lock the door.	[ˌlɒk ðə‿ˈdɔː]	Schließ die Tür ab.
to lock		abschließen
at night	[ət ˈnaɪt]	nachts
night		Nacht
key	[kiː]	Schlüssel
Leave it here.	[ˈliːv‿ɪt ˈhɪə]	Laß es (sie, ihn) hier.
to **leave**		lassen, hinterlassen
to **tell**	[tel]	erzählen, sagen
Switch the light on.	[ˌswɪtʃ ðə ˈlaɪt‿ɒn]	Schalt das Licht an.
to **switch on**		einschalten, andrehen
light		Licht
when *(conj.)*	[wen]	wenn
Switch the light off when you are back.	[ˈswɪtʃ ðə ˈlaɪt‿ɒf ˈwen jʊ‿ə ˈbæk]	Mach das Licht aus, wenn du wieder zu Hause bist.
to **switch off**		ausschalten
to **be back**		wieder zu Hause sein
all night	[ˈɔːl ˈnaɪt]	die ganze Nacht
ladder	[ˈlædə]	Leiter
Can you **open** the door?	[ˌkən jʊ ˈəʊpn ðə ˈdɔː]	Kannst du die Tür aufmachen?
to **open**		öffen, aufmachen
I'm a stranger here.	[aɪm‿ə ˈstreɪndʒə ˌhɪə]	Ich bin hier fremd.
stranger		Fremde(r)
53,1 to **work**	[wɜːk]	arbeiten
53,2 to **remember**	[rɪˈmembə]	sich erinnern
53,3 **meeting**	[ˈmiːtɪŋ]	Treffen
information stand	[ˌɪnfəˈmeɪʃn stænd]	Informationsstand
T-shirt	[ˈtiːˌʃɜːt]	T-Shirt, Hemd

E The storm

54a) to **repair**	[rɪˈpeə]	reparieren
to **show**	[ʃəʊ]	zeigen
Tanja is **asleep** in bed.	[ˈtænjə‿ɪz‿əˈsliːp‿ɪn ˈbed]	Tanja ist im Bett und schläft (fest).
to **be asleep**		(fest) schlafen
to **practise**	[ˈpræktɪs]	üben
difficult	[ˈdɪfɪkəlt]	schwierig
somebody	[ˈsʌmbədɪ]	jemand
Kevin's **still** here.	[ˈkevɪnz‿stɪl ˈhɪə]	Kevin ist noch hier.

	party	[ˈpɑ:tɪ]	Party
	shed	[ʃed]	Schuppen, Gerätehaus
	What's happening here?	[ˈwɒts ˈhæpənɪŋ ˈhɪə]	Was ist hier los?
	to **happen**		geschehen, passieren
	to **take out**	[ˈteɪk‿ˈaʊt]	herausholen, -nehmen
	against	[əˈgenst]	gegen
	to **phone/telephone**	[fəʊn/ˈtelɪˌfəʊn]	telefonieren
	What's going on?	[ˈwɒts gəʊɪŋ‿ˈɒn]	Was ist los?
	exciting	[ɪkˈsaɪtɪŋ]	aufregend, spannend
b)	**really**	[ˈrɪəlɪ]	wirklich
	strong	[strɒŋ]	stark, kräftig
	What are you doing **up there?**	[ˈwɒt‿ə ju:ˈdu:ɪŋ‿ʌp ˈðeə]	Was machst du denn da oben?
	up (there)		(da) oben
	to **hold**	[həʊld]	halten
	loose	[lu:s]	lose, locker
	chimney pot	[ˈtʃɪmnɪ ˌpɒt]	Schornsteinkappe, -kopf
	roof	[ru:f]	Dach
	dangerous	[ˈdeɪndʒrəs]	gefährlich
	You're **crazy!**	[jʊə ˈkreɪzɪ]	Du bist verrückt!
	Come down again!	[kʌm ˈdaʊn‿əˈgən]	Komm' wieder herunter!
	to **come down**		herunterkommen
	again		wieder
	to **climb**	[klaɪm]	klettern, hochsteigen
	fireman (firemen)	[ˈfaɪəmən (ˈfaɪəmen)]	Feuerwehrmann (-männer)
	job	[dʒɒb]	*hier:* Aufgabe
	policewoman	[pəˈli:sˌwʊmən]	Polizistin
	policeman	[pəˈli:smən]	Polizist
	It's going up now.	[ɪts ˈgəʊɪŋ‿ˈʌp naʊ]	Jetzt geht sie (er/es) hoch.
	to **go up**		hochgehen
	Kevin's right.	[ˈkevɪnz ˈraɪt]	Kevin hat recht.
	to **be right**		recht haben
55,1	**missing**	[ˈmɪsɪŋ]	fehlend
55,2	**together**	[təˈgeðə]	zusammen
55,3	**title**	[ˈtaɪtl]	Titel, Überschrift
	part	[pɑ:t]	Teil
55,4	–		
56,5	**farm**	[fɑ:m]	Bauernhof
	family	[ˈfæməlɪ]	Familie
6,⟨6⟩	emergency service	[ɪˈmɜ:dʒensɪ ˈsɜ:vɪs]	Notdienst
	fire	[ˈfaɪə]	Feuer, *hier:* Feuerwehr
	operator	[ˈɒpəreɪtə]	(Telefon-)Vermittlung
57,7	**correct** *(adj.)*	[kəˈrekt]	richtig
	column	[ˈkɒləm]	Spalte
	to **link**	[lɪnk]	verbinden
57,8	–		
57,9	**opposite**	[ˈɒpəzɪt]	Gegenteil
,⟨10⟩	–		

[Ende]

Unit 5

A In and around Bristol

58	**around**	[əˈraʊnd]	um ... herum; herum
a)	the **local** shops	[ðə ˈləʊkl ˈʃɒps]	die hiesigen Geschäfte
	local		Orts-, hiesig, dortig
	post office	[ˈpəʊstˌɒfɪs]	die Post, das Postamt
	corner shop	[ˈkɔ:nə ˌʃɒp]	Laden an der Ecke, ‚Tante-Emma-Laden'

	friendly	[ˈfrendlɪ]	freundlich
	sun	[sʌn]	Sonne
	seaside	[ˈsi:saɪd]	Meeresküste
	fine	[faɪn]	schön, gut
	beach	[bi:tʃ]	Strand
	fun	[fʌn]	Spaß
	price	[praɪs]	Preis
	computer	[kəmˈpju:tə]	Computer
	PC	[ˈpi:ˈsi:]	PC/‚Personal Computer‘
	monitor	[ˈmɒnɪtə]	Monitor, Bildschirm
59b)	**counter**	[ˈkaʊntə]	Ladentisch; Schalter; Theke
	to **sell**	[sel]	verkaufen
	stamp	[stæmp]	Briefmarke
	for example	[fər‿ɪgˈzɑ:mpl]	zum Beispiel
	bread	[bred]	Brot
	fruit	[fru:t]	Obst
	other kinds of food	[ˈʌðə ˈkaɪndz‿əv ˈfu:d]	andere Nahrungsmittel
	kind	[kaɪnd]	Art, Sorte
	butter	[ˈbʌtə]	Butter
	writing paper	[ˈraɪtɪŋ ˌpeɪpə]	Schreibpapier
	to **buy**	[baɪ]	kaufen
	cash-and-carry	[ˈkæʃ‿n ˈkærɪ]	Abholmarkt
c)	**romantic**	[rəʊˈmæntɪk]	romantisch
	a few things	[ə ˈfju: ˈθɪŋz]	ein paar Sachen
	a bottle of milk	[ə ˈbɒtl‿əv ˈmɪlk]	eine Flasche Milch
	a loaf of bread	[ə ˈləʊf‿əv ˈbred]	ein Laib Brot
	loaf/loaves	[ləʊf/ləʊvz]	Laib/Laibe
	half a pound of sugar	[ˈhɑ:f‿ə ˈpaʊnd‿əv ˈʃʊgə]	ein halbes Pfund Zucker
	a pound of apples	[ə ˈpaʊnd‿əv‿ˈæplz]	ein Pfund Äpfel
	a bar of chocolate	[ə ˈbɑ:r‿əv ˈtʃɒklət]	eine Tafel Schokolade
	a packet of tea	[ə ˈpækɪt‿əv ˈti:]	ein Päckchen Tee
	glue	[glu:]	Klebstoff
	pound	[paʊnd]	*engl. Pfund (Geld)*
	change	[tʃeɪndʒ]	*hier:* Wechselgeld
	p	[pi:]	Abkürzung von *penny* und *pence*
59,1	**slogan**	[ˈsləʊgən]	Schlagwort, Slogan
59,2	to **get**	[get]	bekommen
	to **compare**	[kɒmˈpeə]	vergleichen
59,3	–		

some fruit	**etwas** Obst
some stamps	**einige** Briefmarken
a few apples	**ein paar** Äpfel
a bottle of milk	**eine Flasche** Milch
a pound of oranges	**ein Pfund** Orangen
half a pound of butter	**ein halbes Pfund** Butter
a loaf of bread	**ein Laib** Brot
a packet of tea	**ein Päckchen** Tee
a bar of chocolate	**eine Tafel** Schokolade

B Homework for the Morgans and Jenny

60a)	**Granny Smith**	[grænɪ ˈsmɪθ]	*hier:* Apfelsorte
	many	[ˈmenɪ]	viele
	We haven't got any bread.	[ˌwi: ˈhævnt gɒt‿enɪ ˈbred]	Wir haben kein Brot.
	How much?	[ˈhaʊ mʌtʃ]	Wieviel?
	(not) much	[(nɒt) mʌtʃ]	(nicht) viel

b) **traffic**	[ˈtræfɪk]	Verkehr
nothing	[ˈnʌθɪŋ]	nichts
She cannot find anything.	[ʃɪ ˈkænɒt faɪnd‿ˈenɪθɪŋ]	Sie kann nichts finden.
anything		(irgend)etwas
nobody	[ˈnəʊbɒdɪ]	niemand
anybody	[ˈenɪbɒdɪ]	(irgend)jemand

no	**any**	**some**	**every**
nobody	**anybody**	**somebody**	**everybody**
nothing	**anything**	**something**	**everything**

Is **anybody** at home?	Ist **jemand** zu Hause?
Nobody is at home. **Everybody** is in town.	**Niemand** ist zu Hause. **Alle** sind in der Stadt.
But I can see **somebody** at the window.	Ich kann aber **jemanden** am Fenster sehen.
We haven't got **anything** for tea.	Wir haben **nichts** zum Abendessen.
There's **something** in the kitchen.	Da ist **etwas** in der Küche.
But there's **no** milk.	Aber wir haben **keine** Milch.
We can get **some** milk from the corner shop.	Wir können Milch vom Laden an der Ecke holen.

61,1 –		
61,2 –		
61,3 –		
61,4 **awful**	[ˈɔ:fʊl]	schrecklich, furchtbar
car park	[ˈkɑ:ˌpɑ:k]	Parkplatz
62,5 **money**	[ˈmʌnɪ]	Geld
note	[nəʊt]	*hier:* Schein
coin	[kɒɪn]	Münze, Geldstück

These apples are 50p **a pound.**	Diese Äpfel kosten 50p **das Pfund.**
Half a pound of tea, please.	**Ein halbes Pfund** Tee, bitte.
£5 (five pounds), please.	**Fünf Pfund,** bitte.
And **£1** change.	Und **£1** zurück.

C David's new computer

63a) **bank**	[bænk]	Bank
on two days a week	[ɒn ˈtu: ˈdeɪz‿ə ˈwi:k]	zweimal pro Woche
class	[klɑ:s]	Klasse, *hier:* Unterricht
training centre	[ˈtreɪnɪŋ ˌsentə]	Ausbildungszentrum
training		Schulung
clever	[ˈklevə]	schlau, klug
graphics	[ˈgræfɪks]	Grafik
program	[ˈprəʊgræm]	(Computer-)Programm
b) **ad**	[æd]	Anzeige, Inserat, Annonce
offer	[ˈɒfə]	Angebot
Wanted!	[ˈwɒntɪd]	*hier:* Gesucht!
second-hand	[ˈsekənd ˌhænd]	gebraucht
(shop) assistant	[(ˈʃɒp‿)əˈsɪstənt]	Verkäufer(in)
to **offer**	[ˈɒfə]	anbieten
until	[ʌnˈtɪl]	bis
We're very **busy.**	[ˌwɪə ˈverɪ ˈbɪzɪ]	Wir haben viel zu tun.
busy		beschäftigt
See you later.	[si: ju: ˈleɪtə]	Bis später.
Goodbye.	[ˌgʊdˈbaɪ]	Auf Wiedersehen.
63,1 –		
63,2 –		

D At Lawrence Road Computers

64a)	They have **very little time.**	[ðeɪ həv‿ˈverɪ ˌlɪtl ˈtaɪm]	Sie haben sehr wenig Zeit.
	little		wenig
	That's **too much.**	[ðæts ˈtu: ˈmʌtʃ]	Das ist zu viel.
	too		zu
	at that price	[ət ˈðæt ˈpraɪs]	zu diesem Preis
	Very few people are here.	[ˈverɪ fju: ˈpi:pl‿ɑ: ˈhɪə]	Es sind sehr wenig Leute hier.
	few		wenige
	month	[mʌnθ]	Monat
	Excuse me, ...	[ɪkˈskju:z mi:]	Entschuldigung, ...
b)	**software**	[ˈsɒftˌweə]	Software
	I can give you **a little more.**	[aɪ kən ˈgɪv ju:‿ə ˈlɪtl ˈmɔ:]	Ich kann dir ein bißchen mehr geben.
	a little		ein wenig, ein bißchen
	more		mehr
64,1	–		
65,2	–		
65,3	**indirect object**	[ˈɪndaɪrekt‿ˈɒbdʒɪkt]	indirektes Objekt
65,4	**birthday**	[ˈbɜ:θdeɪ]	Geburtstag
	present	[ˈpreznt]	Geschenk
	perhaps	[pəˈhæps]	vielleicht

E On Lundy Island

66	**island**	[ˈaɪlənd]	Insel
a)	to **go to the seaside**	[ˈgəʊ tə ðə ˈsi:saɪd]	ans Meer fahren
	article	[ˈɑ:tɪkl]	Artikel, Aufsatz
	sea	[si:]	Meer
	bird	[bɜ:d]	Vogel
	It is **a long way.**	[ɪt‿ɪz‿ə ˈlɒŋ ˈweɪ]	Es ist weit weg.
	fast	[fɑ:st]	schnell
	train	[treɪn]	Zug
	camera	[ˈkæmərə]	Fotoapparat, Kamera
	binoculars	[bɪˈnɒkjʊləz]	Fernglas
	Nice to meet you.	[ˈnaɪs tə ˈmi:t‿jʊ]	Schön dich kennenzulernen.
	What on earth are you doing?	[ˈwɒt‿ɒn‿ˈɜ:θ‿ə ˈju: ˈdu:ɪŋ]	Was in aller Welt machst du?
	bird-watching	[ˈbɜ:dˌwɒtʃɪŋ]	Vögel beobachten
	How about Lundy Island?	[ˈhaʊ‿əˈbaʊt]	Wie wär's mit der Insel Lundy?
	wonderful	[ˈwʌndəfʊl]	wunderbar, wunderschön
	a **great** idea	[ə ˈgreɪt‿aɪˈdɪə]	eine großartige Idee, eine prima Idee
b)	**famous (for)**	[ˈfeɪməs]	berühmt (für, durch)
	puffin	[ˈpʌfɪn]	Papageientaucher, Lund
67	**map**	[mæp]	Landkarte
	surprise	[səˈpraɪz]	Überraschung
	harbour	[ˈhɑ:bə]	Hafen
	nest	[nest]	Nest
	cliff	[klɪf]	Klippe
	through	[θru:]	durch
	I'm sure **that they're taking eggs** from the nest.	[aɪm ˈʃʊə ðət ðeə ˌteɪkɪŋ ˈegs frəm ðə ˈnest]	Ich bin sicher, daß sie Eier aus dem Nest nehmen.
	that	[ðæt/ðət]	daß
	egg		Ei
	full of	[ˈfʊl‿əv]	voll von, voller
	boat	[bəʊt]	Boot
67,1	–		
67,2	–		
68,3	I've got **another year** at school.	[aɪv gɒt‿əˈnʌðə ˈjɪər‿ət ˈsku:l]	Ich muß noch ein Jahr zur Schule gehen.
	another		noch ein(e)

68,4	**the following sentence**	[ðə ˈfɒləʊɪŋ ˈsentəns]	der folgende Satz
	I'm looking for a second-hand computer.	[aɪm ˈlʊkɪŋ fər‿ə ˈsekəndhænd kəmˈpju:tə]	Ich suche einen gebrauchten Computer.
	to **look for**	[ˈlʊk fə]	suchen
69,5	**diskette**	[dɪsˈket]	Diskette
	to **drink**	[drɪŋk]	trinken
	to **think**	[θɪŋk]	denken
69,6	**a piece of paper**	[ə ˈpi:s‿əv ˈpeɪpə]	ein Stück Papier
9,⟨7⟩	–		

Unit 6

A British schools

70	**British**	[ˈbrɪtɪʃ]	britisch
a)	**most**	[məʊst]	die meisten
	comprehensive school	[ˌkɒmprɪˈhensɪv ˌsku:l]	Gesamtschule
	to be different (from)	[bi: ˈdɪfrənt (frɒm)]	anders als
	pupil	[ˈpju:pl]	Schüler(in)
	jeans *(plural)*	[dʒi:nz]	Jeans
	uniform	[ˈju:nɪfɔ:m]	Uniform
	blazer	[ˈbleɪzə]	Blazer
	badge	[bædʒ]	Abzeichen
	shirt	[ʃɜ:t]	Hemd
	blouse	[blaʊz]	Bluse
	tie	[taɪ]	Krawatte, Schlips
	sometimes	[ˈsʌmtaɪmz]	manchmal
	trousers *(plural)*	[ˈtraʊzəz]	Hose, Hosen
	skirt	[skɜ:t]	Rock
	pullover	[ˈpʊləʊvə]	Pullover
	strict	[strɪkt]	streng
	different *(adj.)*	[ˈdɪfrənt]	verschieden, unterschiedlich
	normally	[ˈnɔ:məlɪ]	normalerweise
	'school dress'	[ˈsku:l ˈdres]	Schulkleidung
b)	**cafeteria**	[kæfəˈtɪərɪə]	Cafeteria
	often	[ˈɒfn]	oft, häufig
	lunch	[lʌntʃ]	Mittagessen
	snack bar	[ˈsnæk ˌbɑ:]	Imbißstube
	usually	[ˈju:ʒʊəlɪ]	gewöhnlich, normalerweise
	how long	[ˈhaʊ ˈlɒŋ]	wie lange
	breakfast	[ˈbrekfəst]	Frühstück
	lesson	[ˈlesn]	(Unterrichts-)Stunde, *hier:* Unterricht
	You are lucky!	[jʊ‿ə ˈlʌkɪ]	Du hast Glück!
	I'd like a cup of tea.	[aɪd‿ˈlaɪk‿ə kʌp‿əv ˈti:]	Ich hätte gern eine Tasse Tee.
	to **like**		gern haben, mögen
	never	[ˈnevə]	nie, niemals
	practice	[ˈpræktɪs]	Übung, Training, *hier:* Probe
	favourite	[ˈfeɪvrɪt]	Lieblings...
	activity	[ækˈtɪvətɪ]	Aktivität, Betätigung; Arbeitsgemeinschaft
	work	[wɜ:k]	Arbeit
	just	[dʒʌst]	nur
	French	[frentʃ]	französisch
71,1	–		
71,2	–		
71,3	–		
71,4	–		

Jenny **always** leaves home at 8 o'clock.	Jenny geht **immer** um 8 Uhr von zu Hause weg.
School is **normally** from 8.45 to 3.45.	Der Unterricht dauert **normalerweise** von 8.45 bis 15.45.
Tanja **usually** has breakfast at 7 o'clock.	Tanja frühstückt **gewöhnlich** um 7 Uhr.
Jenny **often** has lunch at the cafeteria.	Jenny ißt **oft** zu Mittag in der Cafeteria.
Sometimes Jenny hasn't got much homework.	Jenny hat **manchmal** wenig Hausaufgaben.

B At home and at school

72b)	**Tanja does not want to have lunch at school.**	[ˈtænjə dʌz nɒt ˈwɒnt‿tə hæv lʌntʃ‿ət sku:l]	Tanja will nicht in der Schule zu Mittag essen.
	does/doesn't	[dʌz/dʌznt]	*3. Person Sing. von* do
	to **want**		wollen
72,1	–		
73,2	to **correct**	[kəˈrekt]	korrigieren, berichtigen
73,3	–		
73,4	–		

C Tanja's first day at an English school

74b)	**They are at work.**	[ˈðeɪ‿ər‿ət ˈwɜ:k]	Sie arbeiten. Sie sind bei der Arbeit.
	everyone	[ˈevrɪwʌn]	jeder, alle
75,1	–		
75,2	**What else ... ?**	[wɒt‿els]	Was ... sonst (noch)?
75,3	–		
75,4	–		

D The new timetable

76	**timetable**	[ˈtaɪmˌteɪbl]	Stundenplan
a)	**copy**	[ˈkɒpɪ]	Kopie
	on Mondays	[ɒn ˈmʌndɪz]	montags
	Monday	[ˈmʌndɪ]	Montag
	Maths *(Singular)*	[mæθs]	Mathematik
	break	[breɪk]	Pause
	Ms	[mɪz/məz]	Frau *(auch für unverheiratete Frauen)*
	PE (Physical Education)	[ˈpi:ˈi: (ˈfɪzɪkəl‿ˌedju:ˈkeɪʃn)]	Sport
	Biology	[baɪˈɒlɒdʒɪ]	Biologie
	to **love**	[lʌv]	lieben, gern haben, mögen
	subject	[ˈsʌbdʒekt]	(Unterrichts-)Fach
	Geography	[dʒɪˈɒgrəfɪ]	Geographie, Erdkunde
	History	[ˈhɪstrɪ]	Geschichte
	Ugh!	[ɜ:h]	I! Igitt!
	to **hate**	[heɪt]	nicht ausstehen können, hassen
	to **think**	[θɪnk]	denken; glauben, meinen
	boring	[ˈbɔ:rɪŋ]	langweilig
	date	[deɪt]	Datum
	Art	[ɑ:t]	Kunst
	fantastic	[fænˈtæstɪk]	fantastisch
b)	**Tuesday**	[ˈtju:zdɪ]	Dienstag
	Wednesday	[ˈwenzdɪ]	Mittwoch
	Thursday	[ˈθɜ:zdɪ]	Donnerstag
	Assembly	[əˈsemblɪ]	Morgenandacht
	Chemistry	[ˈkemɪstrɪ]	Chemie
	Physics *(Singular)*	[ˈfɪzɪks]	Physik
	Religious Education	[rɪˈlɪdʒəz‿ˌedju:ˈkeɪʃn]	Religion
	Civics *(Singular)*	[ˈsɪvɪks]	Gesellschaftskunde

	Games	[geɪmz]	Sport; Sportnachmittag
	Home Economics *(Singular)*	[ˈhəʊm ˌɪkəˈnɒmɪks]	Hauswirtschaftslehre
77,1	**statement**	[ˈsteɪtmənt]	Feststellung, Aussage
	second	[ˈsekənd]	zweite
77,2	–		
77,[3]	–		

Great!	Prima!/Toll!
I think it's **great!**	Das finde ich toll!
I **like** cats.	Ich mag Katzen (gern).
I **love** salads.	Ich liebe Salate.
That's **fantastic!**	Das ist phantastisch!
The weather is **awful**.	Das Wetter ist scheußlich.
I don't **like** that.	Das mag ich nicht.
I **hate** it.	Das mag ich überhaupt nicht/Das kann ich nicht ausstehen.
Ugh!	I! Igitt!
Oh dear!	O je!
Oh, sorry.	Oh, Entschuldigung.

E School cafeteria or snack bar?

78a)	**menu**	[ˈmenju:]	Speisekarte
	baked beans	[ˈbeɪkt bi:nz]	gebackene Bohnen in Tomatensoße
	sausage	[ˈsɒsɪdʒ]	Wurst
	chips	[tʃɪps]	Pommes frites
	salad	[ˈsæləd]	Salat
	pudding	[ˈpʊdɪŋ]	Pudding
	station	[ˈsteɪʃn]	Bahnhof
	mixed	[mɪkst]	gemischt
	cheese	[tʃi:z]	Käse
	ham	[hæm]	Schinken
	ice-cream	[ˈaɪs ˈkri:m]	Eis
	juice	[dʒu:s]	Saft
78,1	–		
79,2	**order**	[ˈɔ:də]	Reihenfolge
79,3	–		
79,4	to **note down**	[ˈnəʊt‿ˈdaʊn]	notieren, aufschreiben

F A ticket for a pop concert

80	**ticket**	[ˈtɪkət]	(Eintritts-)Karte
	pop music	[ˈpɒp ˌmju:zɪk]	Popmusik
	concert	[ˈkɒnsət]	Konzert
a)	**playground**	[ˈpleɪˌgraʊnd]	Spielplatz, *hier:* Schulhof
	while	[waɪl]	während *(Konj.)*
	to **get**	[get]	holen
	I'd love to come.	[aɪd ˈlʌv tə kʌm]	Ich würde sehr gern kommen.
	It's a **secret.**	[ɪts‿ə ˈsi:krɪt]	Es ist ein Geheimnis.
	to **arrive**	[əˈraɪv]	ankommen
b)	to **take a shower**	[ˈteɪk‿ə ˈʃaʊə]	duschen
	shower		Dusche
	mirror	[ˈmɪrə]	Spiegel
	to **put on make-up**	[ˈpʊt‿ɒn ˈmeɪk‿ʌp]	sich schminken
	to **put on**		auftragen, auflegen
	pocket	[ˈpɒkɪt]	Tasche *(in einem Kleidungsstück)*
81	She **knocks on the door.**	[ʃɪ ˈnɒks‿ɒn ðə ˈdɔ:]	Sie klopft an die Tür.
	to **knock**		klopfen

	to **go out**	[ˌgəʊ ˈaʊt]	ausgehen
	tonight	[təˈnaɪt]	heute abend
	a date	[deɪt]	*hier:* Verabredung
	boyfriend	[bɒɪfrend]	Freund
	Have a good time!	[ˌhæv‿ə ˈgʊd‿ˈtaɪm]	Viel Spaß!
	I can keep a secret.	[ˌaɪ kən ˈki:p‿ə ˈsi:krɪt]	Ich kann ein Geheimnis bewahren.
81,1	–		
81,2	–		
81,3	**difference**	[ˈdɪfrəns]	Unterschied
	between	[bɪˈtwi:n]	zwischen
82,4	**next**		als nächstes
82,5	**I'm hungry.**	[aɪm ˈhʌŋgrɪ]	Ich habe Hunger.
	to **be hungry**		hungrig sein
	I'm thirsty.	[aɪm ˈθɜ:stɪ]	Ich habe Durst.
	to **be thirsty**		durstig sein
	toast	[təʊst]	Toast
	hot	[hɒt]	heiß
83,6	to **be careful with**	[bi: ˈkeəfʊl wɪð]	darauf achten, auf etw. achten
	position	[pəˈsɪʃn]	Position
	adverbial	[ədˈvɜ:bɪəl]	adverbiale Bestimmung
83,7	to **rhyme**	[raɪm]	reimen
83,8	He's the **odd one out.**	[hi:z ðɪ‿ˈɒd wʌn‿ˈaʊt]	Er ist übrig, überzählig, anders.
	odd one out		*hier:* ein nicht dazugehöriges Wort
	meaning	[ˈmi:nɪŋ]	Bedeutung
	form	[fɔ:m]	Form
	to **pronounce**	[prəˈnaʊns]	aussprechen
83,⟨9⟩	to **spend**	[spend]	ausgeben (Geld)

Stopover A ⟨The pond⟩

84	pond	[pɒnd]	Teich
	frog	[frɒg]	Frosch
	building	[ˈbɪldɪŋ]	Gebäude
	technician	[tekˈnɪʃn]	Techniker(in)
	face	[feɪs]	Gesicht
	to build	[bɪld]	bauen
	paper	[ˈpeɪpə]	*hier:* Zeitung
	animal	[ˈænɪməl]	Tier
	opinion	[əˈpɪnjən]	Meinung
	important	[ɪmˈpɔ:tənt]	wichtig
	to agree	[əˈgri:]	zustimmen
	to need	[ni:d]	brauchen
	an aircraft/two aircraft	[ˈeəkrɑ:ft]	ein Flugzeug/zwei Flugzeuge
	to fly	[flaɪ]	fliegen
	environment	[ɪnˈvaɪrənmənt]	Umwelt; Umgebung
	noise	[nɔɪz]	Geräusch, Lärm, Krach
	holidays	[ˈhɒlɪdeɪz]	Ferien, Urlaub
85	European	[ˌjʊərəˈpi:ən]	europäisch; Europäer(in)
	wing	[wɪŋ]	Flügel
	company	[ˈkʌmpənɪ]	Gesellschaft, Firma
	engine	[ˈendʒɪn]	Motor
	airport	[ˈeəpɔ:t]	Flughafen
	satellite	[ˈsætəlaɪt]	Satellit
	to carry	[ˈkærɪ]	tragen, *hier:* übertragen
	map	[mæp]	(Land-)Karte
86a)	to plan	[plæn]	planen
	demonstration	[ˌdemənˈstreɪʃn]	Demonstration
	Write it down!	[ˈraɪt‿ɪt ˈdaʊn]	Schreib es (ihn, sie) auf!
	to change	[tʃeɪndʒ]	(ver-)ändern
	library	[ˈlaɪbrərɪ]	Bücherei, Bibliothek

	headline	[ˈhedlaɪn]	Überschrift, Schlagzeile
	politician	[ˌpɒlɪˈtɪʃn]	Politiker
	including	[ɪnˈklu:dɪŋ]	einschließlich, inklusive
86,1	discussion	[dɪsˈkʌʃn]	Diskussion
	to act	[ækt]	spielen, handeln
87,2	–		
87,3	the pros and cons	[ˈprəʊz‿n ˈkɒnz]	das Für und Wider
	supermarket	[ˈsu:pəmɑ:kɪt]	Supermarkt
	abroad	[əˈbrɔ:d]	im/ins Ausland
87,4	to deal with	[di:l wɪð]	sich befassen/beschäftigen mit

Unit 7

A Croeso i Gymru – Welcome to Wales

	Croeso i Gymru	[ˈkrɔɪsɒ ɪ ˈgɜmrɪ]	Willkommen in Wales *(auf walisisch)*
88a)	**brochure**	[ˈbrəʊʃə]	Broschüre, Prospekt
	Welsh	[welʃ]	walisisch
	You can **enjoy the beautiful scenery.**	[ju: kən‿ɪnˈdʒɔɪ ðə ˈbju:tɪfʊl ˈsi:nərɪ]	Sie können die wunderschöne Landschaft genießen.
	to **enjoy**		genießen
	mountain	[ˈmaʊntən]	Berg
	You can **visit** old **castles.**	[ju: kən ˈvɪzɪt‿əʊld ˈkɑ:slz]	Sie können sich alte Schlösser ansehen.
	to **visit**		besuchen
	castle		Schloß
	capital	[ˈkæpɪtl]	Hauptstadt
	National Park	[ˈnæʃənl ˈpɑ:k]	Nationalpark; Naturschutzgebiet
	sandy	[ˈsændɪ]	sandig
	coast	[kəʊst]	Küste
	Welsh is not English with a **funny accent.**	[ˈwelʃ‿ɪz ˈnɒt‿ˈɪŋglɪʃ wɪð‿ə ˈfʌnɪ‿ˈæksent]	Die walisische Sprache ist nicht Englisch mit komischem Akzent.
	funny		lustig, *hier:* komisch
	accent		Akzent; Aussprache
	Celtic	[ˈkeltɪk]	keltisch
	language	[ˈlæŋgwɪdʒ]	Sprache
	country	[ˈkʌntrɪ]	Land
89b)	**south**	[saʊθ]	Süden, Süd-
	river	[ˈrɪvə]	Fluß
	bridge	[brɪdʒ]	Brücke
	museum	[mjʊˈzi:əm]	Museum
90,1	–		
90,2	**caption**	[ˈkæpʃn]	Bildunterschrift

Tanja is a **German** girl.	Tanja ist ein **deutsches** Mädchen.
Hanover is a city in **Germany.**	Hannover ist eine Großstadt in **Deutschland.**
Mrs Benson is not **French**, she is **English.**	Mrs Benson ist keine **Französin**, sie ist **Engländerin.**
Wales is not a part of **England.**	**Wales** ist nicht ein Teil von **England.**
Wales and **Scotland** are a part of **Great Britain.**	**Wales** und **Schottland** sind Teile **Großbritanniens.**
At some **British** schools pupils must wear school uniform.	In einigen **britischen** Schulen müssen die Schüler Schuluniform tragen.
Switzerland is a beautiful country.	**Die Schweiz** ist ein schönes Land.
Tanja would like to buy a bar of **Swiss** chocolate.	Tanja möchte eine Tafel **Schweizer** Schokolade kaufen.

B Plans for a trip to South Wales

90 **trip**	[trɪp]	Ausflug
She knows quite a lot.	[ʃɪ ˈnəʊz ˈkwaɪt‿ə ˈlɒt]	Sie weiß ziemlich viel.
quite		ziemlich
That's fine with me.	[ðæts ˈfaɪn wɪð ˈmi:]	Das ist mir recht.
Whose bag is this?	[hu:z ˈbæg‿ɪz‿ðɪs]	Wem gehört diese Tasche?
whose		wessen
May I borrow your book?	[meɪ‿aɪ ˈbɒrəʊ jɔ: ˈbʊk]	Darf ich mir dein Buch leihen?
to **borrow**		sich etwas (aus)leihen
We can go **by train.**	[wi: kən ˈgəʊ baɪ ˈtreɪn]	Wir können mit dem Zug fahren.
How can we get from Filton **to** Bristol?	[ˈhaʊ kən wɪ ˈget frəm ˈfɪltən tə ˈbrɪstl]	Wie kommen wir von Filton nach Bristol?
to **get (somewhere)**		(irgendwo) hinkommen
from ... to		von ... nach
Tanja must **catch the train.**	[ˈtænjə məst ˈkætʃ ðə ˈtreɪn]	Tanja muß den Zug erreichen.
to **catch (a train, bus, etc.)**		erreichen (Zug, Bus usw.)
We must **change trains.**	[wɪ məst ˈtʃeɪndʒ ˈtreɪnz]	Wir müssen umsteigen.
to **change (train, bus, etc.)**		umsteigen (Zug, Bus usw.)
Have a look at the castle.	[ˌhæv‿ə ˈlʊk‿ət ðə ˈkɑ:sl]	Schau dir das Schloß an.
to **have a look at**		sich etw. anschauen, ansehen
market	[ˈmɑ:kɪt]	Markt
youth hostel	[ˈju:θ ˌhɒstl]	Jugendherberge
aunt	[ɑ:nt]	Tante
uncle	[ˈʌŋkl]	Onkel
to **live**	[lɪv]	wohnen, leben
super	[ˈsu:pə]	toll, super
91,1 –		
91,2 **dear**	[dɪə]	mein(e) Liebe(r); Liebe(r,s) *(normalerweise nicht übersetzt)*
Hello, dear!		Hallo, Schatz!
Thank you, dear!		Danke.
Dear Kevin,		*(Briefanfang):* Lieber Kevin,
91,3 **schoolbag**	[ˈsku:lbæg]	Schultasche
91,4 –		

How are you today?	**Wie** geht es dir heute?
How many apples would you like?	**Wie viele** Äpfel möchtest du?
How much tea would you like?	**Wieviel** Tee möchtest du?
Who is waiting outside?	**Wer** wartet draußen?
What is Tanja doing at the corner shop?	**Was** macht Tanja beim Laden an der Ecke?
Why are the girls buying apples?	**Warum** kaufen die Mädchen Äpfel?
Where is the farm in Wales?	**Wo** ist die Farm in Wales?
Whose bikes can they borrow?	**Wessen** Fahrräder können sie sich leihen?
Who can they ask?	**Wen** können sie fragen?

C Tanja's letter to her aunt in London

92 **August**	[ˈɔ:gəst]	August
Love	[lʌv]	*hier als Briefschluß:* Herzliche Grüße
93,1 –		
93,2 **normal**	[ˈnɔ:məl]	normal, gewöhnlich
93,3 **over**	[ˈəʊvə]	zu Ende
sweets	[swi:ts]	Bonbons, Süßigkeiten
sister	[ˈsɪstə]	Schwester
93,4 –		

D On time

94 Please **be on time!**	[ˈpli:z bi:‿ɒn ˈtaɪm]	Sei bitte pünktlich!
What's the **exact** time?	[ˈwɒts ði: ɪgˈzækt ˈtaɪm]	Wie spät ist es genau?
The **clock** is on the wall.	[ðə ˈklɒk‿ɪz‿ɒn ðə ˈwɔ:l]	Die Uhr ist an der Wand.

94,1	**timetable**	[ˈtaɪmˌteɪbl]	Fahrplan
94,2	**early**	[ˈɜːlɪ]	früh

What is the time now, please? — Wieviel Uhr ist es jetzt, bitte?
Can you tell me the exact **time,** please? — Können Sie mir bitte die genaue Uhrzeit sagen?
Mr Benson is hurrying. He would like to get to work **early.** — Mr Benson beeilt sich. Er möchte früh am Arbeitsplatz sein.
Tanja must not be **late.** — Tanja darf nicht zu spät kommen.

[E Mr Benson's cake]

95,[1]	lonely	[ˈləʊnlɪ]	einsam
	question tag	[ˈkwestʃən ˌtæg]	Frageanhängsel

F The farm near Llanthony

96a)	**I wake up** early every morning.	[aɪ ˌweɪk‿ʌp ˈɜːlɪ‿ˌevrɪ ˈmɔːnɪŋ]	Ich wache jeden Morgen früh auf.
	to **wake up**		aufwachen
	I get up at 6 o'clock.	[aɪ ˌget‿ˈʌp‿ət ˈsɪks‿əˈklɒk]	Ich stehe um 6 Uhr auf.
	to **get up**		aufstehen
	to **get on a bike**	[get‿ˈɒn]	aufsteigen aufs Fahrrad
	to **cycle**	[ˈsaɪkl]	Fahrrad fahren
	single ticket	[ˈsɪŋgl]	einfache Fahrkarte
	return ticket	[rɪˈtɜːn]	Rückfahrkarte
	platform	[ˈplætfɔːm]	Bahnsteig
	It's raining.	[ɪts ˈreɪnɪŋ]	Es regnet.
	to **rain**		regnen
	hill	[hɪl]	Hügel
	Tanja **is pleased about** the present.	[ˈtænjə‿ɪz ˈpliːzd‿əˈbaʊt ðə ˈpreznt]	Tanja freut sich über das Geschenk.
	to **be pleased about**		sich freuen über
	animal	[ˈænɪməl]	Tier
	sheep *(sing. & plural)*	[ʃiːp]	Schaf(e)
	sheepdog	[ˈʃiːpdɒg]	Schäferhund
97b)	to **sleep**	[sliːp]	schlafen
	barn	[bɑːn]	Scheune
	sleeping bag	[ˈsliːpɪŋˌbæg]	Schlafsack
	happy	[hæpɪ]	glücklich
	comfortable	[ˈkʌmftəbl]	bequem
	dirty	[ˈdɜːtɪ]	schmutzig
	The barn is haunted.	[ðə ˈbɑːn‿ɪz ˈhɔːntɪd]	Es spukt in der Scheune.
	to **laugh**	[lɑːf]	lachen
	Tanja **believes in ghosts.**	[ˈtænjə bɪˈliːvz‿ɪn ˈgəʊsts]	Tanja glaubt an Gespenster.
	to **believe in**		glauben an
	ghost		Gespenst
	to **bark**	[bɑːk]	bellen
	She can hear someone **at the door.**	[ʃɪ kən ˈhɪə ˈsʌmwʌn‿ət ðə ˈdɔː]	Sie kann jemanden an der Tür hören.
	figure	[ˈfɪgə]	*hier:* Gestalt
	to **stand**	[stænd]	stehen
	nightdress	[ˈnaɪtdres]	Nachthemd
	I'm not afraid.	[aɪm ˈnɒt‿əˈfreɪd]	Ich habe keine Angst.
	Good night.	[ˈgʊd ˈnaɪt]	Gute Nacht.
	Sleep well!	[ˈsliːp ˈwel]	Schlaf(t) gut!
	well		gut *(Adverb)*

97,1	**journey**	['dʒɜ:nɪ]	Reise
	in your own words	[ɪn jʊər‿'əʊn 'wɜ:dz]	mit eigenen Worten
	own		eigen
97,2	–		
98,3	–		
98,4	**preposition**	[prepə'zɪʃn]	Präposition, Verhältniswort
98,5	**coach**	[kəʊtʃ]	(Reise-)Bus
99,6	–		
99,7	–		
99,8	**vocabulary**	[vəʊ'kæbjʊlərɪ]	Vokabeln
99,9	–		
99,⟨10⟩	–		

Mr Benson does not normally **take** the girls to school.	Mr Benson **bringt** die Mädchen normalerweise nicht zur Schule.
Mrs Benson **is taking** Tanja to hospital.	Mrs Benson **bringt** Tanja ins Krankenhaus.
Bring me a loaf of bread, please.	**Bring** mir bitte einen Laib Brot mit.
Red **brings** us the newspaper every morning.	Jeden Morgen **bringt** Red uns die Zeitung.

Unit 8

A A visit to Radio Bristol

100	**a visit** to Radio Bristol	[ə 'vɪzɪt‿tə 'reɪdɪəʊ 'brɪstl]	ein Besuch bei Radio Bristol
a)	**twin town**	['twɪn 'taʊn]	Partnerstadt
	guide	[gaɪd]	Führer(in)
	building	['bɪldɪŋ]	Gebäude
	radio station	['reɪdɪəʊ 'steɪʃn]	Rundfunksender
	per cent	[pə'sent]	Prozent
	area	['eərɪə]	Gegend, Gebiet
	to **broadcast**	['brɔ:dkɑ:st]	senden, ausstrahlen
	news	[nju:z]	Nachricht(en)
	event	[ɪ'vent]	Ereignis, Veranstaltung
	important	[ɪm'pɔ:tənt]	wichtig
	to **take place**	['teɪk 'pleɪs]	stattfinden
	competition	[ˌkɒmpə'tɪʃn]	Wettbewerb
	to **win**	[wɪn]	gewinnen
	prize	[praɪz]	Preis
	exhibition	[eksɪ'bɪʃn]	Ausstellung
	open-air pop concert	['əʊpn‿ˌeə 'pɒp 'kɒnsət]	Popkonzert im Freien
b)	**calendar**	['kælɪndə]	Kalender
	winter	['wɪntə]	Winter
	spring	[sprɪŋ]	Frühling
	Cup Final	[ˌkʌp 'faɪnl]	Pokalendspiel
	stadium	['steɪdɪəm]	Stadion
	swimming championships	['swɪmɪŋ 'tʃæmpɪənˌʃɪps]	Meisterschaftskämpfe im Schwimmen
	to **swim**		schwimmen
	championship		Meisterschaft
	summer	['sʌmə]	Sommer
	autumn	['ɔ:təm]	Herbst
	lots of	[lɒts‿əv]	viele (*kurz für:* a lot of)
	powerboat	['paʊəbəʊt]	Rennboot
	October	[ɒk'təʊbə]	Oktober
	Open Day	['əʊpən 'deɪ]	‚Tag der offenen Tür'

100,1	–		
100,2	–		
101c)	**environmental problem**	[ɪnˌvaɪrənˈmentəl ˈprɒbləm]	Umweltproblem
	pollution	[pəˈluːʃən]	Umweltverschmutzung
	swimming baths	[ˈswɪmɪŋ bɑːðz]	Schwimmbad
	bath	[bɑːθ]	Bad
	boat **show**	[ˈbəʊt ˈʃəʊ]	Bootsausstellung
	January	[ˈdʒænjʊərɪ]	Januar
	February	[ˈfebrʊərɪ]	Februar
	March	[mɑːtʃ]	März
	April	[ˈeɪprɪl]	April
	May	[meɪ]	Mai
	June	[dʒuːn]	Juni
	July	[dʒʊˈlaɪ]	Juli
	September	[sepˈtembə]	September
	November	[nəʊˈvembə]	November
	December	[dɪˈsembə]	Dezember
102,1	–		
102,2	–		
102,3	–		

B The nine o'clock news

103a)	He's **older than** Jenny.	[hiːz‿ˈəʊldə ˌðən ˈdʒenɪ]	Er ist älter als Jenny.
b)	**last**	[lɑːst]	letzte
	visitor	[ˈvɪzɪtə]	Besucher
	home	[həʊm]	Heimat
	simple	[sɪmpl]	einfach
103,1	–		
104,2	**sale**	[seɪl]	Verkauf
104,3	–		
104,4	**paragraph**	[ˈpærəˌgrɑːf]	Paragraph, Abschnitt
104,5	–		

C From the station to the Exhibition Centre

105	**bus stop**	[ˈbʌs‿stɒp]	Bushaltestelle
	full	[fʊl]	voll, besetzt, belegt
	to **turn into**	[tɜːn‿ˈɪntʊ]	abbiegen in
	straight on	[ˈstreɪt‿ˌɒn]	geradeaus
	crossroads	[ˈkrɒsrəʊdz]	Kreuzung
	Go past the church.	[ˌgəʊ ˈpɑːst ðə‿ˈtʃɜːtʃ]	Geh an der Kirche vorbei.
	to **cross**	[krɒs]	überqueren
	Go across Queen Square.	[ˌgəʊ‿əˈkrɒs ˈkwiːn skweə]	Geh über den Queenplatz.
	square		Platz
	traffic lights	[ˈtræfɪk laɪts]	Verkehrsampel
	statue	[ˈstætjʊ]	Statue
	down the road	[ˈdaʊn ðə ˈrəʊd]	die Straße entlang
	You can't **miss** it.	[juː ˈkɑːnt ˈmɪs‿ɪt]	Du kannst sie nicht verfehlen.
	to **miss**		verpassen, *hier:* verfehlen
	quick	[kwɪk]	schnell
	to **get into**	[get‿ˈɪntə]	hineinsteigen, -gehen
	seat belt	[ˈsiːtbelt]	Sitzgurt
	to **drive off**	[draɪv‿ˈɒf]	wegfahren, abfahren
	to **drive**	[draɪv]	fahren
	Wendy **is surprised**	[ˈwendɪ‿ɪz‿səˈpraɪzd]	Wendy ist überrascht
	to **be surprised**		überrascht sein
106,1	–		
106,2	**sign**	[saɪn]	Schild; Zeichen

D Saturday afternoon at the Computer Show

107	**nearly**	[ˈnɪəlɪ]	fast
	Good afternoon.	[gʊd‿ɑ:ftəˈnu:n]	Guten Tag.
	lady	[ˈleɪdɪ]	Dame
107,1	–		
108,2	**interview**	[ˈɪntəvju:]	Interview
108,3	–		
108,4	–		

[E The world of the future]

109	world	[wɜ:ld]	Welt
	future	[ˈfju:tʃə]	Zukunft
	probably	[ˈprɒbəblɪ]	wahrscheinlich
	driver	[ˈdraɪvə]	Fahrer(in)
	already	[ɔ:lˈredɪ]	schon
	without	[wɪðˈaʊt]	ohne
	to control	[kənˈtrəʊl]	kontrollieren, steuern
109,[1]	–		
109,[2]	–		
109,[3]	–		

F After the Computer Show

110a)	**already**	[ɔ:lˈredɪ]	schon
	just	[dʒʌst]	gerade, (so)eben
	raincoat	[ˈreɪnkəʊt]	Regenmantel
	umbrella	[ʌmˈbrelə]	Regenschirm
	a bit	[ə ˈbɪt]	ein bißchen
	world	[wɜ:ld]	Welt
	It would be great!	[ɪt ˌwʊd bɪ ˈgreɪt]	Es wäre toll!
	Just imagine!	[dʒʌst‿ɪˈmædʒɪn]	Stell dir vor!
	to **imagine**		sich vorstellen
	result	[rɪˈzʌlt]	Ergebnis
	Never mind!	[ˈnevə ˌmaɪnd]	Das macht nichts!
	flat	[flæt]	Wohnung
	to **run**	[rʌn]	laufen, rennen
b)	**wet**	[wet]	naß
111	**voice**	[vɔɪs]	Stimme
	star	[stɑ:]	Berühmtheit, Star
	winner	[ˈwɪnə]	Gewinner(in)
	announcer	[əˈnaʊnsə]	Ansager(in)
	among	[əˈmʌŋ]	unter
	technology	[tekˈnɒlədʒɪ]	Technologie
	Congratulations!	[kənˌgrætjʊˈleɪʃnz]	Herzlichen Glückwunsch!
111,1	–		
111,2	–		
112,3	–		
112,4	**envelope**	[ˈenvələʊp]	Umschlag, Briefumschlag
112,5	–		
113,6	–		
113,7	–		
113,8	–		
113,9	–		
113,⟨10⟩	to **follow**	[ˈfɒləʊ]	folgen
	route	[ru:t]	Strecke, Route

to **say**	sagen	'Here we are,' Tanja **says**.
to **ask**	fragen	'Have you got everything?' Jenny **asks.**
to **answer**	antworten	'I've got the book,' David **answers.**
to **call**	rufen	Mrs Benson **calls:** 'Please be on time!'
to **laugh**	lachen	'Never mind,' Kevin **laughs**.
to **speak**	sprechen	'Can you **speak** French?'
to **talk to someone**	mit jmd sprechen	I would like to **talk to** Mr Benson.
to **tell**	erzählen, sagen	Kevin **tells** about the party.

Unit 9

A A few more days in Bristol

114	**stay**	[steɪ]	Aufenthalt
	airport	['eəpɔ:t]	Flughafen
	flight	[flaɪt]	Flug
	to **end**	[end]	enden
	to **fly**	[flaɪ]	fliegen
	to **organize**	['ɔ:gənaɪz]	organisieren
	farewell	[ˌfeə'wel]	Abschied
	noisy	['nɔɪzɪ]	*hier:* laut
	to **answer the phone**	['ɑ:nsə ðə 'fəʊn]	ans Telefon gehen
	excited	[ɪk'saɪtɪd]	aufgeregt *(vor Freude)*
	to **discuss**	[dɪ'skʌs]	diskutieren
	barbecue	['bɑ:bɪkju:]	Grillfest
	It's a mess.	[ˌɪts‿ə 'mes]	Es ist ein Durcheinander/Schlamassel.
	mess		Unordnung
	to **tidy up**	['taɪdɪ 'ʌp]	aufräumen
	hard work	['hɑ:d 'wɜ:k]	harte Arbeit
	to **finish**	['fɪnɪʃ]	beenden
114,1	–		
114,2	**almost**	['ɔ:lməʊst]	beinahe; fast

B A party at the Aerospace Club?

115a)	**watch**	['wɒtʃ]	(Armband-)Uhr
	They have invited their friends.	['ðeɪ həv‿ɪn'vaɪtɪd ðeə 'frendz]	Sie haben ihre Freunde eingeladen.
	to **invite**		einladen
	to **need**	[ni:d]	brauchen
b)	**He has not moved the tables into the garden yet.**	['hɪ həz nɒt 'mu:vd ðə 'teɪblz ˌɪntʊ ðə 'gɑ:dn ˌjet]	Er hat die Tische noch nicht in den Garten getragen.
	to **move**		*hier:* hineintragen/hinaustragen
	not ... yet		noch nicht
	hour	['aʊə]	Stunde
116,1	**pronunciation**	[prəˌnʌnsɪ'eɪʃn]	Aussprache
	present perfect	[ˌpreznt 'pɜ:fɪkt]	Perfekt
	past participle	[ˌpɑ:st 'pɑ:tɪsɪpl]	Partizip Perfekt
116,2	**tired**	['taɪəd]	müde
	supper	['sʌpə]	Abendessen
116,3	to **forget**	[fə'get]	vergessen
	That's fine!	[ˌðæts 'faɪn]	Das ist großartig!/Das ist toll!
116,4	–		

armchair	Sessel	**shower**	Dusche
house	Haus	**wall**	Wand, Mauer
(front) door	Haustür	**floor**	Fußboden
back door	Tür (hinter dem Haus)	**shelf/shelves**	Regal(e)
window	Fenster	**cupboard**	Schrank
hall	Flur, Diele	**wardrobe**	Kleiderschrank
living room	Wohnzimmer	**bed**	Bett
dining room	Eßzimmer	**chair**	Stuhl
kitchen	Küche	**table**	Tisch
bedroom	Schlafzimmer	**key**	Schlüssel
bathroom	Badezimmer	**sofa**	Sofa
toilet	Toilette	**desk**	Schreibtisch

C At the barn

117a)	**He has taken them there.**	[hɪ həz ˈteɪkən ðəm ˈðeə]	Er hat sie dorthin gebracht.
	to **take, have/has taken**		
	Nobody has told her about it yet.	[ˈnəʊbɒdɪ həz ˈtəʊld hɜːr‿əˈbaʊt‿ɪt jet]	Niemand hat ihr etwas darüber gesagt.
	to **tell, have/has told**		
	holiday(s)	[ˈhɒlɪdeɪ(z)]	Ferien, Urlaub
	box	[bɒks]	Schachtel, Karton
	I've left them in the car.	[aɪv ˈleft ðem‿ɪn ðə ˈkɑː]	Ich habe sie im Auto gelassen.
	to **leave, have/has left**		
	He has brought a lot of cassettes.	[hɪ həz ˈbrɔːt‿ə lɒt‿əv kəˈsets]	Er hat viele Cassetten mitgebracht.
	to **bring, have/has brought**		
	He has made a poster.	[hɪ həz ˈmeɪd‿ə ˈpəʊstə]	Er hat ein Poster gemacht.
	to **make, have/has made**		
	He has put it up.	[hɪ həz ˈpʊt‿ɪt‿ˈʌp]	Er hat es aufgehängt.
	to **put, have/has put**		
	It has been great.	[ɪt həz biːn ˈgreɪt]	Es ist schön gewesen.
	to **be, have/has been**		
	soon	[suːn]	bald
	Good luck!	[ˈgʊd ˈlʌk]	Viel Glück!
	I have written my name on it.	[aɪv ˈrɪtn maɪ ˈneɪm‿ɒn‿ɪt]	Ich habe meinen Namen darauf geschrieben.
	to **write, have/has written**		
b)	**He has gone up the ladder.**	[hɪ həz gɒn ˈʌp ðə ˈlædə]	Er ist die Leiter hinaufgestiegen.
	to **go, have/has gone**		
	He has found a computer game.	[hɪ həz ˈfaʊnd‿ə kəmˈpjuːtə ˌgeɪm]	Er hat ein Computerspiel gefunden.
	to **find, have/has found**		
	Have you seen my present?	[ˌhæv juː ˌsiːn maɪ ˈpreznt]	Hast du mein Geschenk gesehen?
	to **see, have/has seen**		
	We've forgotten the glasses.	[wiːv‿fəˈgɒtn ðə ˈglɑːs ɪz]	Wir haben die Gläser vergessen.
	to **forget, have/has forgotten**		
	crisps	[krɪsps]	(Kartoffel-)Chips
	Haven't you bought any?	[ˈhævnt‿juː ˈbɔːt‿enɪ]	Hast du keine gekauft?
	to **buy, have/has bought**		
	I've done it!	[aɪv ˈdʌn‿ɪt]	Ich habe es getan/geschafft!
	to **do, have/has done**		

118,1 –
118,2 –
118,3 –

to do	to make	to take
What are you **doing**?	Can you **make a cake?**	He **is taking the car** to work.
Let's **do this job** first.	Tanja must **make breakfast.**	We can walk or **take the bus.**
I must **do my homework.**	Don't **make a noise.**	We must **take a photo** of it.
He can **do the shopping** later.	**Make** a new sentence.	Jenny is **taking a shower.**

D The farewell present

119 **He has come round to the Bensons' house.**	[ˌhɪ həz kʌm ˈraʊnd‿tə ðə ˈbensnz ˈhaʊs]	Er hat bei den Bensons vorbeigeschaut.
to **come, has come**		
poem	[ˈpəʊəm]	Gedicht
riddle	[ˈrɪdl]	Rätsel
joke	[dʒəʊk]	Witz
Drop us a line!	[ˈdrɒp‿əz‿ə ˈlaɪn]	Schreib doch mal!
line		Zeile; Linie
kiss	[kɪs]	Kuß
Kevin goes red in the face.	[ˈkevɪn gəʊz ˈred ɪn ðə ˈfeɪs]	Kevin wird rot im Gesicht.
to **go red**		erröten, rot werden
crowded	[ˈkraʊdɪd]	überfüllt
motor	[ˈməʊtə]	Motor
tram	[træm]	Straßenbahn
to **wish**	[wɪʃ]	wünschen
meadow	[ˈmedəʊ]	Wiese
lamb	[læm]	Lamm
row	[rəʊ]	Reihe
smoke	[sməʊk]	Rauch
noise	[nɔɪz]	Lärm; Geräusch
wood(s)	[wʊd(z)]	*hier:* Wald
sky	[skaɪ]	Himmel
above	[əˈbʌv]	*hier:* oben
There is plenty of room.	[ˌðeər‿ɪz ˈplentɪ‿əv ˌru:m]	Es ist reichlich Platz.
plenty of	[plentɪ ɒf]	viel, eine Menge
cloud	[klaʊd]	Wolke
mouse/mice	[maʊs/meɪs]	Maus/Mäuse
rather	[rɑ:ðə]	ziemlich
tail	[teɪl]	Schwanz
chin	[tʃɪn]	Kinn
ear	[ɪə]	Ohr
tooth/teeth	[tu:θ/ti:θ]	Zahn/Zähne
to **nibble**	[ˈnɪbl]	knabbern
shouldn't (should not)	[ˈʃʊdnt (ʃʊd nɒt)]	sollte(n) nicht
to **touch**	[tʌtʃ]	anrühren; berühren
to **seem**	[si:m]	scheinen
end	[end]	Ende
sad	[sæd]	traurig
anywhere	[ˈenɪweə]	irgendwo
police station	[pəˈli:s‿ˌsteɪʃn]	(Polizei-)Wache
Hands up!	[ˈhændz‿ʌp]	Hände hoch!
rose	[rəʊz]	Rose
violet	[ˈvaɪələt]	Veilchen
sweet	[swi:t]	süß
So are you!	[ˈsəʊ‿ɑ: ˈjʊ]	*hier:* Du auch!
120,1 **expression**	[ɪkˈspreʃn]	Ausdruck
to **hope**	[həʊp]	hoffen
120,2 –		
120,3 to **act**	[ækt]	spielen; handeln

121,4 flower	[flaʊə]	Blume
121,5 noun	[naʊn]	Substantiv, Hauptwort
121,⟨6⟩ octopus	[ˈɒktəpʊs]	Krake
shade	[ʃeɪd]	Schatten
Let us in.	[ˈlet‿əs‿ˈɪn]	Laß(t) uns rein.
below	[bɪˈləʊ]	unter
hideaway	[ˈhaɪdəweɪ]	Versteck
beneath	[bɪˈni:θ]	unter
wave	[weɪv]	Welle
to rest	[rest]	(sich) ausruhen; ruhen
seabed	[ˈsi:ˌbed]	Meeresboden
cave	[keɪv]	Höhle
to dance	[dɑ:ns]	tanzen
We can't be found.	[wɪ ˈkɑ:nt bi: ˈfaʊnd]	Wir können nicht gefunden werden.
to shout	[ʃaʊt]	schreien
coral	[ˈkɒrəl]	Koralle(nriff)
joy	[dʒɔɪ]	Freude
to be safe	[ˈseɪf]	sicher sein
121,⟨7⟩ –		

Stopover B ⟨London⟩

122 coach	[kəʊtʃ]	Reisebus
student	[ˈstju:dənt]	Student, Schüler
the City of London	[ðə ˈsɪtɪ‿əv ˈlʌndən]	*der alte Stadtkern Londons*
record	[ˈrekəd]	Schallplatte
taxi	[ˈtæksɪ]	Taxi
to ask permission	[ˌɑ:sk pəˈmɪʃn]	um Erlaubnis bitten
dome	[dəʊm]	Kuppel
flag	[flæg]	Flagge, Fahne
own	[əʊn]	eigene(s)
123 tower	[ˈtaʊə]	Turm
bell	[bel]	Glocke
accurate	[ˈækjərət]	genau
pendulum	[ˈpendjʊləm]	Pendel
to take off	[ˌteɪk ˈɒf]	ab-, wegnehmen
second	[ˈsekənd]	Sekunde
slow	[sləʊ]	langsam
Beefeater	[ˈbi:fi:tə]	*Wächter im Tower of London*
to guard	[gɑ:d]	bewachen
raven	[ˈreɪvən]	Rabe
only	[ˈəʊnlɪ]	erst

[Unit 10]

A David's ticket to the USA

124 He has won the first prize.	[hɪ həz ˈwʌn ðə ˈfɜ:st ˈpraɪz]	Er hat den ersten Preis gewonnen.
to win, have/has won		
plane ticket	[ˈpleɪn ˌtɪkɪt]	Flugticket
plane		Flugzeug
hotel	[həʊˈtel]	Hotel
restaurant	[ˈrestərɒnt]	Restaurant

	sightseeing tour	[ˈsaɪtsiːɪŋ ˌtʊə]	(Stadt-)Rundfahrt
	They have paid for everything.	[ðaɪ həv ˈpeɪd fər‿ˈevrɪθɪŋ]	Sie haben alles bezahlt.
	to pay, have/has paid		(be-)zahlen
	to take off	[ˈteɪk ˈɒf]	*(Flugzeug:)* starten
124,1	–		
124,2	–		

B Henry Benson

125a)	There were a few surprises.	[ðeə ˌwɜːr‿ə ˈfjuː səˈpraɪzɪz]	Es gab einige Überraschungen.
	to be, was/were		
	We have family in America.	[wɪ həv ˈfæmɪlɪ‿ɪn‿əˈmerɪkə]	Wir haben Verwandte in Amerika.
	many years ago	[ˈmenɪ ˌjɪəz‿əˈgəʊ]	vor vielen Jahren
	to sail, sailed	[seɪl, seɪld]	segeln, segelte
b)	As far as I know, ...	[əz ˈfɑːr‿əz‿aɪ ˈnəʊ]	So weit ich weiß, ...
	No one knows.	[ˈnəʊ ˌwʌn ˈnəʊz]	Das weiß niemand.
	He didn't make enough money.	[hɪ ˈdɪdnt ˌmeɪk‿ɪˈnʌf ˈmʌnɪ]	Er hat nicht genug Geld verdient.
	to make money		Geld verdienen
	to travel	[ˈtrævəl]	reisen
	gold	[gəʊld]	Gold
126,1	expensive	[ɪkˈspensɪv]	teuer
126,2	–		
126,3	yesterday	[ˈjestəˌdeɪ]	gestern

C New York City

127a)	David woke up.	[ˈdeɪvɪd ˌwəʊk‿ˈʌp]	David wachte auf.
	to wake up, woke up		
	Then he knew.	[ˈðen ˌhɪ ˈnjuː]	Dann wußte er es (wieder).
	to know, knew		
	He went to the window.	[hɪ ˈwent‿tə ðə ˈwɪndəʊ]	Er ging ans Fenster.
	to go, went		
	He stood there for a minute.	[hɪ ˈstʊd ðeə fər‿ə ˈmɪnɪt]	Dort stand er einen Moment (lang).
	to stand, stood		
	He ran to the bathroom.	[hɪ ˈræn tə ðə ˈbɑːθrʊm]	Er lief ins Bad(ezimmer).
	to run, ran		
	He had a trip round Manhattan.	[hɪ ˈhæd‿ə ˈtrɪp ˌraʊnd ˌmænˈhætn]	Er machte eine Rundfahrt durch Manhattan.
	to have, had		
	The tour bus drove up.	[ðə ˈtʊə ˌbʌs drəʊv‿ˈʌp]	Der Bus für die Rundfahrt fuhr vor.
	to drive (up), drove (up)		
	David got on.	[ˈdeɪvɪd ˌgɒt‿ˈɒn]	David stieg ein.
	to get (on), got (on)		
	He ate at the restaurant.	[hɪ‿ˈeɪt‿ət ðə ˈrestərɒnt]	Er aß im Restaurant.
	to eat, ate	[iːt, eɪt/et]	
	center	[ˈsentə]	Zentrum *(amerik. Schreibweise)*
b)	David took the boat trip around Manhattan.	[ˈdeɪvɪd ˌtʊk ðə ˈbəʊt‿ˌtrɪp‿əˈraʊnd mænˈhætn]	David machte die Bootsfahrt um Manhattan herum.
	to take, took		
	He bought some postcards.	[hɪ ˈbɔːt səm ˈpəʊstkɑːdz]	Er kaufte einige Postkarten.
	to buy, bought		

He found a place in the park.	[hɪ ˈfaʊnd‿ə ˈpleɪs‿ɪn ðə ˈpɑːk]	Er fand einen Platz im Park.
to find, found		
He sat down.	[hɪ ˈsæt ˈdaʊn]	Er setzte sich.
to sit, sat		
He began to write.	[hɪ bɪˈgæn tə ˈraɪt]	Er fing zu schreiben an.
to begin, began		
to count, counted	[kaʊnt, kaʊntɪd]	zählen, zählte
128,1 –		
128,2 –		
128,3 –		
128,4 –		

D Silicon Valley

129 The hotel bus picked him up.	[ðə ˌhəʊˈtel ˈbʌs pɪkt hɪm‿ˈʌp]	Der Hotelbus holte ihn ab.
to pick up		abholen; aufheben
downtown	[ˌdaʊnˈtaʊn]	in der (Innen-)Stadt
guest	[gest]	Gast
company	[ˈkʌmpənɪ]	Firma, Gesellschaft
department	[dɪˈpɑːtmənt]	Abteilung
popular	[ˈpɒpjʊlə]	beliebt, weitverbreitet
ten miles wide	[ˈten ˈmaɪlz ˈwaɪd]	zehn Meilen breit
mile		Meile *(ca. 1,6 km)*
wide		weit, breit
electronics	[ɪˌlekˈtrɒnɪks]	Elektronik
World War II	[ˈwɜːld ˈwɔː ˈtuː]	der Zweite Weltkrieg
garage	[ˈgærɑːʒ]	Garage
to grow, grew	[grəʊ, gruː]	wachsen, wuchs
inventor	[ɪnˈventə]	Erfinder
transistor	[trænˈzɪstə]	Transistor
microelectronic	[ˌmaɪkrəʊɪlekˈtrɒnɪk]	mikroelektronisch
high-tech	[ˈhaɪ ˈtek]	Spitzentechnologie
communication	[kəˌmjuːnɪˈkeɪʃn]	Kommunikation
to spend, spent	[spend, spent]	*hier:* verbringen, verbrachte
He even understood it.	[hɪ‿ˈiːvən‿ʌnderˈstʊd‿ɪt]	Er verstand es sogar.
to understand, understood		verstehen, verstand
chip	[tʃɪp]	Chip
He met Jan.	[ˌhɪ met ˈdʒæn]	Er traf Jan.
to meet, met		(sich) treffen, traf
130,1 –		
130,2 hardware	[ˈhɑːdweə]	Hardware
130,3 –		

E Jan Benson

131a) He won a trip.	[hɪ ˈwʌn‿ə ˈtrɪp]	Er hat eine Reise gewonnen.
to win, won		
a good sense of humour	[ə ˈgʊd ˌsens‿əv ˈhjuːmə]	viel Sinn für Humor
president of the Benson Corporation	[ˈpresɪdənt‿əv ðə ˈbensn ˌkɔːpəˈreɪʃn]	Geschäftsführer(in) der Firma Benson
president		Präsident(in); Direktor(in); Geschäftsführer(in)
corporation		Gesellschaft, GmbH
business	[bɪznɪs]	Geschäft, Betrieb
Sure!	[ʃʊə]	Sicher!/Klar!
Yep!	[jep]	Ja!/Klar!

	I'm the only employee.	[ˈaɪm ðɪ‿ˈəʊnlɪ‿ɪmplɔɪˈiː]	Ich bin der/die einzige Angestellte.
	the only ...		der/die/das einzige ...
	employee		Angestellte(r)
	to train	[treɪn]	ausbilden
	boss	[bɒs]	Chef, Boß
	to work hard	[hɑːd]	hart arbeiten
	I'm not allowed to do it.	[aɪm ˈnɒt‿əˈlaʊd‿tə ˈduː‿ɪt]	Ich darf es nicht (tun).
	(not) to be allowed to		etwas (nicht) tun dürfen
b)	He told her about the trip.	[hɪ ˈtəʊld hɜːr‿əˈbaʊt ðə ˈtrɪp]	Er hat ihr von der Fahrt erzählt.
	to tell, told		
	schedule	[ˈʃedjuːl/*Am:* ˈskedjuːl]	Programm, Zeitplan
	angry, angrily	[ˈæŋgrɪ, ˈæŋgrɪlɪ]	ärgerlich *(adj. + adv.)*
	You aren't able to see the city.	[juː‿ˈɑːnt‿eɪbl tə ˈsiː ðə ˈsɪtɪ]	Du kannst dir die Stadt nicht ansehen.
	not to be able to		etwas nicht können
	She came back soon.	[ˌʃɪ ˈkeɪm ˈbæk ˈsuːn]	Sie kam bald zurück.
	to come, came		
	smile	[smaɪl]	Lächeln
	customer	[ˈkʌstəmə]	Kunde
	favorite	[ˈfeɪvrɪt]	Lieblings- *(amerik. Schreibweise)*
	happy, happily	[ˈhæpɪ, ˈhæpɪlɪ]	glücklich *(adj. + adv.)*
	grandmother	[ˈgrænˌmʌðə]	Großmutter
131,1	—		
132,2	—		
132,3	—		
132,4	—		

F The party on the beach

133a)	He got a phone call.	[hɪ ˈgɒt‿ə ˈfəʊn ˌkɔːl]	Er bekam einen Anruf.
	grandparents	[ˈgrænˌpeərənts]	Großeltern
	grandfather	[ˈgrænˌfɑːðə]	Großvater
	the whole family	[ðə ˈhəʊl ˈfæmɪlɪ]	die ganze Familie
	if	[ɪf]	wenn, falls
	picnic	[ˈpɪknɪk]	Picknick
	niece	[niːs]	Nichte
	nephew	[ˈnefjuː]	Neffe
	a rock concert	[ə ˈrɒk ˌkɒnsət]	ein Rockkonzert
	to save	[seɪv]	retten
b)	to turn on (a light)	[ˈtɜːn ˈɒn]	(ein Licht) einschalten
	to shut, shut	[ʃʌt]	schließen, schloß
	to choose	[tʃuːz]	wählen
	He's going to quit his job.	[hiːz ˈgəʊɪŋ tə ˈkwɪt hɪz ˈdʒɒb]	Er hat vor, seine Stelle aufzugeben.
	to quit		aufgeben; kündigen
134,1	—		
134,2	—		
134,3	land	[lænd]	Land
	Redwood Forest	[ˈredwʊd ˈfɒrɪst]	Redwood-Wald *(am. Rotholz)*
	It was made for you.	[ɪt wəz ˈmeɪd fə ˈjuː]	Es wurde für dich geschaffen.
	ribbon	[ˈrɪbən]	Band
	highway	[ˈhaɪˌweɪ]	Haupt(verkehrs)straße; Highway
	endless	[ˈendlɪs]	endlos
	skyway	[ˈskaɪˌweɪ]	Himmel, Himmelstraße
	below	[bɪˈləʊ]	unter
	golden	[ˈgəʊldən]	golden
	valley	[ˈvælɪ]	Tal

Alphabetical word list

– Die Zahlen verweisen auf das erstmalige Vorkommen der Wörter,
z.B. **and 1A** 9b) = Unit 1A, Seite 9, Teil b)
abroad StA 87,3 = Stopover A, Seite 87, Übung 3
– Die Grundzahlen, Ordnungszahlen, Wochentage und Monatsnamen sind hier nicht aufgeführt.

A

B

C

class 5C 63a)
classroom 1B 13
clean 3C 36a)
clever 5C 63a)
cliff 5E 67b)
to **climb 4E** 54b)
clock 7D 94
clothes 2A 21c)
cloud 9D 119
club 2C 23
coach *Reisebus* **7F** 98,5
coach *Trainer* **2D** 24
coast 7A 88
coffee 2G 32,2
coin 5B 62,5
coke 2C 23b)
colour 4C 51
column 4E 57,7
to **come 1B** 11b)
to **come down 4E** 54b)
to **come in 1B** 11a)
Come on! 1F 17
comfortable 7F 97b)
⟨communication 10D 129⟩
⟨company 10D 129⟩
⟨company StA 85⟩
to **compare 5A** 59,1
competition 8A 100a)
to **complete 1E** 16,3
comprehension 1F 18,6
comprehensive school 6A 70a)
computer 5A 58a)
concert 6F 80
congratulations 8F 111b)
⟨to control 8E 109⟩
copy 6D 76a)
⟨coral 9D 121,6⟩
corner 2A 21c)
⟨corporation 10E 131a)⟩
to **correct 6B** 73,2
correct (adj) 4E 57,7
⟨to count 10C 127b)⟩
counter 5A 59b)
country 7A 88
crazy 4E 54b)
crisps 9C 117b)
to **cross 8C** 105
crossroads 8C 105
crowded 9D 119
cup 1D 14
Cup Final 8A 100b)
cupboard 2A 21c)
⟨customer 10E 131b)⟩
to **cycle 7F** 96a)

D

Dad 1D 14
⟨to dance 9D 121,6⟩
dangerous 4E 54b)
dark 4D 52a)
date *Datum* **6D** 76a)
date *Verabredung* **6F** 81b)
all **day 3F** 43c)
day 3F 42b)
⟨to deal with StA 87,1⟩
dear 7B 91,2
⟨department 10D 129⟩
to **describe 2B** 22,4
desk 1C 12
dialogue 1F 18,3
difference 6F 82,5
different (from) 6A 70a)
difficult 4E 54a)
dining room 2A 20b)
dirty 7F 97b)
disco 2F 29a)
to **discuss 9A** 114
⟨discussion StA 86⟩
diskette 5E 69,5
to **do 2C** 23,1
docks 2F 29b)
doctor 3D 38b)
does/doesn't 6B 72b)
dog 1E 15
⟨dome StB 122⟩
door 2A 20b)
double 3F 43,2
down 4E 54b)
downstairs 1B 11
⟨downtown 10D 129⟩
drink 3C 36a)
to **drink 5E** 69,5
to **drive (off) 8C** 105
⟨to drive (up) 10C 127a)⟩
⟨driver 8E 109⟩
Drop us a line! 9D 119

E

each 3D 38a)
ear 9D 119
early 7D 94,2
earth 4A 46a)
⟨to eat 10C 127b)⟩
egg 5E 67b)
⟨electronics 10D 129⟩
⟨emergency 4E 56,6⟩
employee 10E 131a)
end 9D 119
to **end 9A** 114
⟨engine StA 85⟩
English 1A 8a)
to **enjoy 7A** 88a)
enough 2G 31a)
envelope 8F 112,4
⟨environment StA 84⟩
environmental 8A 101c)
etc. 3F 44,3
⟨European StA 85⟩
even 2F 29a)
evening 2C 23
event 8A 100a)
every 3A 33
everybody 2C 23a)
everyone 6C 74b)
everything 4A 48,4
exact 7D 94
example 2C 24,2
excited 9A 114
exciting 4E 54a)
to **excuse 5D** 64a)
exercise 1C 12
exercise book 1C 12
exhibition 8A 100a)
⟨expensive 10B 126,1⟩
to **explain 3F** 45,8
expression 9D 120,1
eye 3E 40a)

F

⟨face StA 84⟩
face 9D 119
⟨to fall 2E 28,5⟩
family 4E 56,5
famous 5E 66b)
fan 3A 33
fantastic 6D 76a)
far 3D 38a)
farewell 9A 114
farm 4E 56,5
fast 5E 66a)
father 3A 33,1
favourite 6A 70b)
festival 2F 29a)
to **fetch 3D** 38a)
a **few 5A** 59c)
few 5D 64a)
field 2E 26
figure 7F 97b)
film 4B 50,2
to **find 2C** 23b)
fine 5A 58a)
to **finish 9A** 114
⟨fire 4E 56,6⟩
fireman/men 4E 54b)
first 1F 18,4
first name 1F 18,4
first *zuerst* **3C** 36a)
⟨flag StB 122⟩
flat *Wohnung* **8F** 110a)
flight 9A 114
floor 3D 38b)
flower 9D 121,4
⟨to fly StA 84⟩
to **fly 9A** 114
to **follow 8F** 113,1
following 5E 68,4
food 3C 36a)
football 2C 23b)
for 1C 12
for example 5A 59b)
to **forget 9B** 116,3
form *Form* **6F** 83,8
free 2G 31b)
French 6A 70b)
friend 1E 15
friendly 5A 58a)
⟨frog StA 84⟩
from 1A 8a)
from ... to 7B 90
front door 2A 20b)
fruit 5A 59b)
full 8C 105
full of 5E 67b)
fun 5A 58a)
funny 7A 88a)
⟨future 8E 109⟩

G

game 3A 33
⟨garage 10D 129⟩
garden 1E 15
geography 6D 76a)
German 1A 9c)
to **get 5A** 59,2
to **get into 8C** 105
to **get on 7F** 96a)
to **get to** *hinkommen* **7B** 90
to **get up 7F** 96a)
ghost 7F 97b)
girl 1F 17
girlfriend 2G 31b)
to **give 2C** 23a)
glass 1D 14
glue 5A 59c)
to **go (to) 2C** 23a)
to **go home 3F** 42b)
to **go on 1A** 9c)
to **go out 6F** 81b)
to **go red 9D** 119
to **go shopping 3F** 43c)
⟨gold 10B 125b)⟩
good 2C 23a)
Good afternoon 8D 107
Good luck! 9C 117a)
Good morning 6D 76a)
Good night 7F 97b)
Goodbye 5C 63b)
⟨grandfather 10F 133a)⟩
⟨grandmother 10E 131b)⟩
⟨grandparents 10F 133a)⟩
graphics 5C 63a)
great 5E 66a)
⟨green 2E 28,5⟩
green 4C 51,1
grey 4C 51,1
group 2D 24
⟨to grow 10D 129⟩
⟨to guard StB 123⟩
⟨guest 10D 129⟩
guide 8A 100a)
gym 3A 33

H

half a pound 5A 59c)
half past 3D 38b)
hall *Flur* **2A** 20b)
ham 6E 78a)
hamburger 2F 29c)
hand 3E 40b)
Hands up! 9D 119
⟨to hang 2E 28,5⟩
to **happen 4E** 54a)
⟨happily 10E 131b)⟩
happy 7F 97b)
harbour 5E 67b)
hard 9A 114

⟨hardware 10 D 130,2⟩
to **hate 6 D** 76 a)
haunted 7 F 97 b)
to **have** a coke **2 C** 23 b)
Have a good time! 6 F 81 b)
to **have** a hamburger **2 F** 29 c)
to **have got 2 B** 21 a)
he 1 A 8 a)
⟨headline St A 86⟩
to **hear 4 D** 52 a)
hello 1 A 9 b)
to **help 3 C** 36 b)
her 1 B 11 b)
her *Objektfall* **3 C** 36 b)
here 1 A 9 b)
Here you are. 1 D 14
Hey! 2 E 26,1
Hi! 2 G 31 b)
⟨hideaway 9 D 121,6⟩
⟨high-tech 10 D 129⟩
hill 7 F 96 a)
him 3 C 36 b)
his 1 B 11 a)
history 6 D 76 a)
hockey 2 D 24
to **hold 4 E** 54 b)
⟨holidays St A 84⟩
holiday(s) 9 C 117 a)
home 3 F 42 b)
at **home 1 F** 17
home economics 6 D 76 b)
homework 4 A 46 a)
to **hope 9 D** 120,1
hospital 3 E 40
hot 6 F 82,4
⟨hotel 10 A 124⟩
hour 9 B 115 b)
house 1 B 11 a)
how 1 E 15
how about ... ? 5 E 66 a)
how long? 6 A 70 b)
how many? 2 B 21 b)
how much? 5 B 60 a)
hungry 6 F 82,4
to **hurry (up) 3 D** 38 a)

I

I 1 A 9 c)
I'd like to 2 C 23 a)
I'd love to 6 F 80 a)
I'm 1 A 9 c)
ice-cream 6 E 78 a)
idea 2 C 23 a)
⟨if 2 E 28,5⟩
⟨if 10 F 133 a)⟩
to **imagine 8 F** 110 a)
⟨important St A 84⟩
important 8 A 100 a)
in 1 7
in front of 1 E 15
⟨including St A 86⟩
indirect object 5 D 65,3
indoor 3 A 33
information 4 D 53,3
information stand 4 D 53,3
interested in 2 F 29 b)
interesting 2 F 29 d)
interview 8 D 108,2
into 2 G 31 a)
⟨inventor 10 D 129⟩
invitation 4 B 49
to **invite 9 B** 115 b)
is 1 7
island 5 E 66
isn't 1 A 9 b)
it 1 7
It's me. 1 E 15
its 4 D 52 b)

J

jeans 6 A 70 a)
job *Arbeit* **2 D** 24
job *Aufgabe* **4 E** 54 b)
to **join 2 D** 24
joke 9 D 119
journey 7 F 97,1
⟨joy 9 D 121,6⟩
judo 3 A 33
juice 6 E 78 a)
Just a minute! 3 D 38 a)
just *gerade* **8 F** 110 a)
just *nur* **6 A** 70 b)

K

to **keep 3 C** 36 a)
key 4 D 52 b)
kiss 9 D 119
kitchen 2 A 20 b)
to **knock 6 F** 81 b)
to **know 4 A** 48,4

L

ladder 4 D 52 b)
lady 8 D 107
lamb 9 D 119
⟨land 10 F 134,3⟩
language 7 A 88 a)
large 2 F 29 a)
last 8 B 103 b)
late 1 D 14
later 3 D 38 a)
to **laugh 7 F** 97 b)
to **learn 3 A** 33
to **leave** *lassen* **4 D** 52 b)
to **leave** *verlassen* **5 E** 67 b)
on the **left 2 A** 19 a)
to turn **left 8 C** 105
leg 3 D 38 b)
lesson 6 A 70 b)
let's 2 C 23 a)
letter *Brief* **3 D** 38 a)
letter *Buchstabe* **3 F** 43,2
⟨library St A 86⟩
to **lie 3 F** 43 c)
light 4 D 52 b)
like 2 A 19 a)
to **like 6 A** 70 b)
Drop us **line! 9 D** 119
to **link 4 E** 57,7
list 4 B 49
to **listen (to) 1 A** 12,4
a **little 5 D** 64 b)
little 1 B 11 a)
little *wenig* **5 D** 64 a)
to **live 7 B** 90
living room 2 A 20 b)
loaf/loaves 5 A 59 c)
local 5 A 58 a)
to **lock 4 D** 52 b)
⟨lonely 7 E 95,1⟩
long 3 B 35,4
a **long way** *weit* **5 E** 66 a)
to **look 1 A** 12,4
to **look at 1 E** 15
to have **a look at 7 B** 90
to **look for 5 E** 68,4
loose 4 E 54 b)
lorry 2 A 19 a)
a **lot of 2 A** 19 a)
lots of 8 A 100 b)
to **love 6 D** 76 a)
love *Schatz* **4 B** 49
love *Viele Grüße* **7 C** 92
lovely 1 E 15
lucky 6 A 70 b)
lunch 6 A 70 b)

M

magazine 4 D 52 a)
to **make 2 C** 23,1
to **make a cake 4 A** 46 a)
⟨to make money 10 B 125 b)⟩
to **make up 2 A** 20
make-up 6 F 80 b)
man/men 1 F 18,6
many 5 B 60 a)
map 5 E 67 b)
market 7 B 90
to **match 6 B** 72,1
match *Spiel* **3 C** 36 a)
maths 6 D 76 a)
What's the **matter? 3 D** 38 b)
may 3 B 34 b)
Me, too. 8 F 110
meadow 9 D 119
meaning 6 F 83,8
to **meet 1 D** 14
meeting 4 D 53,3
member 3 A 33
menu 6 E 78 a)
mess 9 A 114
message 4 D 52
⟨microelectronic 10 D 129⟩
⟨mile 10 D 129⟩
milk 1 D 14
minute 2 C 23 a)
mirror 6 F 80 b)
to **miss** *verfehlen* **8 C** 105
missing 4 E 55,1
mixed 6 E 78 a)
modern 2 G 31 b)
Just a **moment. 4 B** 49
at the **moment 2 D** 24
on **Mondays 6 D** 76 a)
money 5 B 62,5
monitor 5 A 58 a)
month 5 D 64 a)
more 5 D 64 b)
in the **morning 3 F** 43 c)
most 6 A 70 a)
mother 3 E 40 a)
motor 9 D 119
mountain 7 A 88 a)
mouse/mice 9 D 119
to **move 3 D** 38 b)
Mr 1 A 8 a)
Mrs 1 A 8 a)
Ms 6 D 76 a)
much 5 B 60 a)
Mum 1 B 11 b)
museum 7 A 89 b)
music 2 F 29 c)
must/mustn't 3 B 34 b)
my 1 A 9 b)

N

name 1 A 9 c)
nasty 4 D 52 a)
National Park 7 A 88 a)
near 2 G 31 a)
nearly 8 D 107
to **need 9 B** 115 b)
⟨to need St A 84⟩
needn't 3 B 34 a)
neighbour 1 F 17
⟨nephew 10 F 133 a)⟩
nest 5 E 67 b)
never 6 A 70 b)
Never mind! 8 F 110 a)
new 1 C 12
news 8 A 100 a)
newspaper 2 C 23 a)
the **next 2 G** 31 a)
next door 4 B 49
next to 1 B 11 a)
to **nibble 9 D** 119
nice 1 B 11 a)
⟨niece 10 F 133 a)⟩
at **night 4 D** 52 b)
all **night 4 D** 52 b)
nightdress 7 F 97 b)
no 1 A 9 b)
no *keine* **2 A** 19 a)
⟨no one 10 B 125 b)⟩
nobody 5 B 60 b)
⟨noise St A 84⟩
noise 9 A 114
noisy 9 A 114 a)
normal 7 C 93,2
normally 6 A 70 a)
not 1 A 10,1 b)
not ... yet 9 B 116 b)
to **note down 6 E** 79,4
note *Schein* **5 B** 62,5

ote *Zettel* **1 C** 12
otebook 1 C 12
othing (else) 5 B 60 b)
otice-board 3 C 36 a)
oun 9 D 121,5
ow 2 A 20
umber *Nummer* **2 A** 19 a)
umber *Zahl* **4 C** 51
urse 3 E 40

)

'clock 3 D 38 a)
dd one out 6 F 83,8
f 1 D 14
f course 1 E 15
ffer 5 C 63 b)
ɔ **offer 5 C** 63 b)
ften 6 A 70 b)
h 1 B 11 a)
)h dear! 3 F 42 b)
)K 1 A 9 b)
ld 1 C 12
n 1 C 12
n time 7 D 94
n TV 2 C 23 a)
nly 2 A 21 c)
the **only** 10 E 131 a)⟩
pen 2 D 24
ɔ **open 4 D** 52 b)
)pen Day 8 A 100 b)
pen-air 8 A 100 a)
operator 4 E 56,6⟩
opinion St A 84⟩
pposite 4 E 57,9
r 1 D 14
range 1 C 12
range *Farbe* **4 C** 51,1
rder *Reihenfolge* **6 E** 79,2
o **organize 9 A** 114 b)
ther 2 A 21 c)
)ther kinds of 5 A 59 b)
Ouch! 3 D 38 b)
)ur 1 B 11 a)
)ut 4 D 52 a)
)utdoor 3 A 33
outdoors 3 A 33
)utside 3 F 42 a)
over 3 E 40 a)
)ver *zu Ende* **7 C** 93,3
over there 2 E 26
Over to you! 1 A 9 c)
own 7 F 97,1

P

p (pence) 5 A 59 c)
packet 5 A 59 c)
page 1 E 15,1
painful 3 E 40 b)
pair 3 F 45,7
⟨paper St A 84⟩
paragraph 8 B 104,4
park 2 F 29 a)
part 4 E 55,3
partner 1 E 15,1
party 4 E 54 a)
half **past 3 D** 38 b)
past *vorbei an* **8 C** 105
patient 3 E 40
⟨to pay 10 A 124⟩
PC 5 A 58 a)
PE (Physical Education) 6 D 76 a)
pen 1 C 12
pencil 1 C 12
⟨pendulum St B 123⟩
people 2 F 29 a)
per cent 8 A 100 a)
perhaps 5 D 65,4
⟨permission St B 122⟩
phone 4 B 49
photo 1 E 15
phrase 3 A 33,2
physics 6 D 76 b)
⟨to pick up 10 D 129⟩
⟨picnic 10 F 133 a)⟩
picture 1 E 15,1
piece 1 D 14
pink 4 C 51,1
place 2 A 21 c)
plan 4 B 50,2
⟨to plan St A 86⟩
⟨plane 10 A 124⟩
⟨plane ticket 10 A 124⟩
plate 1 C 12
platform 7 F 96 a)
to **play 2 C** 23 b)
player 3 C 36 a)
playground 6 F 80 a)
please 1 A 9 b)
pleased 7 F 96 a)
plenty (of) 9 D 119
plural 2 A 19,1
pocket 6 F 80 b)
poem 9 D 119
police 4 D 52
policeman 4 E 54 b)
policewoman 4 E 54 b)
police station 9 D 119
⟨politician St A 86⟩
pollution 8 A 101 c)
⟨pond St A 84⟩
pop concert 6 F 80
⟨popular 10 D 129⟩
position 6 F 83,6
post office 5 A 58 a)
postcard 4 A 48,5
poster 2 A 21 c)
pound *Geld* **5 A** 59 c)
pound *Gewicht* **5 A** 59 c)
powerboat 8 A 101 b)
practice 6 A 70 b)
to **practise 4 E** 54 a)
preposition 7 F 98,4
present 5 D 65,4
present perfect 9 B 116,1
⟨president 10 E 131 a)⟩
price 5 A 58 a)
prize 8 A 100 a)
⟨probably 8 E 109⟩
problem 8 A 101 c)
program 5 C 63 a)
programme 2 C 23 a)
pronoun 3 C 37,4
to **pronounce 6 F** 83,8
pronunciation 9 B 116,1
⟨the pros and cons St A 87,1⟩
pudding 6 E 78 a)
puffin 5 E 66 b)
pullover 6 A 70 a)
pupil 6 A 70 a)
purple 4 C 51,1
to **put 1 A** 9 b)
to **put in 2 C** 23,1
to **put on 3 F** 42 b)
to **put up 4 A** 47 b)

Q

a **quarter past 3 D** 38 a)
a **quarter to 3 D** 38 b)
question 2 F 30,2
⟨question tag 7 E 95,1⟩
quick 8 C 105
quiet 2 A 19 a)
⟨to quit 10 F 133 b)⟩
quite 7 B 90
quiz 1 F 18,4

R

radio 2 A 21 c)
on the **radio 2 C** 23 a)
radio station 8 A 100 a)
to **rain 7 F** 96 a)
⟨rainbow 4 C 51,2⟩
raincoat 8 F 110 a)
⟨raven St B 123⟩
RE (Religious Education) 6 D 76 b)
to **read 3 C** 36 a)
ready 3 D 38 a)
really 4 E 54 b)
⟨record St B 122⟩
red 1 F 17
⟨redwood 10 F 134,3⟩
to **remember 4 D** 53,2
to **repair 4 E** 54 a)
⟨to rest 9 D 121,6⟩
⟨restaurant 10 A 124⟩
result 8 F 110 a)
to **retell 9 A** 115,2
return ticket 7 F 96 a)
to **rhyme 6 F** 83,7
riddle 9 D 119
to **ride 7 B** 90
right 2 F 30,1
to be **right 4 E** 54 b)
on the **right 2 A** 19 a)
to turn **right 8 C** 105
to **ring 4 B** 49
river 7 A 89 b)
road 2 A 19
⟨a rock concert 10 F 133 a)⟩
role 3 D 39,5
role play 3 B 35,3
romantic 5 A 59 c)
roof 4 E 54 b)
room 1 B 11 a)
rose 9 D 119
round 3 E 40 b)
route 8 F 113,1
row 9 D 119
rules 3 C 36 a)
to **run 8 F** 110 a)

S

David'**s** *Genitiv* **1 B** 11 a)
sad 9 D 119
⟨safe 9 D 121,6⟩
⟨to sail 10 B 125 a)⟩
salad 6 E 78 a)
sale 8 B 103,2
sandwich 1 D 14
sandy 7 A 88 a)
⟨satellite St A 85⟩
sausage 6 E 78 a)
⟨to save 10 F 133 a)⟩
saxophone 2 A 21 c)
to **say 1 A** 12,4
scenery 7 A 88 a)
⟨schedule 10 E 131 b)⟩
(to) **school 3 E** 40 b)
school 2 A 21 c)
school book 2 A 21 c)
school dress 6 A 70 a)
schoolbag 7 B 91,3
score 3 D 38 b)
sea 5 E 66 a)
⟨seabed 9 D 121,6⟩
seaside 5 A 58 a)
seat 2 G 31 b)
seat belt 8 C 105
⟨second St B 123⟩
second *zweiter* **6 D** 77,1
second-hand 5 C 63 b)
secret 6 F 80 a)
to **see 2 C** 23 a)
See you later. 5 C 63 b)
to **seem 9 D** 119
to **sell 5 A** 59 b)
⟨sense of humour 10 E 131 a)⟩
sentence 2 C 23,1
⟨service 4 E 56,6⟩
⟨shade 9 D 121,6⟩
she 1 A 8 a)
shed 4 D 54 a)
sheep 7 F 96 a)
sheepdog 7 F 96 a)
shelf/shelves 2 A 21 c)
ship 2 F 29 b)
shirt 6 A 70 a)
shoe 2 A 21 c)
shop 2 F 29 d)
shop assistant 5 C 63 b)
shopping centre 2 F 29 d)
short 3 B 35,2
⟨should 2 E 28,5⟩
shouldn't 9 D 119

⟨to shout 9D 121,6⟩
to **show 4E** 54a)
show 8A 101c)
shower 6F 80b)
to **shut 4D** 52a)
⟨sightseeing tour 10A 124⟩
sign 8C 106,2
simple 8B 103b)
⟨to sing 2E 28,5⟩
⟨to sing along 4C 51,2⟩
single ticket 7F 96a)
sister 7C 93,3
to **sit 1D** 14
to **sit down 2G** 31b)
skirt 6A 70a)
sky 9D 119
to **sleep 7F** 97b)
Sleep well! 7F 97b)
sleeping bag 7F 97b)
slogan 5A 59,1
⟨slow St B 123⟩
small 1B 11c)
⟨smile 10E 131b)⟩
smoke 9D 119
snack 2F 29c)
snack bar 6C 75,1
so *also* **3D** 38a)
so *wirklich* **4B** 49
sofa 2A 20b)
software 5D 64b)
some 2A 19a)
somebody 4E 54a)
someone 7F 97b)
something 2C 23,1
sometimes 6A 70b)
⟨song 2E 28,5⟩
soon 9C 117a)
I'm **sorry 2D** 24
south 7A 89b)
to **speak 3F** 43c)
speaking 4B 49
special 4D 52a)
spectator 3C 36a)
to **spell 3F** 42a)
⟨to spend 6F 83,9⟩
sport(s) 2C 23a)
sports centre 2D 24
sports field 2E 26
sprained 3E 40a)
spring 8A 100b)
square 8C 105
stadium 8A 100b)
stamp 5A 59b)
stand 4E 53,3
to **stand 7F** 97b)
star 8F 111b)
to **start 3A** 33
statement 6D 77,1
station 6E 78a)
statue 8C 105
stay 9A 114
to **stay 3E** 40b)
steamer 2F 29b)
still *noch* **4E** 54a)
to **stop 3D** 38b)
storm 4B 49
story 6F 82,4
straight on 8C 105
stranger 4D 52b)
street 2A 19a)
strict 6A 70a)
strong 4E 54b)
⟨student St B 122⟩
subject 6D 76a)
suburb 2A 19a)
sugar 1D 14
suitcase 1A 9b)
summer 8A 100b)
sun 5A 58a)
super 7B 90
⟨supermarket St A 87,1⟩
supper 9B 116,2
I'm **sure 2D** 24
⟨Sure! 10E 131a)⟩
surprise 5E 67b)
surprised 8C 105
sweet 9D 119
sweets 7C 93,3
to **swim 8A** 100b)
swimming baths 8A 101c)
swimming championships 8A 100b)
Swiss 1A 9c)
to **switch off 4D** 52b)
to **switch on 4D** 52b)

T

table 1D 14
table-tennis 2C 23b)
to **take a bus 3D** 38a)
to **take a shower 6F** 80b)
⟨to take off St B 123⟩
⟨to take off 10A 124⟩
to **take out 4E** 54a)
to **take place 8A** 100a)
to **talk about 3B** 34a)
to **talk to 3A** 33
tall 9D 119
tea 1D 14
tea-time 1B 11b)
teacher 1A 9b)
team 2D 24
⟨technician St A 84⟩
technology 8F 111b)
teeth 9D 119
to **(tele)phone 4E** 54a)
telephone 4B 49
to **tell 4D** 52b)
tennis 2C 23a)
text 2A 20
than 8B 103a)
Thanks a lot. 4A 47b)
Thanks. 1B 11a)
that 2C 23a)
that *daß* **5E** 67b)
the 1A 9b)
their 1E 15
them 3C 36b)
then 3D 38b)
there 2D 24
there are 2A 19a)
there is 1C 12
⟨there'd be 2E 28,5⟩
these 2E 26
they 1E 15
thing 2A 21c)
to **think 5E** 69,5
thirsty 6F 82,4
this 1 7
this evening 2C 23a)
those 2E 26
through 5E 67b)
ticket 6F 80
tidy 9A 114b)
to **tidy up 9A** 114
tie 6A 70a)
time 2F 29c)
What **time is it? 3D** 39,4
timetable *Fahrplan* **7D** 94,1
timetable *Stundenplan* **6D** 76
tired 9B 116,2
title 4E 55,3
to 2C 23a)
toast 6F 82,4
today 2G 31a)
together 4E 55,2
toilet 1B 11a)
tomorrow 3F 43c)
tonight 6F 81b)
too *auch* **1A** 8a)
too much 5D 64a)
to **touch 9D** 119
tourist 2G 31b)
⟨tower St B 123⟩
in **town 1F** 17
town 1F 17
traffic 5B 60b)
traffic lights 8C 105
train 5E 66a)
by **train 7B** 90
⟨to train 10E 131a)⟩
training 5C 63a)
tram 9D 119
⟨transistor 10D 129⟩
⟨to travel 10B 125b)⟩
tree 1E 15
trip 7B 90
trousers 6A 70a)
to **try 3D** 38b)
T-shirt 4D 53,3
to turn into 8C 105
TV 2A 20b)
twin town 8A 100a)

U

umbrella 8F 110a)
uncle 7B 90
under 1E 15
⟨to understand 10D 129⟩
unhappy 3F 43c)
uniform 6A 70a)
unit 1 7
until 5C 63b)
up 4E 54b)
upstairs 1B 11
us 2G 31b)
to **use 3C** 36a)
usually 6A 70b)

V

verb 2C 23,1
very 2A 21c)
violet 9D 119
visit 8A 100
to **visit 7A** 88a)
visitor 8B 103b)
voice 8F 111b)
volleyball 2D 24

W

to **wait (for) 3F** 42a)
waiting room 3E 40
waitress 2G 31b)
to **wake up 7F** 96a)
to **walk 3E** 40a)
wall 2A 21c)
to **want 6B** 72b)
Wanted! 5C 63b)
wardrobe 2A 21c)
watch 9B 115a)
to **watch 2C** 23a)
⟨wave 9D 121,6⟩
way 4B 49
on the **way 4B** 49
we 1B 11a)
to **wear 3A** 33
weather 4B 49
week 3F 42b)
weekend 4D 52a)
to **welcome 1** 7
well *(adv.)* **7F** 97b)
well, *nun, tja* **3D** 38b)
Welsh 7A 88a)
West 2A 19a)
wet 8F 110b)
what? 1A 9c)
what about ... ? 2G 31a)
what else ... ? 6C 74b)
what on earth ... ? 5E 66a)
What's the matter? 3D 38b)
when? 3F 43,1
when *(conj.)* **4D** 52b)
where? 1A 9c)
while 6F 80a)
white 3C 36b)
who? 1E 15
⟨the whole family 10F 133a)⟩
whose? 7B 90
Why (not)? 3A 33
⟨wide 10D 129⟩
to **win 8A** 100a)
wind 4D 52a)
window 2A 20b)
⟨wing St A 85⟩
winner 8F 111b)
winter 8A 100b)
to **wish 9D** 119
with 1E 15
⟨without 8E 109⟩
woman/women 3E 40a)

wonderful 5 E 66 a)
wood(s) *Wald* **9 D** 121
word 3 A 33,2
work 6 A 70 b)
at **work 6 C** 74 b)
to **work 4 D** 53,1
⟨world 8 E 109⟩
world 8 F 110 a)
to **worry 4 B** 49
would like to 2 D 24
wrist 3 E 40 b)
to **write 3 D** 38 a)
⟨Write it down! St A 86⟩
writing paper 5 E 59 b)
wrong 2 F 30,1
to be **wrong with 3 D** 38 b)

Y

year 5 E 68,3
yellow 4 C 51,1
⟨Yep! 10 E 131 a)⟩
yes 1 A 9 b)
⟨yesterday 10 B 126,3⟩
yet 9 B 115 b)
you 1 A 9 c)
young 2 F 29 a)
your 1 A 9 b)
youth club 2 C 23
youth hostel 7 B 90

List of names

Boys' names

Andy ['ændɪ]
Ben [ben]
David ['deɪvɪd]
⟨George⟩ [dʒɔ:dʒ]
⟨Harold⟩ ['hærəld]
⟨Henry⟩ ['henrɪ]
Jack [dʒæk]
Jeff [dʒef]
Jim [dʒɪm]
John [dʒɒn]
Kevin ['kevɪn]
Patrick ['pætrɪk]
Peter ['pi:tə]
Rajiv ['rædʒɪv]
Roger ['rɒdʒə]
⟨Scott⟩ [skɒt]
Terry ['terɪ]
Tom [tɒm]
Tony ['təʊnɪ]
William ['wɪljəm]

Girls' names

Barbara ['bɑ:brə]
Carol ['kærəl]
⟨Carrie⟩ ['kærɪ]
⟨Jan⟩ [dʒæn]
Jenny ['dʒenɪ]
Melanie ['melənɪ]
Nivruti [nɪv'ru:tɪ]
Pamela/Pam ['pæmələ/pæm]
Sandra ['sɑ:ndrə/'sændrə]
Sharon ['ʃærən]
Susan ['su:zn]
Tanja ['tænjə/'tɑ:njə]
Wendy ['wendɪ]

Surnames

Benson ['bensn]
Black [blæk]
Brown [braʊn]
⟨Chang⟩ [tʃæŋ]
Dale [deɪl]
Davey ['deɪvɪ]
Eliot ['elɪət]
Finch [fɪntʃ]
Fletcher ['fletʃə]
Fox [fɒks]
Gossip ['gɒsɪp]
Grey [greɪ]
Hall [hɔ:l]
Hart [hɑ:t]
King [kɪŋ]
⟨Kramer⟩ ['kreɪmə]
Long [lɒŋ]
Mead [mi:d]
Mee [mi:]
Morgan ['mɔ:gən]
Ottaway ['ɒtəweɪ]
Phillips ['fɪlɪps]
Pratap ['prætæp]
Prichard ['prɪtʃəd/'prɪtʃɑ:d]
⟨Shockley⟩ ['ʃɒklɪ]
Smith [smɪθ]
Taylor ['teɪlə]
White [waɪt]
Wilkinson ['wɪlkɪnsən]
Wilson ['wɪlsn]

Geographical names

Abergavenny [ˌæbəgə'venɪ]
⟨America⟩ [ə'merɪkə]
⟨the Atlantic⟩ [ðɪ ət'læntɪk]
Avon ['eɪvən]
Bath [bɑ:θ]
Brecon Beacons ['brekən 'bi:kənz]
Bristol ['brɪstl]
Broadmead ['brɔ:d'mi:d]
California [kælɪ'fɔ:nɪə]
⟨Canada⟩ ['kænədə]
Cardiff ['kɑ:dɪf]
Carmarthen [kə'mɑ:ðn]
Devon ['devən]
England ['ɪŋglənd]
Filton ['fɪltən]
⟨France⟩ [frɑ:ns]
Germany ['dʒɜ:mənɪ]
Gower ['gaʊə]
Great Britain [ˌgreɪt 'brɪtən]
Hanover ['hænəʊvə]
Heathrow ['hi:θrəʊ]
Horfield ['hɔ:fi:ld]
Jenny's Cove ['dʒenɪz 'kəʊv]
⟨Liverpool⟩ ['lɪvəˌpʊl]
Llanthony [læn'təʊnɪ]
London ['lʌndən]
Lundy Island ['lʌndɪ 'aɪlənd]
⟨Manhattan⟩ [ˌmæn'hætn]
⟨Monterey⟩ [ˌmɒntə'reɪ]
New York [ˌnju: 'jɔ:k]
Newport ['nju:pɔ:t]
⟨Palo Alto⟩ ['pæləʊ 'æltəʊ]
Pembroke ['pembrəʊk]
⟨San Francisco⟩ [ˌsæn frən'sɪskəʊ]
⟨San Jose⟩ [ˌsæn həʊ'zeɪ]
Scotland ['skɒtlənd]
Southmead ['saʊθmi:d]
⟨Spain⟩ [speɪn]
Switzerland ['swɪtsələnd]
the USA [ðəˌju:es'eɪ]
Wales [weɪlz]
⟨Washington D.C.⟩ ['wɒʃɪŋtən 'di: 'si:]
Westbury ['wesbərɪ]
⟨Westminster⟩ ['westmɪnstə]
Weston-super-Mare ['westən su:pə 'meə]

Other names

Aerospace Club
['eərəspeɪs 'klʌb]
⟨Airbus⟩ ['eəbʌs]
Ashton Park
['æʃtən 'pɑ:k]
⟨Big Ben⟩ [ˌbɪg 'ben]
Bristol Rovers
['brɪstl 'rəʊvəz]
British Aerospace
['brɪtɪʃ 'eərəspeɪs]
⟨Buckingham Palace⟩
['bʌkiŋəm 'pælɪs]
⟨Central Park⟩
['sentrəl 'pɑ:k]
Clifton Downs
['klɪftən 'daʊnz]
CompuStar
['kɒmpju:ˌstɑ:]
Corn Street ['kɔ:n ˌstri:t]
Granny Smith
[ˌgrænɪ 'smɪθ]
the Gulf Stream
[ðə 'gʌlf stri:m]
⟨Hewlett-Packard⟩
['hju:lɪt 'pækəd]
⟨Houses of Parliament⟩
['haʊzɪz‿əv
'pɑ:ləmənt]
Kitty ['kɪtɪ]
Lawrence Road
['lɒrəns 'rəʊd]
⟨Nelson's Column⟩
['nelsənz 'kɒləm]
Neptune ['neptju:n]
⟨Oxford Street⟩
['ɒksfəd 'stri:t]
⟨ProNet⟩ ['prəʊ'net]
Red [red]
Redcliffe Bridge
['redklɪf 'brɪdʒ]
Redcliffe Way
['redklɪf 'weɪ]
⟨Redwood Forest⟩
['redwʊd 'fɒrɪst]
River Severn ['rɪvə 'sevən]
Severn Bridge
['sevən 'brɪdʒ]
Ship Street ['ʃɪp ˌstri:t]
Silicon Valley
['sɪlɪkən 'vælɪ]
Small Street ['ʃmɔ:l
ˌstri:t]
⟨St James's Park⟩
[snt 'dʒeɪmzɪz 'pɑ:k]
⟨St Martin-in-the-Fields⟩
[snt 'mɑ:tɪn‿ɪn ðə
'fi:ldz]
⟨St Paul's Cathedral⟩
[snt 'pɔ:lz kə'θi:drəl]
Station Road
['steɪʃn 'rəʊd]
⟨Statue of Liberty⟩
['stætju:‿əv 'lɪbətɪ]
⟨Tower Bridge⟩
['taʊə 'brɪdʒ]
Tower of London
['taʊər‿əv 'lʌndən]
⟨Trafalgar Square⟩
[trə'fælgə 'skweə]
⟨Westminster Bridge⟩
['westmɪnstə 'brɪdʒ]
⟨World Trade Center⟩
[ˌwɜ:ld 'treɪd 'sentə]
York Road ['jɔ:k 'rəʊd]

Bildquellen:
Umschlag: Fee Sprachreisen, Stuttgart; Gestaltung: Dieter Gebhardt, Asperg.
Stuart Amor, Stuttgart: S. 89 u. re.; S. 106 mi.; S. 136 mi.
Barnaby's Picture Library, London: S. 84; S. 106 u.; S. 136 li.
Klaus Bauer, Stuttgart: S. 96 o.
Bavaria Bildagentur GmbH, Gauting: S. 127 mi. li. und u.
British Aerospace, Britsol: S. 85 o., mi. und u.
Richard Open – Camera Press, London: S. 75 li.
J. Allan Cash Ltd., London: S. 29 mi. li. und u.; S. 95; S. 122; S. 129 o. re. und u. re.; S. 123 o. li und u. re.
Alan Cossey, Bristol: S. 7 u. li.; S. 58 o. re. und u. re.
Dieter Gebhardt, Asperg: S. 62; S. 103; S. 109; S. 137
Philip Hewitt, Stuttgart: S. 96 u. li. und u. re.
Klett-Kartographie/Krüger (Karten): S. 216
Jon Mather, Calverley: S. 69 li. und re.
H. Münzing, Renningen: S. 105; S. 124
Picturepoint, London: S. 122 li.; S. 123 o. re., mi. und u. li.; S. 127 o., o. re.; S. 133
Punch Publications Ltd., London: S. 39
Tony Stone Worldwide: S. 70
© The Telegraph Magazine, London: S. 87 li. und re.
Norman Thelwell, 'Top Dog', Methuen Associated Book Publishers, London: S. 18, 55
Derek Thrippleton, York: S. 58 o. li. S. 79
Transglobe Agency: S. 126
Viewfinder Colour Photo Library, Bristol: S. 7 o., mi. und u. mi.; S. 29 o. und m. r.
H. Wendler, The Image Bank: S. 134

Textquellen:
Sing a rainbow, S. 51. Originaltext und Musik Arthur Hamilton © Copyright 1955 by MARK VII MUSIC CHAPPELL-MORRIS, Ltd./London/ CHAPPELL & CO. GmbH, Hamburg 13
Mice, S. 119 by Rose Fylemann is reproduced by permission of The Society of Authors
Bell & Hyman/Unwin Hyman, part of Harper Collins Publishers poem by Irene Thompson from THE BOOK OF A THOUSAND POEMS, *'The Town Child'* (12 lines, arranged as 24 lines).
Octopus's garden, S. 121, Richard Starkey, Starling Music, Deutschland, Österreich, Eaton Music, Köln
This land is your land, S. 134 by Woody Guthrie © Ludlow Music Inc. Für Deutschland, Österreich und die Schweiz: Essex Musikvertrieb GmbH, Köln

⟨Useful phrases in class⟩

• What you can say to your friends or to the teacher

• Good morning, Mr/Mrs/Miss …	Guten Morgen …
Good-bye.	Auf Wiedersehen.
Thanks. Thank you (very much).	Danke. Vielen Dank.
• I'm sorry.	Tut mir leid.
I'm sorry I'm late.	Tut mir leid, daß ich mich verspätet habe.
I'm not feeling well.	Ich fühle mich nicht gut.
Can I open the window?	Darf ich das Fenster aufmachen?
• What's this in English/German?	Was heißt dies auf englisch/deutsch?
Can I say: …?	Kann ich sagen: …?
What does … mean?	Was bedeutet …?
• Can I ask a question, please?	Kann ich bitte eine Frage stellen?
How do you do this exercise?	Wie macht man/geht diese Übung?
Can you help me, please?	Können Sie/Kannst du mir bitte helfen?
This question is difficult.	Diese Frage ist schwierig.
I don't know the answer.	Ich weiß die Antwort nicht.
Is this right?	Ist das richtig?
I don't think this is right/wrong.	Ich glaube nicht, daß dies richtig/falsch ist.
Can you repeat the question/sentence?	Können Sie/Kannst du die Frage/den Satz wiederholen?
I don't understand this word/sentence.	Ich verstehe dieses Wort/diesen Satz nicht.
Pardon?	Wie bitte?
Can you write it on the board?	Können Sie es an die Tafel schreiben?
• Can we read this story?	Können wir diese Geschichte bitte lesen?
Let's act the story.	Wir möchten die Geschichte spielen.
Can we sing a song?	Können wir ein Lied singen?
• What must we do for homework?	Was haben wir als Hausaufgabe auf?

• What the teacher may say to you

• Open your books at page …	Öffnet eure Bücher auf Seite …
Turn to page …	Schlagt Seite … auf.
Read the text on page …	Lies den Text auf Seite …
• Please fetch me some chalk.	Bitte hol mir Kreide.
Would you collect the exercise books/worksheets/workbooks?	Würdest du bitte die Übungshefte/Arbeitsblätter/Arbeitsbücher einsammeln?
Do this exercise for homework.	Macht diese Übung als Hausaufgabe.
Write the answers/sentences in your exercise book/on the board.	Schreibt die Antworten in eure Übungshefte/an die Tafel.
• That's right. That's wrong.	Das ist richtig. Das ist falsch.
Good. Very good. That's good.	Gut! Sehr gut! Das ist gut.
That's not very good. Try again.	Das ist nicht sehr gut. Versuch es noch einmal.
That's better. Well done.	Das ist besser. Gut gemacht.
• Be quiet.	Seid ruhig.
Sit down, please.	Setzt euch bitte.
Please speak up.	Sprich lauter bitte.

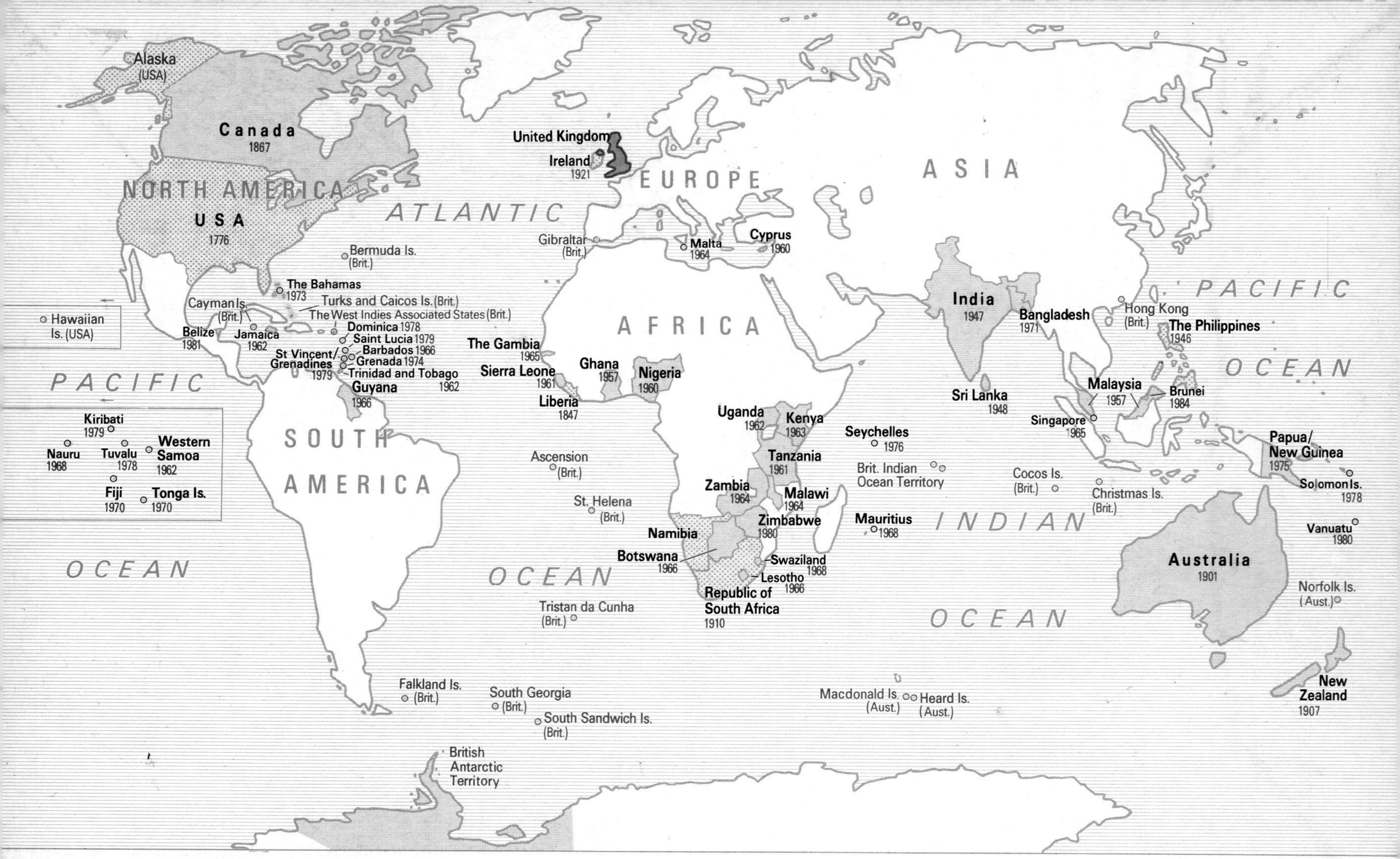

Britain and the World

- English-speaking countries
- Independent Commonwealth members (mostly English-speaking)
- 1974 Year of founding as an independent state